FLYING CARPETS, FLYING WINGS

For Ben —
This is an airplane
journey you won't
want to miss!

Barbara H. Schultz

Other books by the same author:

Pancho: The Biography of Florence Lowe Barnes

Wedell Williams Air Service

FLYING CARPETS, FLYING WINGS

THE BIOGRAPHY OF MOYE W. STEPHENS

Barbara H. Schultz

Little Buttes Publishing Co.

Library of Congress Catalogue Card Number
2010917717

ISBN – 978-0-9652181-2-2

Published in the United States by
Little Buttes Publishing Co.
PO Box 2043
Lancaster, CA 93539

Cover design by Todd Schultz; photos courtesy of Moye F. Stephens and Katy Ranaldi.

For Moye Francisco Stephens,
a loving son.

Moye F. Stephens stands in front of the Northrop N-1M flying wing that his father flew. The location was Silver Hills, the Smithsonian Air and Space Museum's restoration facility. Photo courtesy of Moye F. Stephens.

In December 1930, Richard Halliburton and Moye Stephens departed Grand Central Airport in the Flying Carpet. They would return eighteen months later after completing an around-the-world flight. Photo courtesy of Moye F. Stephens.

PREFACE

I had the privilege of meeting Moye Stephens in 1989 while researching a biography about Pancho Barnes. During the course of the interview, I discovered that Moye was a true pioneer of aviation. His knowledge and relationships during the 1920s and 1930s painted an exciting era of flying. The barnstorming pilots of Clover, Rogers, Venice, and De Mille Fields came to life through his descriptions. Learning about his involvement in the *Flying Carpet* around-the-world flight and Northrop Corporation's first flying wing was fascinating. Moye had a lot to say about Pancho too! "Certainly, Pancho could cuss like a trooper when the occasion demanded, but that was only one aspect of a much larger and more important whole. A warmer and more generous person never lived."

The same could be said about Moye. Confident, charming and sincere are words that describe this distinguished gentleman whose charismatic presence filled the room as he spoke. His knowledge of aviation history added depth and understanding to its early development. In 1984, Moye completed an autobiography, *Whither the Wild Blue Yonder*, a title reflective of the ever tightening control and concurrent loss of freedom of flight. Sadly, his manuscript ended before he ventured around the world as Richard Halliburton's pilot in the *Flying Carpet* and later, his involvement with Northrop Corporation. "That would take another volume or two," he told me, "and I'm far too old to do that."

Much has been written about Richard Halliburton's *Flying Carpet* saga but not from the pilot's perspective nor through any factual commentary. Several books describe the beginnings of Northrop Corporation. Their references to the role Moye played are sparse. They do not give him credit for the organizational skills and investment contacts he provided to make Jack Northrop's vision for a flying wing a reality. The title for Moye's biography, *Flying*

Carpets, Flying Wings, represents a more balanced and comprehensive narrative of Moye's participation in aviation.

Flying Carpets, Flying Wings is based, in part, on Moye's original autobiography. Throughout the text, the reader will find direct quotes from Moye that are not footnoted for the sake of simplicity. They give credence to additional research and allow Moye a voice in his biography. Because there is a potential for confusion in identifying important associates of Moye, Dick Ranaldi is referred to as Dick and Richard Halliburton is referred to as Richard. Technically, Moye W. Stephens should be followed by a Jr. It is not used here as the suffix was never used by him or in any other reference to him (with the exception of some society column articles in the 1930s). Many of the places visited by Richard and Moye during the world flight retain the spelling used at the time of the adventure.

During the process of researching Moye's involvement with the early airlines, I discovered additional information which is not included in the biography. One such item was the Transcontinental Air Transport Handbook belonging to Moye's son. Although lengthy, I felt the history buff would enjoy reading it and have included its contents in the Appendix.

Please enjoy Moye's story.

ACKNOWLEDGEMENTS

The extensive research for *Flying Carpets, Flying Wings* has taken place over several years. Moye's son, Moye Francisco Stephens, and his wife Cecile have extended me every courtesy in my search for original materials and photos. Words cannot express how grateful I am for their generosity in allowing me access to the maps created in London and those purchased in France, India, and Singapore for the *Flying Carpet*'s round-the-world flight. The charts have proved invaluable to depict the voyage accurately. More importantly, I was given access to Moye's autobiography, his letters to his parents and grandparents during the round-the world flight, and a wonderful photo collection. Moye's biography would not have been comprehensive without them.

Moye's nephew Steve LeFever and his wife Cathy have also given me access to their family photos. Dick Ranaldi's daughters and Vance Breese's son supplied valuable information to enhance Moye's story. Most generous, Katy Ranaldi gave me access to her father's photo albums and other memorabilia. Northrop test pilots Max Stanley, John Meyers, and Bob Cardenas gave me facts relevant to Moye and their personal reflections about him. They all remembered Moye as an excellent test pilot and gentleman of the highest order. Roy Wolford, an employee of Northrop for 60 years, was a crucial source of the early flying wing days. John Underwood helped supply photos and information he collected in his association with Moye and Inez. Ron Gilliam lent me his written and taped interviews which he initiated while living next door to Moye and Inez in Ensenada. The Davis-Monthan Airfield Register developed by Gary Hyatt was a superior resource for information on the many aviation notables who were integral to Moye's early flying. Sabine Mueller provided substantive information about Elly Beinhorn.

Richard Halliburton's collection at Princeton which included

Moye's logbook from London to Cairo, Eugene Biscailuz's collection from the University of Southern California, the David Hatfield Collection in the Museum of Flight archives, the John K. Northrop-Richard W. Millar Aviation Collection at Occidental University, Roy Wolford's Collection at Harvey Mudd College, and the Mohave Museum of History and Arts have all provided essential information. Several books were used for additional information and validation of facts. Halliburton's *Flying Carpet* and *Richard Halliburton,* the story of his life as told in letters to his parents, Cortese's *Royal Road,* Max's *Horizon Chasers,* and Cole's *Their Eyes on the Sky* were secondary sources for the round-the world flight. Texts used for Moye's involvement with Northrop were Anderson's *Northrop: An Aeronautical History*, Coleman's original notes as well as his book, *Jack Northrop and the Flying Wing,* and Allen's *The Northrop Story 1929-1939*. Other texts that I found integral to Moye's life were Beinhorn's *Flying Girl*, De Sibour's *Flying Gypsies*, and Seabrook's *Air Journey* and *The White Monk of Timbuctoo.*

Special thanks are extended to my husband Phil and literary friend Gerry Max whose suggestions and perceptive comments gave clarity to the project. Gerry's own work gave me a necessary insight into Halliburton's character. He is a true historian and genuine inspiration. Phil spent many hours editing the manuscript, providing technical advice where needed, and helping select photographs. Many other individuals and sources enriched the content of Moye's biography and are listed appropriately in the bibliography. My sincere appreciation is extended to all.

I would be remiss if I did not acknowledge those early pilots who dedicated their lives to the advancement of aviation. They were on the 'ground floor' at an exciting time in aviation history - designing state-of-the-art aircraft, organizing airline and aircraft companies, analyzing weather conditions, configuring air-to-ground communication systems, and making concerted efforts to convince the public that flying was an essential part of the future. As you read Moye's biography, you'll discover how the lives of these innovative men and women intertwined as their passion for flying advanced aeronautics.

CONTENTS

A group of aviation enthusiasts from the original Rogers Airport on Wilshire Boulevard. L to R: 'Slim' Maves, Robby Robinson, Dana Boller, Reeves Darling, unknown, and Al Morgan in the white overalls. Sterling Boller is the young boy on the airplane. Photo courtesy of the Museum of Flight.

1

THE INSPIRATION

After weeks of foregoing ice cream sodas at the local drug store, Moye Stephens and Bill Moore managed to save five dollars apiece for an airplane ride. They woke early that highly anticipated Saturday morning, threw on their clothes, and ran the distance to Rogers Airport in record time. The airport manager did his best to calm the energized seventeen-year-olds as he presented them with waivers to sign and fitted them with helmets and goggles. Donning the well-used equipment, Bill and Moye envisioned themselves as ace aviators. Their strut out to the airplane gave the appearance of seasoned veterans ready for another mission.   Following instructions from the pilot, they clambered into the front cockpit and cinched their belts tight. Their excitement grew as the engine roared to life.

The bumpy take-off role down the hard-packed dirt runway proved of little consequence to the two boys. It simply signaled a prelude to something magnificent. When the plane's wheels left the ground, sheer joy replaced memories of the impossibility of this moment. Both wanted to stand up, wave their arms, and shout, "Look at us! We're flying!"

"As Wilshire's two-lane width of asphalt grew distant,"

Moye later recalled, "I was filled with an intense exhilaration paradoxically coupled with snug serenity. This was the ultimate experience! Despite the authoritative voice of the engine, the rigging wires whistled in tune to the airplane's movements. The exposed rocker arms of the OX-5 blurred with the rapidity of their action. "

Once they reached cruising altitude, the vacant expanse between Santa Monica Boulevard on the north, Baldwin Hills on the south, Beverly Hills on the west, and Vine Street on the east - an area of approximately 20 square miles – surprised Moye and Bill. They had no idea how much land lay vacant near their homes. Except for the La Brea Tar Pits, just east of the airport, and a forest of oil wells to the north, a sparse scattering of farm buildings appeared the sole encroachment on the air field. Today, only the tar pits remain; gone are the airport, oil wells, farm buildings, and airfield.

The aerial view of the coastline off Santa Monica was impressive. The cloudless blue sky gave way to an endless ocean of dancing waves and flickering brilliance. The airplane seemed to float above it, guided by the special talents of the pilot and the commanding power of the engine. As the plane turned homeward at the shoreline, Moye sensed the flight coming to an end. Before the airplane completed its landing roll-out, he began to contemplate how to arrange for another flight.

A simple plan materialized. With the help of fellow high school senior Fritz Ripley, Moye would bring a number of paying passengers to the airport in exchange for a free ride. Anxious to present his idea to Rogers' manager, he barely made it through the next day's classes. The following afternoon, Moye was pleasantly surprised to find the manager so receptive. Within minutes, the two settled on twelve passengers - six trips with two passengers each - in exchange for a five minute flight for Moye and Fritz. Two days before high school graduation ceremonies, they arrived at the field with twelve passengers in tow to claim their reward. This second flight reaffirmed Moye's desire to fly. He just needed to figure out the economics of becoming a pilot.

The Stephens' family lineage possessed respected leaders,

2

able lawyers, and smart investors. Colonel William Henry Stephens gained a reputation as a superior Civil War field officer and a trustworthy lawyer. As a member of the 6th Tennessee Infantry Regiment, Colonel Stephens survived the Battle of Shiloh, one of the bloodiest battles of the war. In his history of the 6th Regiment, Robert Gates praised Colonel Stephens. "Col. Stephens deserves great credit for the skill displayed in bringing the regiment to such a high degree of efficiency. He possessed the genius of command to an eminent degree and succeeded in infusing his spirit of discipline and pride into the regiment." These qualities became an intrinsic part of the Stephens pedigree. 1

In 1868, Colonel Stephens migrated west. At the time, the southern United States had begun the long process of coping with reconstruction efforts dictated by Congress. The grueling ordeal proved lengthy as families struggled to achieve some semblance of their lives prior to the conflict. When their efforts failed, they abandoned their homes and left the south in hopes of a better life elsewhere. California, with its excellent weather and abundance of land, promised prosperity. The Colonel and his family, including his son Albert, wife Matilde, and their son William, settled in southern California. The elder Stephens purchased a large tract of land in colorful San Gabriel, the oldest settlement in Los Angeles County. An ardent horticulturist, he planted groves of orange trees. He enjoyed working the land until his death in 1887.

Albert, who had practiced law with his father in Tennessee, maintained a law office near downtown Los Angeles and specialized in water litigation. Elected to the Los Angeles County bench in 1877, he sat as a probate judge. In 1888, he assisted in the founding of the Los Angeles Bar Association and served as a trustee of the organization as well as its first president. Judge Albert Stephens had four sons, William, Albert Jr., Moye, and Ray, who would become partners in the family law firm after graduating from law school. They also became associates in the Albert M. Stephens Company which invested in real estate throughout southern California. Shortly after the Colonel's death, the company purchased 2,100 acres in the Sierra Madre foothills above the small town of Lordsburg, renamed La Verne in 1912. 2

Referred to as the Mile-High Ranch, the property became known as one of the finest ranches in Southern California. The hillside property contained 60 acres of orange orchards, 300 acres devoted to range land for the cattle, and five reservoirs. Eight homes of various sizes covered the ranch. Architect Theodore Criley Jr. designed the main house; Harold W. Grieve served as the interior decorator. Redwood paneling, a twelve-foot ceiling, oak plank floor, and a massive fireplace gave the living room a rustic, yet elegant, feel. Overhanging the canyon, a small alcove or *hikia* held a seven-foot square divan surrounded by floor-to-ceiling windows. The large divan served as an overflow area for ranch guests. The

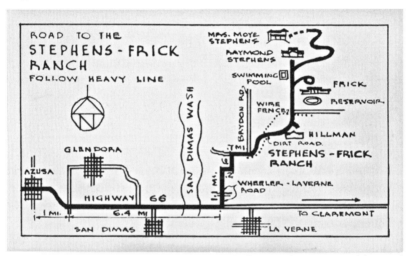

Stephens' family members occupied four of seven additional homes; ranch employees lived in three. Other structures included two horse barns with fourteen box stalls, miscellaneous sheds for tools and tractors, a blacksmith's shop, swimming pool, and tennis courts. 3

Albert's third son, Moye Wicks, did not have the luxury of his father's support for a law educationas did his brothers. Judge Stephens demanded total subservience. Moye Sr., although respectful, possessed an independence unacceptable to the Judge. As a result, Moye put himself through school and then joined the law firm. Attending Stanford, he met Mary Hendricks, an English and education major. They were married in 1905. Their first son,

THE INSPIRATION

The Moye W. Stephens family circa 1918. From left to right - Trow, Mary, Moye Jr., Suzanne, and Moye Sr. Photo courtesy of Steve LeFever.

Moye Jr., was born on February 21, 1906. Following tradition, his parents gave him his father's name. Some assurance that he would possess the stalwart character of his predecessors presumably accompanied their selection.

The Stephens family lived in a modest apartment at 508 South Serrano Street in Los Angeles' Wilshire District until they could afford a more opulent home. Their second residence was located at 920 Kings Road in West Hollywood. Situated on two acres, the estate proved a wonderful place for entertaining and the growing Stephens' family. Moye's sister Suzanne was born in 1910; brother Trowbridge, in 1913. The estate boasted a 100-bird aviary, tennis courts, and well-manicured grounds.

Reserved and not one to act on impulse, Moye Sr. stressed how respect was based on reputation and appearances. "Who you are and what you represent is key to success." An avid outdoorsman, he often took his sons on hunting trips into the Angeles Forest, never failing to pack out at least one deer. Trow

The 100-bird aviary is visible in the top right corner of the Stephens' family estate on Kings Road. Photo courtesy of Steve LeFevre.

and Moye excelled at shooting pistols, rifles, and shotguns. At the age of twelve, Moye won top honors at an informal rifle competition for boys under eighteen sponsored by the Dyas Sporting Goods Store. All five of his shots hit the black and could have been covered by a quarter. Moye Sr. encouraged his sons to participate in sports when they entered school. They joined the swim team and played football at Hollywood High School. Suzanne, under the wing of her mother, attended Marlborough School, the oldest independent girl's school in southern California.

Moye's mother Mary, nicknamed Brickie by her grandson because of the resemblance of her bright red hair to the brick hearth, was warm, outgoing, and much more approachable than her husband. She loved discussing politics and knew more about baseball than most. A woman devoted to family and tradition, Mary set a table for 28 each Christmas. Everyone came, bearing gifts to exchange after an incredible Yule feast. When her grandchildren were old enough, she enjoyed taking them to baseball games or on road trips during their summer vacations. Her grandsons remember Brickie as someone who was more than their grandmother; she became their mentor. 4

THE INSPIRATION

Moye's first encounter with aviation occurred at the 1910 Dominguez Air Meet, the first American aviation exhibition for heavier-than-air vehicles. Famous aviators came from as far away as France to perform in front of the grandstands in their linen and wood birds. Included on the pilot roster were Glenn Curtiss, Louis Paulhan, Lincoln Beachy, and Roy Knabenshue. Though Moye's father attempted to explain the historic significance to his four-year-old son, the excitement and astonished exclamations of their fellow spectators were an eloquent commentary in themselves. Unforgettably, the distinctive smell of burnt castor oil and the drone of airplane engines lingered in their senses for many years. Moye's mother latter commented that Dominguez "left its mark" on her son. In his twilight years, Moye could close his eyes and summon visions of primitive flying machines sailing past the grandstand. His most vivid image was a sleek monoplane designed by Louis Bleriot.

During the latter part of America's entry into World War I, Moye hurried his lunches at Virgil Elementary School to spend time in the library pursuing accounts of air battles taking place in Europe. He unearthed the names of Guynemer, Rickenbacker, Immelmann, Von Richtofen, and Udet. By the time Moye entered Hollywood High, the Allies and Germans had signed the armistice and material on flying became harder to find. In spite of the scarcity, Moye found enough worthwhile information in the school's library to keep his interest alive for the next three years. The introduction of aviation into the movies added an element of romance to Moye's fascination with the sport. Comedies and serials incorporated flying scenes to generate more excitement. *A Dash through the Clouds, the Sky Pirate,* and Mary Pickford's *The Girl of Yesterday* were among the more popular. Films produced during the war attempted to describe the conflict. Their titles reflected their content – *Berlin vs. America, Flying with the Marines*, and the *Zeppelin's Last Raid.* Many others followed the war - *The Great Air Robbery, A Cowboy Ace,* and *With Wings Outspread.* 5

Moye completed the required number of credits to graduate high school by his junior year. Believing their son too young to enter college, his parents insisted he attend a post-graduate year at Hollywood High. The permanent custody of a recently purchased Model T made his parent's decision much more agreeable. Giving the additional year at Hollywood some thought, Moye saw an opportunity to please his parents and himself. He would attend classes in the morning and take flying lessons in the afternoon. His father, however, displayed little enthusiasm for his son's plan.

The inherent risks of flying provided Moye Sr. with a reason for rejecting his son's afternoon activities. On August 2, 1920, Moye Sr. witnessed an airplane crash that resulted in the deaths of Ormer Locklear and Milton *Skeets* Elliott. Locklear and Elliott became close friends while serving in the United States Air Service during WWI. Besides their regular Army duties, Locklear, Elliot, and Shirley Short developed a technique for wing-walking and plane changing to a high degree of expertise. Locklear's skills at wing walking may have originated when military experts wanted to determine how to mount a machine gun on the plane's wing without increasing wind resistance. Locklear proved that, no matter where he walked on the wing, his position did not affect the airplane's operation. 6

Following their discharge in 1919, Locklear, Elliott, and Short joined forces with promoter William H. Pickens to tour the country as the Locklear Flying Circus. Elliot and Short flew the planes while Locklear transferred from one to the other. Locklear may not have been the first man to leave the cockpit of an airplane in flight, to clamber from wingtip to wingtip, but he was certainly the first to bring the feat to popular attention. The fame the Locklear Flying Circus achieved eventually brought them to Hollywood where Locklear starred in two films, *The Great Air Robbery* and *Skyway Man*.

The final airplane scene in *Skyway Man* called for a night flight culminating in a spin illuminated by ground-based searchlights. At 2,000 feet, with Elliott as a passenger, Locklear ignited flares attached to the plane's outer wing struts and entered the spin. At five hundred feet above the field, the ground crew neglected to turn the lights off, the signal for Locklear to start his recovery. Inexplicably, they stayed on until less than one hundred feet remained between the plane and the ground, too late to pull the airplane out of its dive. Locklear dove into an oil sump near the southeast corner of Third Street and Crescent Avenue near the Stephens' home. The fiery explosion and ghastly spectacle deeply disturbed Moye Sr. His son's hopeful suggestion of how to fill his free afternoons struck no sympathetic chord in his father. His reply left little doubt.

"Son, in view of my feeling about flying, I couldn't pay for your lessons with a clear conscience. If you want to learn to fly, you're going to have to wait until you can do it on your own." His polite response masked his belief, and that of most of his generation, that flying was a fool-hardy venture.

To occupy his summer, Moye's parents arranged a trip to Europe through the high school. He went, although reluctantly, resigned to enduring an undetermined period of time before any hope of realizing his ambition occurred.

Vice Principal Forster led the group of Hollywood High School students through Europe with a comprehensive agenda of historic sites. They boarded trains for Paris, Lucerne, Salzburg, Madrid, Rome, Amsterdam, and other major cities. Walking tours conducted by informed guides enriched the students' class lectures and textbook assignments. They visited cathedrals, monuments, and other artistic and architectural gems; on rare occasions, Moye caught a glimpse of an airplane overhead which always delighted him. On August 24, 1923, the SS Montlaurier, with Forster and students aboard, docked in Quebec. Their final destination, Los Angeles' Union Station, was made by train.

Moye found it difficult to concentrate during his post-graduate year. Mild autumn weather reminded him of the exciting possibilities waiting beyond the confining classroom. On a day when the breeze just stirred the tops of the elms, he glanced over at the artistic endeavors of Harry Rosselot seated next to him. The wealth of authentic detail in Harry's airplane drawing intrigued Moye. Catching up with him after class, Moye learned that Harry spent a great deal of time at Rogers Airport. Surprised, Moye believed it would be presumptuous of him to hang around the airport without being invited - not the activity for a proper gentleman. Further, he discovered that Harry knew the pilots and mechanics on a first name basis and had even been allowed to sit in a cockpit. Moye, attempting to hide his growing excitement, asked Harry if he could accompany him to the airport. He had a car and could drive them. Harry, happy to help, arranged to meet Moye after school the next day.

On the drive to the airport, Moye, playing for effect, told Harry that he had flown twice but Harry wasn't impressed. He said he flew all the time. Moye made another attempt. Pointing to the southwest corner of De Mille Field No 1, he stated matter-of-factly, "Back in 1918, I saw an airplane land there just before they built the airport. I don't live very far from here and I was out hunting ground squirrels in the stubble fields. The two men in the ship got out and seemed to be waiting for somebody. I let the pilot shoot my .22."

Harry told Moye that the plane must have been either a Jenny or a Canuck and recognized the pilots from Moye's description. "If it was a Canuck, it was probably Mr. De Mille and Al Wilson. Al was his pilot. Mr. De Mille couldn't get a ship in the U.S. during the war so Al found a cracked-up Canuck in Canada for him. They had it rebuilt and Al taught him to fly. Al's a hot stunt pilot."

Moye's aspirations of achieving status with Harry verged on failure. His classmate seemed to possess far more knowledge about aviation than he did. Moye could only hope that he would be fortunate enough to be welcomed at Rogers Airport in the same manner as Harry.

2

ROGERS AIRPORT

Three flying fields made up Rogers Airport. In early 1919, Cecil B. De Mille, pilot and motion picture producer, formed the Mercury Aviation Company located at De Mille Field No. 1. The field consisted of 40 acres of leased land on the southwest corner of Crescent (now Fairfax) and Melrose Avenues. As business expanded, De Mille opened Field No. 2 on the northwest corner of Crescent and Wilshire. Near the same time, Emory Rogers and Sidney Chaplin, Charlie's half-brother, created Chaplin Aerodrome on the southwest side of Wilshire opposite De Mille No. 2. Emory and Sidney also operated a flight service from Wilmington, California to Catalina Island. In 1920, Sidney, more involved in Charlie's movie interests than aviation, sold his half to Emory who then purchased De Mille's share of Mercury and formed Rogers Aircraft Incorporated. With the purchase of George Stephenson's Pacific Airplane and Supply, a company involved in general aircraft remanufacture, repair, and service, Rogers Aircraft became a full service aviation business.

One of the company's first airplane modifications involved

Above, De Mille Field No. 2 on a typical Sunday. Below, Chaplin Field, Mercury Aviation, and a field full of Jennys. Photos courtesy of Katy Ranaldi.

replacing the 100 hp Hall Scott A-7A with a 200 hp Hall Scott L-6 in film director Victor Fleming's Standard J-1. Looking for more power from their own airplanes, Rogers changed out the 90 hp OX5s in his Standards with A-7A motors. 1

ROGERS AIRPORT

Emory Rogers managed his various businesses from a small, two-room wooden building that fronted Crescent Avenue. Four corrugated steel hangars sat along the northern boundary of the rectangular field. Six or seven airplanes, mostly Jennys, were typically parked on either side of the structures. A network of ruts, mementos from the passage of innumerable tailskids, scarred the unpaved take-off area. On the flight line, clearly visible to passing traffic, Rogers placed three of his Standard J-1s in hopes of attracting paying passengers. Behind the office, facing Wilshire, Clara and Tex Newland operated a lunch stand. The modest establishment offered home-cooking at its best – meatloaf and mashed potatoes, cabbage rolls, and creamy rice pudding. The Newlands, always friendly, provided ample support to the pilots.

Just after he bought Pacific Airplane and Supply, Emory Rogers met an untimely death. Sunday afternoon, November 27, 1921, Rogers Airport hosted its customary air show. Grounded from a suspected attack of malaria, Emory allowed one of his pilots to compete against Remy Remlin in the day's feature race. When Remlin's Nieuport 28 bested Emory's Standard C-1, he was infuriated. He lost no time in challenging Remlin to another race. They made one turn just west of La Brea Tar Pits when Emory either blacked out or pulled up into an accelerated stall and crashed, dying instantly. 2

Following his death, Emory's mother struggled to keep the airport open as a tribute to her son. The visible volume of business barely covered the overhead. Few individuals signed up for flying lessons; charter flights were scarce. The main source of income came from five dollar local sight-seeing hops. Skywriting contracts later obtained by manager Jim Webster improved their economic condition considerably. Webster's Fokker D-VII, a German WWI fighter, kept busy in the skies over Los Angeles, advertising events and local businesses.

Webster, a tall, slim man, was an unusually animated speaker. When describing an airplane maneuver, he used his entire body to imitate the action. His arms flew up and down in tune to the side to side movement of his body. His facial expressions ranged from surprise to concentration. Often his exchanges bordered on the satiric, perhaps a shield for a soft heart. He was never seen without his cloth cap, somewhat soiled and pulled low over his ears. It was Webster who had given Moye a free flight in exchange for 12 paying customers.

Arriving at Rogers Airport, Harry and Moye located Webster behind his office. He was discussing the day's events with Eddie Bellande, the pilot responsible for Bill Moore and Moye's first airplane ride. Bellande remembered Moye and claimed he wasn't surprised to see him again based on Moye's previous enthusiasm for flying. The great Glenn Curtiss taught Bellande to fly in 1915. During WWI, he became a naval instructor at Pensacola. His relaxed manner undoubtedly contributed to his recognized ability as a first rate flight instructor. The only time his 'feathers were ruffled' was when a conversation made light of his thinning light brown hair.

While chatting with Webster and Bellande, Moye noticed Webster glancing towards Wilshire Boulevard. Webster's interest became apparent when he commented to Bellande. "Eddie, the traffic seems to be building up out there. What do you say to jazzing the road. You might take Harry and Moye with you."

Harry indicated profound approval. Moye concurred even though he was completely in the dark about what the flight entailed. On the way to the ship, he pulled Harry aside to find out what 'jazzing' the road meant. "When there are enough cars on the road to make it worthwhile," Harry responded, "a pilot flies back and forth over the road at a low altitude in hopes of attracting some spectators. Before long, they're able to drum up some passenger hops."

The flight proved daunting for the two adolescents. At 100 feet, Bellande leveled off to gain speed and then put the Standard into a smooth sixty-degree left bank to line up on Wilshire, just clearing the boulevard's palm trees in the process. The astonished expressions from the people below were quite apparent.

"The remainder of the all-too-short flight was conducted at a height of around 50 feet," recalled Moye. "We paralleled a stretch of the road adjacent to the airport, crisscrossing it a number of times. At that low altitude, the sixty-five mile an hour speed of the airplane seemed electric as we sped past the cars below. It was

14

tremendously more rewarding than flying at higher altitudes."

Upon landing, Moye was allowed to sit in the cockpit of Ted Young's Jenny as long as he didn't touch anything. Moye, readily agreeing to the condition, cautiously climbed into the revered cockpit. Nestling down into the pilot's seat, Moye's day became richer. Time stopped as he imagined himself airborne, controlling his own craft with competent ease. If Harry and Burgess F. *Bud* Creeth had not intervened the reverie might have lasted indefinitely.

Creeth exemplified the public's image of the aviator. He was tall, lean, debonair, and sported an eyebrow mustache. During WWI, he belonged to the 838th Aero Squadron, 5th Pursuit Group in France. Always ready to share his enthusiasm for flying, he offered to take Harry and Moye on a tour of the field. They followed him to one of the hangars that served as a shop. Compared to the quiet of the airfield, they found mechanics and a few pilots industriously engaged in four or five separate projects. One mechanic carefully brushed dope on new fabric covering the fuselage of Creeth's project, a wartime French Nieuport 28 pursuit plane. Bellande worked diligently stitching unbleached linen on the Nieuport's wing. Gil Budwig assisted a mechanic with the Fokker D-VII installing sky writing equipment. Two more mechanics labored on OX-5 engines.

Bud Creeth. Photo courtesy of John Underwood.

The men cheerfully bantered as they went about their tasks. The only exception was mechanic Fritz Mathews, a giant of a man. He needed little assistance to swing an 800 pound engine onto a stand. As he lectured the two boys on the dangers of going aloft, Moye discovered that Fritz possessed no fondness for flying. Fritz and his brother flew during the war but when a fatal crash ended his brother's life, Fritz vowed to never fly again. He saw no positive value that could come from piloting a plane. Fritz's argument nor an incident that Moye witnessed earlier could discourage him from pursuing his goal of becoming a pilot.

Playing in the Stephens' backyard, a loud boom startled thirteen-year-old Moye, brother Trow, two young cousins, Jeff Stephens and Don Frick, and a next door neighbor, Don Dodge. The five adolescents scrambled into the street to get a view of what Moye suspected to be an airplane crash. Unable to see anything, they ran south down Kings Road until it dead-ended near De Mille Field No. 1. Just beyond the dead-end, in the open fields, lay the crumpled remains of a Jenny.

Reaching the wreck, the boys saw a ship up on its nose, the radiator partially buried in the sandy field. The tail dangled from the nearly vertical fuselage. The impact had driven the motor back through the fire wall, pushing the ruptured gasoline tank into the lap of the pilot. A passenger wandered dazed, blood streaming from a cut on his forehead.

Fearful of what gory remains he might see, Moye recalled how reluctant he felt to look at the pilot. He persevered, however, discovering the pilot to be unconscious. Together, he and the others tried desperately to remove him from the cockpit before spilling fuel could ignite. They tugged at the exposed engine in a vain attempt to pull it away from the trapped pilot. Much to their relief, personnel from the airport arrived and quickly freed the pilot with the proper tools and manpower. Moye remembered his overwhelming sense of helplessness at the time, a feeling that never diminished no matter how many crashes he witnessed.

In the weeks that followed Moye's rewarding visit to Rogers Airport, he took every opportunity to repeat the experience. In return for odd jobs, pilots gave him rides in their airplanes. Bellande flew him in W. E. Thomas's Jenny after Moye had applied fresh coats of varnish to the plane's wings. Thomas, a Los Angeles automobile dealer, had given Bellande driving lessons in exchange for flying lessons. Byron Morgan, the author of scenarios for a popular series of automobile racing pictures starring Wallace Reid, was another pilot who took Moye aloft. Although the pilots that Moye met on the field came from varied backgrounds, they enjoyed an easy camaraderie that seemed to be the outgrowth of a strong but unspoken allegiance. At the time, Moye could only vaguely sense its nature. Maturity would allow him to appreciate the solid bond of friendship.

In his later years, Moye reflected on what flying meant to him in those early days. "The flying game," he recalled, "demanded payment for the favors it conferred. The fortunate gained a degree of skill and diligence; the inept, the reckless, and those abandoned by whatever gods guided their destinies paid the ultimate price. Pilots whose experience dated from the war years or earlier, played the game long enough to lose friends and acquaintances in fiery crashes. Each knew, without words, that the ineffable fulfillment binding him to his calling was shared irrevocably by all. It set them infinitely apart from groundlings which, in the absence of an adequate means of expression, remained forever incapable of comprehending the substance of their bitter-sweet bondage."

The young Moye viewed pilots as demigods who devoted little time to inquisitive youngsters. The friendly indulgence the pilots at Rogers accorded him and his friends seemed a revelation. He thought they saw something of themselves in their young following. Besides Harry Rosselot and Moye, the retinue of young enthusiasts included Red Ruthven and Dick Ranaldi who washed dishes at Newland's lunch stand. Dick, five feet two inches tall and weighing less than 110 pounds fully clothed, elected to drop out of high school at the beginning of his freshman year. Moye did his best to dissuade his bright young friend by reciting the familiar platitudes regarding the importance of a solid education. As it turned out, Ranaldi had the matter well in hand. "Don't give it a second thought," he curtly explained. "I've gone around to see all my teachers and told them when they learn something new to give me a ring."

Dick's warm personality and sparkling sense of humor endeared him to the pilots who frequented the stand. From the tales he heard, Dick absorbed a sizeable fund of aviation lore - one rivaling even that of Harry Rosselot. His newly acquired knowledge proved an unqualified source of satisfaction for him. "Boy, we sure missed the boat," he told Moye during one of his visits to the diner. "Why couldn't we have started coming out here when Emory Rogers was still alive? Every weekend they had something special going on to attract a crowd - races, stunts, movie stars - all sorts of excitement."

Dick's enthusiasm for aviation almost ended his career as a dishwasher. Every time an airplane engine fired up, he grabbed a plate and towel, practically rubbing off the plate's ornamental trim as he rushed to the door to watch the plane take off. Tex Newland solved the situation by cutting a make-shift window in the wall above the sink.

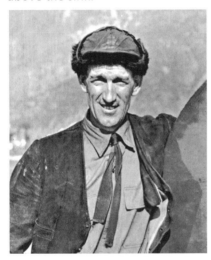

Doc Whitney. Photo courtesy of John Underwood.

With the exception of Frederic C. 'Doc' Whitney, the old pros at Rogers were in their late twenties or early thirties. Doc, fifty-five at the time Moye met him, claimed the same age when he retired from TWA ten years later. Indeed, his grey hair, steady grey eyes, leathery face, and lanky frame made him appear ageless. A former Texas cowpuncher, Doc bought a cracked-up pusher airplane prior to the war. After he rebuilt it, he taught himself how to fly and would have joined the war effort were it not for his need for glasses. Before Venice Airport closed in 1923, he and Harry Crawford did passenger hops; at Rogers, he piloted for A. H. Hayes, the owner of an L-6 Pacific Standard. 3

No one equaled Gil *Buddy* Budwig's ability to write a message across the sky. One of the smoothest pilots with whom Moye had the pleasure to fly, Budwig earned his wings in 1916 at the Curtiss Exhibition Company School in Buffalo, New York. Migrating to California in 1920, he brought a resume that included stunting, flying the mail, instructing, test flying, and co-founding the Queens Aerial Transportation Company. He partnered with Fred D. Hoyt at the Venice Airport where they concentrated on commercial flying and flight testing for local aircraft companies such as Loughead (Lockheed) Brothers. Budwig became Los Angeles banker L. C. Brand's personal pilot until 1924 when he formed the Budwig Radio Company. In 1927, Hoyt joined Lloyd Stearman's company as sales manager and chief test pilot. His involvement with the company ended abruptly in January 1928, however. Ferrying a Model C-2B to Varney Airlines in Idaho, a severe ice storm south of Boise forced an emergency landing. Hoyt survived the crash but froze to death waiting to be rescued. 4

Maurice *Loop* Murphy, a former Air Corps pilot, flew a single seat Thomas Morse Scout SC-4, affectionately referred to as a *Tommy*. Although he went by *Loop*, he preferred the snap roll which he performed with astonishing frequency. He often parked his plane on the flight line in an attempt to lure passers-by into the clutches of a salesman hawking sight-seeing tickets. When Rogers Airport relocated in early 1924, Murphy moved to Clover Field in Santa Monica and decided to recover the *Tommy*. Removing the fabric, he discovered that the stresses imposed by the snap rolls caused the bolt holes in the wooden spars' wing root fittings to elongate. The slots had increased to a size several times the diameter of the bolts. Murphy sold the plane.

Leo Nomis worked in Hollywood as a general stuntman, stunt pilot, and actor. Apart from his singular confidence, Leo possessed a keen sense of humor along with a modest dignity. His face, a tally of numerous disastrous encounters with an assortment of uncompromising objects, gave rise to many barroom stories. Despite his conspicuous scars confined to the bridge of his nose and forehead, the rest of his chiseled face remained unblemished.

As a young man, Leo succumbed to the allure of life with a traveling carnival. Joining a troupe, he performed loops with a bicycle. The feat began on a narrow track high above the ground which curved to ground level and then curved up and over to complete the loop. One foggy night, Leo skidded off the top of the loop. While recovering from minor injuries, he learned to dive into a net from atop a lofty ladder. The routine consisted of a headfirst plunge, with a last minute tuck to insure landing on his shoulders and back. Stakes, topped with vicious looking points, surrounded the net. To create more death-defying drama, Leo gradually extended the ladder to a height of one hundred and five feet. During his first performance at this height, as gusting winds caused the ladder to sway more than usual, Leo plummeted toward the net to set a new record. His attempt proved successful despite the few broken bones he suffered when the net broke.

Not long after being released from the hospital, Leo decided to become a hot air balloon parachutist with a troupe that toured county fairs. His job required him to grab a trapeze attached to a parachute, itself attached to the ascending balloon. Leo didn't fare much better with this new occupation than with his previous ones. During one ascension, the rising balloon drug him across the kerosene stove used to inflate the balloon. Spilled kerosene soaked his shirt; a spark from the stove set him on fire. Too high to let go of the trapeze, he held on until he reached an altitude sufficient to pull the parachute's rip cord, burning all the while. A waiting ambulance sped Leo, with a severely burned back, to the hospital.

Recovered from his burns, Leo chose a more conservative vocation. He took up dirt track auto racing at county fairs but quickly discovered that pilots who performed at the fairs in their biplanes received a higher salary. Before World War I, Leo had completed a course of flight instruction which enabled him to instruct for the Army. He survived one serious crash while in the Air Corps. In an intentional spin, the drain plug to the motor's oil sump loosened, fogging his goggles with a mist of leaking oil. To retain visibility, Leo lifted his goggles just as the plug dropped out completely. The gush of hot oil blinded him but somehow he managed to regain normal flight. Having no idea of his altitude, other than the certainty that it was decreasing rapidly, Leo quickly initiated a desperate plan of action to save himself. He attempted to maintain a glide path by listening to the sound of the rigging wires. As his speed increased, the pitch amplified; as it decreased, the pitch lessened. The technique made it possible to keep from either over speeding or entering a stall. A very ragged, porpoising descent resulted. He would never know how much his efforts helped, if at all, except that he survived the crash.

In 1922, Leo participated in De Mille's film *Manslaughter.* The movie starred Thomas Meighan and Leatrice Joy. Leo doubled for Miss Joy who causes the death of a motorcycle officer as she flees from prosecution. The scene called for Leo to spin Joy's car, stopping it in the middle of the road so the officer would crash into it. When the original motorcycle stuntman realized the danger involved, he quit. Leo promptly volunteered to do both stunts.

Despite De Mille's directions to impact the car at 25 mph, Leo wanted to reach a speed of 45 mph, fast enough to be thrown over the hood and on to mattresses positioned on the other side of the vehicle. Rugged braces welded to the motorcycle prevented its front from collapsing and hooking him with one of the handle bars. Just before the impact, Leo stiffened his arms, allowing them to act as levers and provide sufficient lift to propel him forward. His plan succeeded; he neatly cleared the car and the mattresses, breaking a collar bone and adding another gash to his head.

One early Saturday morning, Leo took Moye up in his Jenny and introduced him to aerobatic maneuvers. Spectacular wing-overs, loops, and spins intensified Moye's desire to become a pilot. Waiting until some future date seemed unbearable to the seventeen-year-old. Six years of college, an indefinite term as a destitute neophyte in the law firm, marriage, and the probable financial burden of raising a family relegated flying to wishful thinking. The dismal prospect of delaying flight lessons called for immediate measures of some desperation.

With one month left before completing his studies at Hollywood High, Moye approached Bellande to unburden the frustrations he faced in his quest to learn how to fly. Bellande listened patiently and, as Moye sat opposite him in a state of total defeat, suggested that he approach Jim Webster with the following proposal. Moye would trade working on the field for flight instruction. Bellande believed that Webster would agree to this exchange. The idea seemed plausible to Moye.

The 'great' Leo Nomis. Photo courtesy of Katy Ranaldi.

Near the end of that same day Moye waited until Webster's office emptied. Entering the dusty little cubbyhole, he found Webster tilted back in his desk chair, hands clasped behind his head.

He appeared distant.. Not wishing to disturb him, but having spent the entire day preparing to present his proposition, Moye let the words tumble out uncontrollably. "Jim, I've simply got to learn how to fly!"

"Look," Moye continued in earnest, "I'm free every week day afternoon and all day Saturday and Sunday. I'm a hard worker and I've had quite a bit of experience with tools so I could do almost any kind of work you give me and I wouldn't need to be paid in cash because I would take my pay in flying time and I wouldn't mind working after. . ."

The thud of Webster's chair hitting the wooden floor abruptly ended Moye's passionate outpouring. The manager's response sounded edgy with impatience. "Okay! Okay! When can you start?"

"Today," Moye stammered. "How much flying time do I get for my work?"

Webster, now presenting himself as a canny business man, explained the rigors of his strict requirements as an employer and the wide scope of Moye's possible duties. They would range from virtual beast of burden to quasi-mechanic. Webster professed commiseration over the paltriness of Moye's prospective remuneration. Costs limited it to one minute of instruction for each hour of labor. Each fifteen hour accumulated work credit entitled Moye to a fifteen minute lesson. Once he realized that becoming a pilot was within reach, Webster could not have set forth unacceptable conditions.

By the end of the day, Moye had earned two and a half minutes of flying time. He arrived home and settled down long enough to do some figuring. Despite Webster's self-image, he discovered a fact certainly not overlooked by his new boss. Based upon the current rate of $25.00 an hour for instruction, Moye would earn the equivalent of almost 42 cents an hour, more than generally paid for demanding work. In the end, Moye would fare even better. Bellande invariably stretched the fifteen minute lesson to a half hour. No doubt fully aware of Bellande's shortcomings as a timekeeper, Webster chose not to challenge the discrepancy.

Webster insisted upon one prerequisite to Moye's flight

training. His father needed to sign a written release. A man of his word, his father couldn't refuse. The senior Stephens told his son earlier that, if he wanted to fly, he would have to wait until he could do it on his own. Moye's sincere commitment and talent for bargaining accomplished just that. Presented with the facts, his father offered no argument, signed the document, and Moye's goal became a reality.

Handing Webster the signed permission, Moye asked if the rumors of Rogers Airport relocating were true. Webster replied in the affirmative. The new location would be on the northwest corner of Western Avenue and Ballona (now El Segundo) Boulevard. Captain G. Allan Hancock, from whom they leased the airport property, had notified Webster that the lease would not be renewed following its expiration at the end of December. Hancock intended to subdivide the land.

The relocation of Rogers Airport caused Moye to reconsider his agreement with Webster. The distance required a daily round-trip of thirty miles, considerably more than the mile and a half to the Wilshire-Crescent site. Again, Moye thought about his future as he weighed the advantages and disadvantages of continuing his flying lessons with Bellande. Established since earliest recollection, studying law and becoming a member of the family law firm had been his singular goal. The idea of replacing a law career with one in aviation was nonexistent. In the end, Moye thought he could have the best of both worlds. A lawyer's salary would afford him the opportunity to continue flying and eventually enable him to purchase his own airplane. He would continue his relationship with Webster at the new field and, in nine months, if all went as planned, he would enter Stanford University with a pilot's license.

Compared to the Wilshire location, the new Western Avenue airfield was less than geographically desirable. A deep gully curving through the field restricted flying operations to one north-south strip paralleling Western and another east-west landing area following Ballona. With a westerly wind, pilots flew off the east-west runway. The column of tall eucalyptus trees along Western Avenue, however, made landing to the west difficult. Because the field sloped downhill from north to south and eucalyptus trees lined

Ballona, a northerly landing proved risky for the best pilot. As a result, landing downhill with an almost direct cross-wind or landing through the high trees along Ballona remained the only viable choices. They all presented a considerable combination of pitfalls, especially for a novice in an era before brakes. How he responded to these landing challenges contributed to and increased Moye's piloting skills.

Moye's first flying lesson took place a few days before Rogers officially ceased operations at the Wilshire-Crescent site. Bellande invited Moye to accompany him on a routine test flight in one of the Standards. Referred to as an indoctrination flight, it would not count against Moye's flight time credits. Even so, Bellande followed an instructor's customary practice of occupying the front cockpit in order to give directions to Moye by means of hand signals. As the Standard lifted off, Moye exuded confidence. He felt handling an airplane would pose no problems for him. In a favorite childhood daydream, Moye envisions the pilot of an airplane becoming incapacitated. He masterfully takes over for him and brings the ship in for a perfect three-point landing. Anxious to demonstrate his ability as a natural born pilot, Moye believed that Bellande will be impressed and realize his new student requires only a meager amount of dual before being counted as a pilot.

When Bellande signaled for him to take over, Moye found coordinating the controls not as simple as he thought. He became frustrated as he struggled to compensate for too much or too little of any one control aspect. After approximately ten minutes, Bellande shook the stick to indicate he had the controls. Moye felt certain that Bellande would tell him to forget about flying and concentrate on becoming a lawyer.

Back on the ground, Moye, now miserable, waited for the blow to fall. Instead, Bellande explained the trick of easing aileron forces with the rudder and commented that the first regular lesson would be from the new field. Moye found an empty hangar to ponder his next move. Belonging to a social order whose expectations loomed high, his emotional disappointment was not unexpected. Many hours of flight would pass before Moye felt secure with his piloting skills.

3

FLYING LESSONS

With Eddie Bellande as his flight instructor, Moye's training would be exceptional. Bellande possessed undeniable patience and irrefutable talent in the air. As both men walked toward the flight-line at the new Rogers Airport, Bellande preached his gospel about the art of flying. "The real guts of flying are based on what goes on or does not go on, in the head of the pilot. The more gifted you are in developing a feel for the plane, the faster you will learn to fly. Speed is control. If you're fast, you'll last."

Bellande rattled off other sayings Moye took to heart.

"Never bet your life on the odds of your engine not quitting. It's enough that the damn things do. Every flight should be made with the attitude that the engine can demonstrate the soundness of Murphy's Law at any instant. Always have in sight an area suitable for landing that can be reached in a power-out glide. You will hear it said that in a forced landing, a good landing is any landing you can walk away from. It hardly seems likely the genius who dreamed up the saying first sought the opinions of very many airplane owners. I hope you will come to accept their view that the only good landing under any circumstances is one that you can fly away from."

Reaching the airplane, Bellande said, "I'll pass along more

Charismatic Eddie Bellande.
Katy Ranaldi image.

gems of wisdom from time to time but for now, we'd better get cracking."

Moye's frame of mind bore little resemblance to that during his indoctrination flight. Analyzing his mistakes, his overconfidence gave way to humility. By the end of his first thirty minute lesson, Moye performed level flight and turns well enough for Bellande to introduce him to take-offs and landings their next session.

"Landings are one of the toughest parts of learning to handle an airplane, so the sooner we get started on them, the better." Bellande explained. "You can't make landings without air work, so most of your air work practice will take care of itself in the process."

Following that first lesson, Moye blissfully began earning credit for the next. He had been averaging four hours a day after school and eight hours a day on the weekends but now that his post-graduate year was completed, he worked a minimum of eight hours every day. He couldn't have been happier. Mechanics taught him how to rebuild wings and perform routine engine maintenance and top overhauls. Entries in his logbook accumulated quickly flying with Bellande and anyone else that offered to take him aloft. Just two weeks into summer, Moye had made half a dozen landings in a stubble field adjacent to Rogers. Bellande chose the field to give Moye the opportunity to land into the wind with no obstructions. These six landings convinced Bellande that Moye possessed enough skill to tackle the perverse north-south runway of the airport. Once again, his landings reflected his growing competence with the airplane.

Although Moye felt he was ready to solo after only four hours of flight time, Bellande insisted that he learn the procedure for wing-overs and spin recovery, the only deviations from straight and level flight that Fritz Mathews permitted in the Standard. Robbie Robinson had torn the wings off one a year before. He believed that diving an airplane could cure deafness and made a valiant effort to cure a passenger with this affliction. Sadly, no one survived the crash to give a report.

After Moye became proficient with spins and wing-overs, Bellande presented him with a seemingly insurmountable hurdle. He could not solo until he became a man. Taking him at his word, Moye gave considerable thought about violating the lessons of his youth. His parents instilled a belief in premarital abstinence and its importance to a successful marriage. Moye's love and respect for them induced him to please them unconditionally. This included attending Kramer's Dancing Academy on South Grand Avenue every two weeks. Wearing stiff Eton collars that pinched their necks, black ties, and dark blue serge suits, the boys were required to follow strict rules. Mr. Kramer instructed the boys to approach prospective partners, seated primly in chairs arranged along the walls, with a proper bow. Carrying clean handkerchiefs so not to stain their partner's gown, they then asked for 'the pleasure of the dance'. They could not cut across the dance floor to accomplish this task. They were required to walk around the floor to reach the girls. Moye thought his and the other teenagers' parents "were possibly motivated by some latent tribal compulsion to foster continuing consanguinity" in requiring their attendance at Kramer's. 1

At this juncture in his life, Moye decided that flying took precedence over propriety. Finding someone with whom to fulfill Bellande's request seemed another matter. Moye did not know a single female that would be inclined to cooperate. He spent an entire week arguing his deplorable status with Bellande. Then, possibly as a conciliatory measure, Bellande arranged an evening of dinner and dancing at Culver City's Green Mill Night Club. He persuaded a young woman in her mid-twenties to be Moye's date. Palmer Nichols, a former student of Bellande's, and the two girls Nichols and Bellande escorted, made up the rest of the party. Moye enjoyed himself despite being reminded to talk about something other than flying. When his date suggested he call her, Moye was flattered. If Moye thought Bellande possessed an ulterior motive for the evening, he quickly dismissed the idea. The girl seemed much too nice - and nice girls have morals. Moye never did call the girl. He thought his efforts to sustain a conversation with an older woman would prove disastrous.

The impasse between Bellande and Moye lasted a total of two weeks. Much to Moye's surprise – and relief – the stalemate ended suddenly. Taxiing to the flight line following a routine lesson, Moye reflected morosely on the tribulations of chastity. Dejected, he prepared to cut the switch when Bellande stopped him and pronounced the golden words as he jumped from the cockpit to the tarmac, "Okay. Take her around."

A sudden surge of emotion swept away Moye's low spirits. Bellande barely cleared the take-off area as Moye powered up the lumbering Standard to match his zeal.

"I was filled with a very special sense of superiority from my lofty vantage, looking down on the mundane and what seemed insignificant. My destiny was in my hands alone. I would have continued contemplating the essence of flight but Bellande did just tell me, *take it around*."

Bud Creeth greeted Moye with a warm handshake and an understanding smile as he climbed from the cockpit, gestures which spoke volumes. After eight hours of flight time, Moye became a member of the intimate fraternity of pilots. Here, a wordy initiation would have been meaningless.

As he looked back toward the flight line, the once ugly duckling known as a Standard J-1 transformed into the finest-looking airplane known to man. Such was his first solo flight. Even after accumulating thousands of hours of flight time, the milestone remained a magnificent memory.

Moye, proud of his accomplishment, wanted to share its significance with his friends. The following day, he persuaded Palmer Nichols to fly with him. Palmer thanked him for the ride but didn't seem impressed. The intrepid Fritz Ripley placed himself in the passenger seat a few days later. Determined to demonstrate his expertise to the limits of his ability, Moye decided to conclude the flight with a wing-over and a spin. The maneuvers resulted in a

Moye, bursting with pride and confidence, took his father flying in the Standard. Photo courtesy of Steve Lefever.

substandard performance. Moye didn't generate enough speed in his dive and the wing-over degenerated into a sloppy half roll at the top. The plane hung there, in the open sky, inverted. This, in itself, injured Moye's pride, but to make matters worse, he had fallen partially out of the cockpit. As he clung to the top of the stick, falling dust and gravel enveloped him. Mercifully, Fritz appeared too engrossed in the stunt to notice Moye hanging helplessly behind him. After what seemed an eternity, the ship's forward section fell below the horizon and Moye regained his seat. He chose not to attempt a spin. Fritz's polite appreciation of the flight proved disappointing to Moye.

A former high school football teammate, Ward Poulson, became Moye's next passenger who also took the flight quite matter-of-factly. Frustrated with his inability to impress his friends, Moye thought his chances would improve with a female passenger aboard, provided he could summon up enough courage to approach one with an invitation. Alice Reynolds, a frequent dancing partner at Kramer's Dancing School, seemed the most promising choice. Moye felt more at ease with Allie than other girls he knew. When asked, she accepted without hesitation. Alice found the series of wing-overs and six-turn spin thrilling but her response left Moye's stature unchanged or so it appeared to him. Harry Rosselot, whom Moye fruitlessly strove to impress during his first trip to Rogers, gave Moye a lukewarm reaction upon landing. Moye's father consented to fly with him despite his dim view of the sport. Moye hoped that his father would regard his skills as masterful. Foul weather dashed that optimism. Shortly after take-off, low lying stratus clouds forced Moye to return to the airport.

Mid-summer, the engine on Moye's Model T ceased operating which threatened his job and flying opportunities. Creeth, living just four blocks from the Stephens' home, offered Moye a lift to and from work until the Ford was repaired. A graduate of the Colorado School of Mines, Creeth hoped to capitalize on his wartime experiences and begin an air service with new Curtiss *Orioles* powered by 150 hp Curtiss K-6 engines. The superior performing *Orioles* incorporated plywood monocoque fuselages. Damage to a conventional fuselage, stick and wire construction, could be repaired at a minimum cost; a damaged monocoque structure demanded scrapping. A run of mishaps on the part of Creeth's pilots put him out of business. As a result, he took a position at Rogers as sales manager and test pilot to pay off his outstanding debt on the *Orioles*.

Just after Rogers moved to the Western Avenue site, Osmond T. Belcher, owner of Belcher Manufacturing Company, offered Creeth a job testing his new cabin monoplane, the *California*. Constructed with a novel form of plywood in which the center ply consisted of thin corrugated strips of wood, identical wooden strips interwoven into a sheet and pressed flat formed the outer piles. The finished product, referred to as a basket-weave style, was extremely light and strong. A full-cantilevered high wing gave the palatial air liner an exceptionally clean line. Powered by a 200 hp Hall Scott L-6, the monoplane promised to be a high performance craft. After completion of a successful test program, Belcher planned to go into production and distribute the ship nationally. [2]

Tempted to accept without hesitation, Creeth asked for a

few days to consider Belcher's offer. The fact that the position offered Creeth a way out of his financial straits made it very attractive. Visible features of the plane, however, gave rise to several questions. Most dealt with the designer's phobia regarding metal. Belcher avoided using metal wherever possible. The elevators and rudder were actuated by wooden push-pull rods. The wing attached to the fuselage by numerous windings of cord wrapped around the upper longerons and impregnated with aircraft dope to provide tautness. A strong possibility existed that portions of the ship not open to inspection possessed similar anomalies.

The *California* neared completion about the time Moye started riding with Creeth. During the round-trip to Rogers, Creeth unburdened his doubts and hopes concerning the impending test program. He knew the dangers, some expected, but the ones undisclosed made him apprehensive. Belcher, however, advanced persuasive arguments in support of his unusual practices. Confident of his abilities, Creeth accepted the job, continuing to work at Rogers until the project required his full-time participation. On days when Creeth was at the test site, Moye picked up hot lunches at the airport lunch stand and flew them to the mile square, open stubble field southwest of Inglewood, later designated as Mines Field (now Los Angeles International Airport). He found performing useful work as a pilot extremely rewarding regardless of the relative unimportance of the tasks.

The test program proceeded satisfactorily until the *California* developed aileron flutter during take-off. Creeth had just cleared a barbed wire fence and overhead telephone line at the western edge of the field when the ailerons began vibrating. A thorough investigation revealed that the aileron controls were improperly rigged. After rigging them correctly, Creeth made several test flights and found the flutter concern resolved. He then flew the *California* to Rogers Airport in preparation for an official demonstration flight. Along with plenty of press, hundreds gathered that Sunday - July 27, 1924. Creeth picked up Moye as usual en route to the airport. Moye recalled the excitement his friend displayed. "The ship could not fail to be an outstanding success," Creeth boasted. Listening to his enthusiastic outpouring,

Moye cheered up. He felt no one could be more deserving of that sometimes elusive stroke of good fortune. 3

Normal operations ensued at Rogers while Belcher's crew readied the *California* for a mid-afternoon test run. The field crew pushed the three Standards out of their hangars, hoisted their tails onto the bed of the flat-rack, and towed them to the flight line. Anticipating brisk weekend business, Moye washed motors and lubricated overheads. The task would be repeated during the day, frequently with engines running. Budwig, Bellande, and Doc Whitney seldom left their cockpits to accommodate the line of passengers waiting for a short hop around the field. Moye, always on the run, loading and unloading passengers, accompanied by the often repeated, "Get the ladder, Moye!"

At mid-day, the passenger hops halted. No one wanted to miss the feature attraction. The roar of the *California*'s powerful motor announced the start of the eagerly awaited event. Mr. and Mrs. Belcher, their son, and the shop superintendent sat in the passenger compartment. When the plane reached the take-off area, the superintendent climbed out to help turn the airplane into the wind. Before he could hop back in, Creeth pushed the throttle forward and took off. The ship climbed impressively into the sky. After completing a circuit of the airport, the *California* turned directly toward the field to prepare for a low approach down the runway to demonstrate its superlative speed.

Approaching with breath-taking swiftness, disaster struck. The once stable wing-tips suddenly blurred - aileron flutter! Moye, horrified, saw a burst of splinters erupt from a sizable outer portion of the left wing's trailing edge. Almost simultaneously, the ship rolled viciously to the left. In an effort to lose speed and diminish the flutter, Moye thought that Creeth may have attempted to pull up. As the roll whipped into an inverted position, the ship's nose dropped. The *California* plunged into the ground not more than 75 yards from where Moye stood. It all happened in the space of a heart beat.

Stunned by the spectacle, Moye rushed to help his friend. As he neared the crash, reason refused to let him absorb the excruciatingly painful scene. The impact had driven the cabin forward, enveloping the engine. The plywood fuselage had exploded into fragments, scattering in all directions. The four passengers, including Creeth, lay like rag dolls in a relatively clear area. Moye knelt at his friend's side wanting to breathe life into him, so buoyant just minutes before. Many years later, Moye remembered the anguish he felt. In one brief instant, a good friend disappeared forever. Never before had Moye experienced such strong emotions. In an attempt to deal with Creeth's death, Moye immersed himself in work and flying for the rest of the summer. His dedication and persistance as a student pilot resulted in Bellande officially designating Moye a pilot. He received the following document on September 12, 1924.

TO WHOM IT MAY CONCERN: The bearer Moye W. Stephens whose photograph and signature appear below, has completed the regular course in flying at Rogers Airport and having passed the required texts is judged capable of flying and operating a heaveir than air machine (aircraft). Moye F. Stephens collection.

FLYING LESSONS

Fall weather cooled southern California and Moye began preparations to enter Stanford University with mixed feelings. He looked forward to starting this next stage of his life but, at the same time, was nostalgic about leaving behind a way of life that had taught him so much. He could not defer the inevitable though. His upbringing had been purposeful and his future determined. In October 1924, Moye said good-bye to his family and drove north to Palo Alto, his home for the next four years.

An apt pupil, Moye excelled in his studies but never welcomed the school terms with open arms. He viewed them as essential periods of resignation to be endured in the name of education and a college degree. Anticipating holidays and sports provided his only reprieve from the grind of academics. During high school, he had participated in boxing, water polo, and, as a second string tackle, football. The latter was at the request of his father. When Moye tried out for Stanford's freshman football team, he was content to be selected for the second string *grays.* This allowed him to sit out most of the season and avoid being kicked, pummeled, and literally ground into the dirt, something he found distasteful. Still, he found the pep talk from coach Andy Kerr prophetic.

"In view of the numbers gathered here today to try out for the team, it is obvious the majority will not make it. Those of you who do not must in no way feel wanting. The properties needed to be a top flight football player may not be those needed to reach the top in other pursuits. Remember, there were football stars who failed miserably as pilots during the war. And, on the other hand, there were football dropouts who became combat aces."

When the football season ended, Moye turned to polo. He believed his experience riding horses at the La Verne ranch gave him a basis for being accepted. Moye joined the ROTC Field Artillery Unit, a prerequisite to becoming a member of the polo team. Army officers selected new remounts for the Stanford ROTC detachment on the basis of their adaptability to polo. The team's older horses then retired to less glamorous functions, serving as mounts for the officers or as draft animals to pull the limbers attached to the caissons and French field pieces in military exercises.

Before participating on the field, Moye sat atop a horse

anchored in the center of the practice cage, hitting a willow ball to develop accuracy and power. Weeks later, he participated with the team on a limited basis. For the remainder of his freshman year and during most of his sophomore year, Moye trained with the other beginners. He eventually advanced to the first team, realizing that no amount of tedious preparation could be viewed as excessive in light of the ultimate rewards of a good game. No other sport offered the satisfaction, both in variety and intensity, than polo when played by skilled contestants. The game required teamwork equal to that of other team sports, but not only between teammates. A rider established a very special relationship with his mount. Moye described his admiration of the game "as the enchantment imparted by a symphony". It could be surmised that Moye found significant similarities between polo and flying.

Moye joined Delta Theta Phi, a law fraternity, and Alpha Delta Phi, an academic fraternity, as a freshman. Founded as a literary society in 1832, Alpha Delta Phi evolved into one of the most distinguished of the original American college fraternities. The principle purpose they espoused focused on the moral, social and intellectual development of its members. Perhaps his membership in the fraternity motivated Moye to write the short story, *Ghosts of the Air*. He co-authored it with roommate Jim Hiatt. Published by the Popular Fiction Publishing Company, the story centers around a dare devil stunt man who offends everyone at the air field with his contemptuous reticence and brutish manners. Returning from his last performance, he falls to his death during an unappreciated cross-country wing-walking. The pilot who has grown to loathe him returns to the field without him. Later, the pilot is consumed with the stuntman's ghost and jumps to his death. [4]

The summer of 1925, having completed his freshman year, Moye accompanied his family to Hawaii. They boarded the *President Taft* in San Francisco on June 27 and arrived in Honolulu July 3. Nearly one month was spent on the islands before the *City of Los Angeles* returned them to the mainland. The remainder of his summer, Moye gave flight instruction and passenger hops, worked in the shop, and was presented with an attractive airplane rental agreement by Jim Webster. [5]

36

Dick Ranaldi was just a boy - 14 years old - when he learned to fly. Photo courtesy of Katy Ranaldi.

Following Creeth's death, his mother experienced difficulty collecting the indemnity arranged for her should her son be killed while testing the *California*. When Moye told his father of the situation, Moye Sr. expedited securing payment for Mrs. Creeth. In appreciation, Webster volunteered to rent Moye his Standards for five dollars an hour, a generous offer and one close to Webster's actual cost. Moye's increased allowance since enrolling at Stanford and money earned working for Webster allowed him to take advantage of this arrangement. He frequently flew the short distance to Clover Field to visit former Rogers' pilots – Leo Nomis, Byron Morgan, Loop Murphy, Victor Fleming, and Dick Ranaldi.

Dick had given up his job dishwashing at Rogers to look after Leo's airplanes when he moved to Clover. An excellent opportunity, Leo taught him the basic of mechanics. Dick learned quickly and began accompanying Leo and other stunt pilots to picture locations. On most of these flights, he handled the controls while the pilot enjoyed a smoke. One day, after a shoot, Leo signaled Dick to take over. Halfway through the cigarette, Leo noticed how smooth and steady his young apprentice flew. He motioned for a series of turns that Dick executed flawlessly. "This kid's doing a fine job," thought Leo. "Somebody ought to give him some landings and solo him." Landing at Clover, Leo gave Dick ten landings, one right after the other, and bestowed the title of pilot upon him.

The following day, Dick announced that he needed to build his flying time and was going to teach his pal Al Morgan to fly. Leo, a cautious businessman, asked Dick if his prospective student had any money. He did - $5 for a half hour lesson. After the allotted thirty minutes, Dick declared Al a pilot. Between the two of them, they had 90 minutes of flying time and 10 landings. Al, the son of a UCLA professor, was a tall, good-looking young man whose deceptively sober bearing led Dick to nickname him *Deke*, short for Deacon. His droll sense of dry, deadpan humor acted as a foil to Dick's sparkling wit. When Dick introduced Moye to Al, they formed a lasting friendship.

Clover Airfield was developed by the city of Santa Monica in early 1922. The field's purpose was two-fold. The Army Air Service Reserve unit located its hangars on the northeast corner of the field; a row of thirteen small civilian hangars extended westward along the northern boundary and housed a variety of commercial businesses. Kenneth Montee, one of the original tenants, served as an instructor at Kelly Field during the war. He taught his brothers, Harold and Ralph, and his father, J. W. *Dad* Montee, to fly. Together, they operated the K. W. Montee Aircraft Company specializing in "Aerial Survey, Oblique Photography, and Custom Built Aircraft" and any other flying operation that could turn an honest dollar. Al Wilson, though primarily a stunt pilot, engaged in buying and selling airplanes. Bob Lloyd, who previously worked for B. H. Delay at Delay's Venice airfield, owned the lunch stand, operated a service station for airplanes, and participated in exhibition flying. 6

Several aircraft manufacturing companies set up shop at

Clover. Lloyd Stearman assembled his prototypes in Fred Hoyt's hangar. L. Morton Bach designed his own aircraft as well as provided general aviation maintenance and gave rides in his Standard J-1 nicknamed *King Tut*. Douglas Aircraft Company achieved the most success as a serious aeronautical enterprise at Clover. The factory, located on the corner of Wilshire Boulevard and 26th Street, manufactured their designs and towed them, minus wings, to the Clover Field hangar for final assembly and test flying. 7

The majority of Clover's civilian residents were former barnstormers. They earned this moniker due to their similarity to barnstorming actors who traveled through the rural areas of America staging performances. Conventional theaters didn't exist so actors settled for barns to display their talents. Pilots, existing on the meager returns of passenger hops and stunting exhibitions, performed in small town cow pastures and hayfields. Many hoped for a stable career in aviation but those opportunities were few. As a result, their love of flying relegated them to a vagabond's existence. By 1926, fixed base operations in the larger metropolitan areas offered an adequate income. Clover Field was no exception. A steady income could be earned from flying charters, passenger hops, flight instruction, and what became the most conspicuous activity on the field - stunt flying. 8

By 1925, Clover Field became known as the center for exhibition and stunt flying. Leo Nomis, Frank Clarke, Al Wilson, Art Goebel, E. L. *Remmy* Remlin, and Frank *Swede* Tomick, reputedly the foremost stunt pilots of the era, resided at Clover. Al Johnson, Speed Osborne, Ivan Unger, Spider Matlock, Stub Campbell, Gladys Ingle, Gladys Roy, and Ethel Dare specialized in the art of wing-walking, plane changing, and parachuting over the field. All the wing-walkers distinguished themselves with unique feats. Gladys Ingle, the most accomplished of them, changed planes in mid-air and shot an arrow at a target from the top wing of a Curtiss Jenny. Billed as the *Flying Witch* and the first woman to change planes in the air, Ethel Dare specialized in the Iron Jaw Spin. Tossed around by the slipstream, she twirled from the end of the rope using a special mouthpiece clinched tightly between her teeth. 9

The aerial photo shows the Clover Field civilian hangars along the north of the field. Photo courtesy of Katy Ranaldi.

Stunt flying became popular as part of public exhibitions and in motion pictures. Motion picture stunting comprised special newsreel episodes and film sequences. Stunts for newsreel episodes were customarily dreamed up by stunt men and sold to Pathe News through two of their cameramen, Joe Johnson and Sam Greenwald. Most were pure, harebrained dare-deviltry. Frank Clarke changed planes while hand-cuffed; Al Wilson clung to a strut while Gil Budwig looped several times; and Wilson also performed a double plane change. Some ended tragically; a few provided amusement to highlight a plot. Frank Clarke and Al Wilson performed just the kind of scenario that directors loved. Clarke flew low over the front lawn of the Wilshire Avenue Ambassador Hotel to allow Wilson to exit the airplane by parachute. Newsreel cameramen, and reporters, stood ready. Clad in a business suit, helmet, goggles, and parachute, Wilson climbed out onto the wing and waited for Clarke's signal to pull the rip cord. The timing was critical to insure the chute opening and pulling him from the plane at the right altitude. This precision provided greater accuracy in pinpointing the chosen landing spot.

After landing, Wilson removed the parachute, opened a suitcase strapped in front of his body, and took out a straw hat to replace his helmet and goggles. With the parachute bundled under one arm and the suitcase in the opposite hand, he made his way to the hotel's reception desk trailed by a cortege of newsmen. He gave a short speech to the reporters about what would certainly become the future for hotel arrivals. As luck would have it, the proposed stunt failed to result in the free room Wilson expected.

Instances in which stuntmen's skills proved worthwhile seemed rare. From time to time, an airplane's wheel fell off when a mechanic overlooked installing the cotter pin which secured the wheel to the axle. Jerry Phillips, a Clover Field pilot, lost a wheel in just this manner. He learned of the dilemma on final approach. Phillips did not overlook the significance of Ivan Unger atop the hump in the landing area holding a tire over his head. Executing a missed approach, he gained altitude to ponder the problem. Meanwhile, Unger boarded another Jenny to attempt a rescue. As his pilot approached to secure a position alongside Phillips' Jenny, Unger made his way out along the leading edge of the right lower wing. Reaching the outer strut, he climbed to the upper wing and, bolstering his legs against the cabane struts, stood erect. Phillips maneuvered his plane into position to enable Unger to transfer planes. Once in place, the weight of the replacement wheel and tire became unwieldy in the slipstream making it impossible for Unger to slide it onto the axle. The two planes maneuvered into position and Unger transferred back to his Jenny. Next, Al Johnson went aloft with a wheel minus the tire. Successful in his attempt, he sat on the leading edge of the lower wing with his shoe against the end of the axle to hold the wheel in place for the remainder of the flight.

Speed Osborne performed an even more dramatic example of a plane rescue. Bob Lloyd took Jackie Dare aloft for an exhibition parachute jump in Bach's *King Tut*. The regulation exhibition parachute, packed in a sack, hung below the leading edge of the wing. Normally, the momentum of the parachutist's fall forced the parachute from the sack. Jackie's slight build, however, did not provide enough weight to pull the chute out. After jumping, Jackie dangled helplessly below the airplane.

The continued drag on the left wing alerted Lloyd that Jackie and the parachute had not separated from the airplane. He could only imagine the young girl's fruitless and exhaustive efforts to climb back on the wing. Fuel starvation would ultimately force Lloyd to land with probable fatal consequences to the imperiled girl. Osborne volunteered to do a rescue. Transferring to *King Tut*, he attempted to pull the girl back onto the wing without success. After several futile attempts, Osborne worked his way into the cockpit to confer with Lloyd. They determined that if Osborne could loosen the chute, Lloyd could position the plane to provide a safe landing spot for Jackie. When ready, Osborne signaled to release the chute and Lloyd throttled back. Their united efforts worked perfectly. Jackie landed in the center of Clover Field, shaken emotionally but otherwise unhurt.

By the time Moye returned to Stanford in the fall, his bank account showed sufficient funds remaining to pay for flying during school breaks. He took advantage of the holidays to keep proficient until a ruptured appendix side lined him at the beginning of the 1926 spring term. Surgery forced him to withdraw from school and return home to convalesce. After several weeks of confinement, Moye felt well enough to make a trip to Clover. The evening before, he called Leo Nomis to make certain he would be on the field the next day. Leo's cordial response evoked visions of a warm reunion. When Moye arrived, he found members of the Thirteen Black Cats stunt team, Al Johnson, Ivan Unger, and Speed Osborne, along with Rupert McCallister, an Australian edition of a remittance man, seated cross-legged in front of Leo's hangar intensely engrossed in a game of red dog poker. Dick Ranaldi, Al Morgan, and Leo were observing. Spotting Moye, Leo shouted out, "Here's Moye. Maybe we can get him to take Otie's girl for that stunt ride!" 10

Having been grounded for some weeks, Moye enthusiastically agreed to take the girl up in Leo's Jenny. Dick and Moye went off to find Otie's girl accompanied by puzzling boos from the remaining pilots. Moye thought their heckling was aimed at him but couldn't understand what he had done to deserve their ridicule. Once airborne, Moye forgot the incident and performed several aerobatic maneuvers much to the young girl's delight. Taxiing toward Leo's hangar, he noticed a military-style line of Clover pilots closely observing him. As Moye and Otie helped the beaming passenger from the Jenny, the group surrounded the ship making an elaborate show of examining it in every detail. They strummed flying wires, thumped struts, kicked tires, and shook the stabilizer and wing tips. They also diligently moved all the control surfaces through their entire arcs of travel. *Speed* Osborne even climbed to the upper wing and inspected the cabane struts and wires, a routine second nature to a wing-walker and plane changer.

Mystified by the meticulous examination, Moye boldly asked, "All right, fellas. I hardly think my splendid example of flying has had time to take effect. What's up?" Leo tentatively replied that they were curious to see how the ship would stand up under ham-fisted piloting.

"The subtle intimation cuts me to the quick," Moye replied indignantly. "If it hadn't been for the well-known Stephens' feather touch, that fugitive from the Flying Junkman would have fallen apart for sure. But why the sudden interest?" 11

"It's strange that you should mention Balboni," Leo responded. "Several weeks ago, I was taking off from the infield of the Culver City board track when the motor quit just as I reached the banked end. I may have stretched the glide a mite to clear the rail or I may have dropped it just a wee bit, but the landing gear came up through the lower wings. I thought about selling the ship to Balboni but after Ranaldi and I talked it over, we decided we could fix it. The wings were the most trouble. We had to find spars from salvaged wings damaged nearer their tips and cut their inner ends to match the good outer portions of my spars. We've just finished recovering the wings. It's too bad you can't see the job we did splicing the spars and replacing the broken ribs. It looks like the patch-up turned out to be okay after all."

Leo's explanation gave clarity to the pilots' earlier booing. They felt Leo was taking advantage of Moye, using him as a test pilot for his patched up Jenny. After that incident, Moye made a habit of asking questions about the recent history of an airplane before stunting, even if it belonged to a friend. Performing aerobatics required the structural integrity of a plane to be sound. For Moye, the condition of his aircraft remained a critical concern, even more so when he began transporting passengers.

4

CLOVER FIELD AND A *TOMMY*

At the time of the impromptu test flight in Leo's Jenny, Moye made a final transition from Rogers to Clover. It made sense. The three pilots that meant the most to him, Leo Nomis, Al Morgan, and Dick Ranaldi, were based at Clover. Moye acted as a stabilizing force between Al and Dick. His reserved demeanor belied a great sense of humor and propensity for enjoying himself. He would never think of squashing Ranaldi's hair-brain schemes, although he definitely assessed the risk factors involved before participating. Al and Dick would look to Moye for advice as their careers continued to connect in the future.

Leo Nomis added his unique style of mentoring to keep Moye, Al, and Dick safe in the skies over southern California. The three young flyers maintained a great respect for Leo's ability and experience. He never lectured them but attempted to advise them in a less than subtle manner. When one of them did something Leo considered too risky, he laughed derisively and delivered a comment to the effect that it was always possible to tell a greenhorn by the cockeyed way he flew. On the other hand, the

Leo Nomis' Jenny at Clover. Moye and Dick had many memories of Leo's exploits in this airplane. Photo courtesy of Katy Ranaldi.

three never clearly understood what Leo considered exceeding the bounds of acceptable flight. He intentionally cracked up airplanes for the movies or pulled off daredevil performances just for the hell of it. Not knowing what Leo might consider going too far served to restrain the three from attempting the unknown and losing his approval.

Leo thought nothing of the inherent risks of having Moye test his Jenny after its sloppy repairs. He engaged Dick in a contest of short take-offs in which they took turns flying the Jenny. Each take-off started from a standstill at a point opposite the row of hangars along the northern boundary of the field. Reaching hangar level, they gained speed and executed a right hand climbing turn over the hangars and the eucalyptus trees behind them. The object of the contest was to see who could make the turn in the shortest distance from the starting point. The boys declared Leo the winner after an outstandingly short effort, from take-off to landing, complete with eucalyptus boughs hanging from this landing gear.

Leo's habit of executing a slanting dive across his hangar roof was, to Moye, a brash temptation of fate. On one occasion, Leo slightly misjudged his pull-out, crashing in front of his hangar. Al, Moye, and Dick rushed to the scene and pulled Leo, reeking of alcohol, from the crumpled Jenny. Much to their relief, a large gash in his forehead appeared to be his only injury. They drove him home and turned him over to his wife Jerry. As they left, they heard him mumbling something about being hit over the head with a bottle of gin.

Not only did Leo take the three young pilots under his wing, he sold Moye his first airplane, a single-seat Thomas Morse Scout S-4-C. Designed and manufactured as an advanced trainer in 1917, the *Tommy*'s postwar civilian use consisted of exhibition flying, training, or sports flying. When Leo purchased the airplane, the olive drab paint scheme made the plane appear insignificant. Repainting the spritely biplane a brilliant emerald green made a lasting impression compared to the unimaginative finish on Rogers' Standards. Leo flaunted his *Tommy* proudly. After moving to Clover, Leo flew the biplane very little, keeping it carefully sheltered in one of his two hangars. On the day Moye debuted as a test pilot in Leo's Jenny, he dropped by Leo's hangar to see if he wanted to sell the *Tommy*. He did – for $400. Moye told him it was as good as sold.

That evening, Moye discussed the purchase with his father. Moye Sr. seemed more concerned with the practicality of a one-seat airplane than the actual purchase of the plane itself. Moye produced a number of arguments for buying the *Tommy*. Acceding at last, his father promised to take a look at Moye's savings account passbook the next morning. They would discuss the matter further when he returned home. The wait proved unbearable for Moye. Did he have enough? If he didn't, would his father consider giving him a loan? The $400 check presented to him by his father answered his question. Only partially aware that his father would not deprive him from pursuing his passion, Moye always wondered how much his savings account actually totaled.

Within hours of receiving the money, Moye became the proud owner of his first airplane! His stance, with chest puffed up and an ear-to-ear grin, said it all!

A French-designed Le Rhone rotary motor provided the power for the *Tommy*. Some pilots considered airplanes equipped with rotary engines difficult to fly. Moye didn't agree. The pilot just

Moye's first airplane, a Thomas Morse Scout known affectionately as a 'Tommy'. Photo courtesy of Katy Ranaldi.

needed to understand how they worked and compensate with their responses. The spinning engine acted as a gyroscope. Because of the gyroscopic precession encountered during maneuvers, a turn to the left tended to force the nose up. A turn to the right forced the nose down. Abrupt maneuvers made the precession phenomena more apparent.

The motor's crankcase and cylinders rotated around the crankshaft with a propeller bolted to the front of the case; the crankshaft bolted stationary to the airplane. The 80 hp Le Rhone included a unique induction-lubrication system. Gasoline and air combined in a 'mixing valve' and fed into the motor's hollow crankshaft. The lubricant, castor oil, fed into the crankshaft from the oil tank. Individual intake pipes leading from the crankcase to the intake valve ports drew the fuel-air-lubricant concoction into the crankcase and cylinders. Tiny globules of castor oil suspended in the mixture provided the total internal lubrication.

A quadrant in the cockpit controlled the fuel-air charge with two, side-by-side levers. A tall lever regulated the flow of gasoline and a short one governed the air intake. The supply of castor oil was adjusted in the cockpit by means of a visible drip valve. After the pilot opened both levers one quarter travel, the mechanic hand propped the engine. With the engine running, the levers were juggled to deliver the maximum rpm, 1210 for a Le Rhone in first class condition. The low, maximum rpm necessitated an oversized propeller to absorb the power.

Satisfied with the engine output, the pilot cut the single magneto ignition by means of an auxiliary switch on the control stick known as the 'blipper button' or 'burp switch'. The momentum of the whirling engine kept it spinning for some time before it slowed to a stop. When the motor slowed to the equivalent of idling speed in a fixed engine, a momentary blip of the blipper button picked it up and kept it from stopping. A series of on-off blips maintained idling speed. Taxiing rpm was attained by sustaining the 'on' periods for an appropriate length of time.

Take-off and the remainder of the flight required maximum rpm. Any attempt to reduce power for prolonged periods by means

Moye was incredibly proud to take possession of the Thomas Morse Scout. Photo courtesy of the Museum of Flight.

of the levers created a disproportionate ratio of castor oil to fuel-air charge and resulted in fouled spark plugs. Judicious blipping slowed the engine for approach and landing. After an 'off' period, switching to 'on' induced a slight roll to the left, a reaction to the inertia of the motor.

The landing characteristics of the *Tommy* received serious criticism. With an excessively far aft center of gravity, any slight deviation from a straight roll-out resulted in a ground loop. In addition, the small rudder provided a marginal amount of control upon landing, even more so with a strong crosswind. The *Tommy*'s lack of brakes did not reduce the potential for ground loops either. Compared to the Jenny or Standard, the biplane's light stick forces surprised Moye. The sensitivity of its controls virtually transformed the airplane into an extension of the pilot's body. The *Tommy* gave Moye an entirely different perspective on the art of flight. Although 'on cloud nine' after his first flight in his new plane, when asked what he thought about the experience, Moye could only response with, "It sure handled nicely."

Although the *Tommy* and other airplanes of the era may have received criticism, the government did not require certification of aircraft until 1926. Even with regulations in place, many designers and manufacturers felt official approval to be an optional consideration. Pilots simply overlooked the shortcomings of their planes and adjusted their flying to accommodate any inadequacies.

One very interesting summer day, Moye discovered that the single seat arrangement of the *Tommy* did not necessarily bar carrying more than the pilot aloft. The occasion involved a black pilot by the name of Julian who planned a transcontinental flight - the first by a black flyer. Despite arranging a departure date and place, Julian did not have an airplane. To resolve the problem, he approached Leo and proposed buying his Jenny with the gate receipts charged at the epic event. Admission would be one dollar per person to watch Julian take off from a large field on Western Avenue just south of Century Boulevard. Leo agreed but remained conservatively optimistic about the revenue that would be collected.

On the day of the flight, Dick Ranaldi flew Leo's Jenny to the designated take-off spot. He would return to Clover with Leo in Victor Fleming's Standard. At least a dozen other pilots from Clover planned to tag along as witnesses to Julian's departure. As Moye taxied out to join the aerial procession, Ivan Unger ran alongside the *Tommy,* waving his thumb in the air. Gasping as he ran, Unger managed to yell out, "Have you got room for a hitch-hiker?" Moye motioned for him to hop on. Although he lacked helmet, goggles, or other protective flying paraphernalia, Unger seated himself unconcernedly on the leading edge of the left lower wing. For security, he wedged his right thigh between the front spar and the double flying wires that angled up to the top of the front strut. His lower legs dangled below the wing. Moye took the veteran stuntman's willingness to ride along with him as a compliment as well as a boost to his status as a pilot.

The arrival of the parade of airplanes at the event site sparked a near disastrous and immediate end to the projected record flight. As the ships landed, the crowd broke through the meager restraints and rushed onto the field. Swarms of excited curiosity seekers surrounded the planes as they attempted to come to a complete stop. It seemed a miracle that no one was decapitated by a whirling prop. Spectators climbing onto wings and pressing toward the cockpits imprisoned the pilots in their planes. Only by yelling and fist-waving did the pilots manage to inch themselves from their cockpits and to the ground. Once there, they asked their passengers to guard the planes so souvenir hunters would not dismantle them.

"Wow!" the irrepressible Dick exclaimed as he appraised the situation. "You could get lost in this tangle and wander around for days. If we get separated and I'm able to find my way out of here, I'll send back a St. Bernard - but without the cask. You characters have been drinking bathtub gin for so long you wouldn't know what to do with first class brandy if it was waved under your noses in crystal goblets. Brandy or no Brandy, the pooch would come in handy as a guide dog if you can't figure out a way to unsnarl the airplanes. But, for now, it's your shindig, Leo. You got any ideas?"

Leo's response indicated no ready solution, stating that

Julian seemed to be the key to the problem. Until he took off, nobody else could. The entire situation seemed out of control. People crashing through the gates prevented the collection of admission fees. Without the money to pay Leo, Julian's chances of making his record flight seemed impossible. The frenzy of the crowd caused him to fear for his life if he didn't depart by airplane. The Clover pilots seemed equally concerned. Leo quickly made a decision. He gave Julian permission to take off but, after circling the field, he would land at Clover. Hopefully, Julian's departure would calm the disorderly crowd.

Hubert Fauntleroy Julian, an early aviator, was known as the Black Eagle of Harlem. Queen Mary Archives photo.

As Leo explained his plan to the other pilots, Julian walked over to the Jenny, climbed into the cockpit, and shouted to the crowd that they needed to clear the take-off area. He also asked the crowd to wish him well as he discoursed on the good fortune of those privileged to witness the start of what would prove an event of tremendous significance.

The Clover pilots, preparing to follow Julian's take-off roll with their own, cranked their engines and, with the help of wing-walkers, inched their way into position behind the Jenny. As the advancing wave of humanity began rolling away on either side of the course, the aircraft began moving slowly forward. A few stragglers remained at the far end of the field as Julian pushed the throttle forward and sped down the uncomfortably narrow lane. The instant before his ship lifted off, one inordinately myopic spectator dove to the ground just as the Jenny's right wing passed over him. Fighting wake turbulence and churning dust, the remaining ships departed in quick succession before the tide rolled back.

Landing at Clover, Julian thanked Leo profusely for his efforts and then beat a hasty retreat. Julian reemerged for a short time in 1931 as a member of the nation's first black precision flying troupe - the Five Blackbirds. William J. Powell and James Herman Banning, both black aviators, started the troupe in 1929 after founding the Bessie Coleman Aero Club at Los Angeles' Eastside Airport. Powell included Julian in his flying act until he realized that the flamboyant Julian was nothing more than a scam artist and an incompetent pilot. In contradiction to Powell's assessment of Julian's flying skills, he became the first black pilot to fly the Atlantic. The 1929 flight took place two years after Lindbergh's success. The young man came to mind when Moye, in 1935, saw a newspaper article regarding a Hubert Fauntleroy Julian, heralded as the "Black Eagle" of Ethiopian Emperor Haile Selassie's Air Force. 1

The summer of 1926 marked two milestones for Moye, the purchase of an airplane and joining the ranks of movie pilots. The WWI movie *Corporal Kate*, a Paramount release starring Vera Reynolds and Kenneth Thompson, set the backdrop for Moye's first motion picture flying job. One scene called for a Sopwith Camel or a close approximation. Leo, in charge of the flying segments, decided that Moye's Thomas Morse Scout would serve the purpose. Moye also piloted Victor Fleming's L-6 Standard, with the larger 200 hp engine, in another scene. The Standard substituted for a German Rumpler. Leading a three ship formation, Moye simulated a bombing attack on a French village. Leo and Frank Clarke flew as pursuit escorts. Leo flew to Moye's right in Fleming's custom-built 180 hp Hisso-powered biplane designed by Edward M. Fisk, a pioneer builder whose aeronautical activities in Venice dated back to 1911. Frank Clarke took up the left wingman position in an International, another Fisk product, powered by a 90 hp OX5. 2

The day of the flight sequence, director Paul Sloan briefed the pilots in front of Leo's hangar. As Sloan departed for the site of the attack, Fleming drove onto the field in his Duisenberg touring car with close friend and noted director Howard Hawks. Fleming, a reserved man, commanded attention when he spoke. Addressing the two pilots who would fly his airplanes, he spoke with an almost macabre tenor.

"Leo, you and Moye were practically standing on top of my Jenny at Rogers Airport when it suffered an unkind fate at the hands of Deed Levy three years ago. I don't know that there is any particular relationship between you two and close proximity to my flying equipment, but please bear in mind any Jonahesque actions today would wipe me out, aeronautically speaking."

A set on the De Mille Culver City studio just north of Baldwin Hills served as the French village. As the pilots approached from the south over the hills, they needed to maintain a high enough altitude to permit a dive long enough in duration to satisfy filming requirements. After their pull-out over the village, explosives strategically placed throughout the set would be touched off to simulate aerial bomb explosions.

Moye circled the studio once to signal the film crew that the three planes were about to make their approach. Throttling back to 50% power, he entered a dive. On the ground, the powder monkeys, their hands poised on the generator plungers, watched the descent of the ships to determine when to set off the blasts. Their timing was critical to prevent a hazardous situation as Ormer Locklear's fatal dependence on non-flying ground personnel had revealed. With the dive underway, Moye realized that a 50 per cent power setting would not permit him to stabilize the speed of the airplane. He began inching the power back to give Leo and Frank a chance to adapt to the change of speed. The drag of the wind milling propeller, combined with the Standard's aerodynamic untidiness, slowed the ship so effectively that the difference in momentum pulled Moye forward in his seat. Leo and Frank fought to remain in formation by fishtailing to slow their speed while Moye concentrated on the correct moment to pull out of the dive. Anticipating a premature blast, he winced as he flew over the set. Much to his relief, the ground crew had done their job. Only Clarke's departure from the formation gave Moye some concern.

Taxiing up to Leo's hangar, he saw Clarke fuming quietly. The twitching of his moustache let everyone know his state of mind. Clarke, with an intimidating glare, demanded to know why Moye throttled back during the dive. Moye could understand Clarke's annoyance about struggling to stay in formation but had no explanation for the intensity of his emotional outburst. Moye apologized and explained his need to lose power in the Standard. Fleming would never forgive him if he crashed. Fleming, leaning against the wing of his airplane, listened to the exchange. He patted the Standard familiarly as he matter-of-factly agreed with Moye's assumption. "Of that you may be sure, my friend. I would have expressly neglected to send flowers to your funeral."

"Lay off the kid, Frank." Leo, also puzzled by Clarke's disturbance, replied. "If Vic will excuse the term, that *box kite* was going too fast. Moye couldn't have done anything else. Anyhow, we finished the dive and the studio can probably buy the shot in spite of our ragged formation."

"So what!" Clarke angrily replied. "That's no skin off my ass! But you've got another thing coming if you don't believe I could have damn well lost a sizable patch when my ailerons gave out during the maneuvering to stay behind that frigging Standard. As far as your worry about the shot is concerned, I didn't lose aileron control until we were pulling up. I had to come home using the rudder to keep the wings level."

Leo, fumbling in a pocket of his leather jacket, produced a crumpled pack of Lucky Strikes. He offered one to Clarke, took one himself and, in a conciliatory gesture, lit both. "In any case," he said, "we all came out of it with our posteriors intact - which is more than could be said if the Standard started falling apart."

Somewhat mollified, Clarke led the way to the International. Evidently, two horns in the aileron control system bent over in such a way to prevent them from being very effective. Fishtailing or swinging the plane's tail from side to side by kicking the rudder back and forth called for abrupt, vigorous use of opposite aileron. The design of the aileron horns on the International simply proved deficient for the drastic maneuvering.

Moye's second flying role in *Corporal Kate* revolved around a parting scene between the heroine and the hero beside the "Sopwith Camel". The studio prepared Moye's *Tommy* by painting the Allied tricolor roundel in water paints on either side of the fuselage. The plane's bright emerald green paint would disappear in the black and white photography. In Moye's scenario, the two stars hug in a farewell embrace after which the hero climbs into the airplane, buckles his helmet's chin strap, and pulls down his goggles. At this point, the director cuts the action to allow Moye to replace the actor in the cockpit. As the shooting resumes, Moye takes off and performs a chandelle as a parting salute to the forlorn sweetheart, tearfully watching her hero depart.

Director Sloan chose the far western end of Clover Field for the scene. Little used, the area suffered a moderate growth of weeds. As a precautionary measure, Moye explored the route on foot to uncover any possible surprises hidden in the grass such as ditches, holes, rocks, and discarded hard objects. Finding nothing, he proceeded to take-off. As he accelerated down the field, Moye felt the drag of the weeds on the landing gear but concluded all would be well once the ship lifted off. Airborne, he leveled off to pick up speed for a steep climbing turn but the airplane refused to accelerate. If he entered a climb, the plane's decreasing speed would put it dangerously close to stalling.

Frank Clarke - premier stunt pilot. Katy Ranaldi photo.

Not wanting to disappoint the director or to endanger himself, Moye questioned why the airplane responded in such an uncharacteristic manner. He then remembered the tumbleweeds ignored during his exploration of the take-off area and pictured them packed against the wire cross-bracing of the landing gear, between the spreader bar and the bottom of the fuselage. Their drag would explain the lack of the ship's acceleration. Moye also feared that the tumbleweeds, absorbing unburned oil, would ignite from an exhaust spark. He decided it best to land. Moye was able to put the plane into a steep turn and side-slip in for a quick landing. While he and Leo dislodged the compacted tumbleweeds, Moye learned that his brief flight provided enough footage for the hero's parting scene to satisfy the director. Moye received $25 for flying the L-6 Standard, $25 for the rental of the *Tommy,* and $25 for flying it. The pay seemed a bonus to the experience of actively participating in a movie.

In time, Frank Clarke smoothed his ruffled feathers. Not a person who made friends easily, his peers considered him something of a loner. His aloofness did not extend to the female sex, however. His successes in this connection proved noteworthy, not at all surprising in view of his exceptional physical attributes. A powerfully built man, he resembled Clark Gable and doubled in several films for the actor. His chiseled features, more regular than the actor's, exuded a greater masculinity. When it came to flying and stunting, his fellow pilots considered Clarke the best of the best.

Clarke claimed his ancestry to be a mixture of Anglo-American, Italian, and, proudly, American Indian. Raised on a cattle ranch in California's San Joaquin Valley, an exhibition by Glenn Curtiss and Charles Hamilton at a Fresno county fair inspired him to learn how to fly. In 1918, at the age of 17, Clarke traded airplane maintenance and part time wing-walking for flying lessons at the Venice Airport. According to rumors, he invited his stepfather to be his first passenger after soloing and then charged the unsuspecting gentleman ten dollars for the ride. He spent the rest of the day offering joy rides to a succession of paying passengers. Clarke became recognized as an outstanding stunt pilot in a surprisingly short time. When the renowned Ormer Locklear and his pilots, *Skeets* Elliot and Shirley Short, arrived on the local scene in July 1919, Clarke possessed a well established reputation. [3]

Locklear stood alone as the great wing-walker/stunt pilot until Clarke, Al Wilson, and Wally Timm perfected the art. Much to the chagrin of Locklear's manager William Pickens, the three began duplicating Locklear's aerial feats and creating their own. When they worked together, Clarke and Timm did the flying and Wilson changed planes. One of Clarke's most notable movie exploits during his early career occurred when a script called for a take-off from Pacific Electric's roof in downtown Los Angeles. A crew disassembled and hoisted Clarke's L-4 Canuck to the top of the twelve story structure for the filming. In order for the reassembled airplane to clear the surrounding parapet, studio carpenters constructed a narrow wooden runway slightly higher than the low wall. When the authorities learned of the project, they reacted with an emphatic veto forcing the director to alter the script. The changes included filming the flight preliminaries and the take-off roll but stopping short of the actual lift-off. That would be edited in later. All proceeded according to plan with one exception. Clarke failed to cut the power and abort the take-off. The Canuck lumbered down the wooden runway, staggered off the end, and settled alarmingly before gaining adequate speed to fly.

The police quickly surrounded Clarke's airplane, handcuffs ready, when he landed at Rogers Airport. Defending his actions, he explained that the tailskid was not going to stop the plane in time to prevent it from tumbling off the edge of the building and into the crowded street below. He insisted that he had no choice but to complete the take-off. Finding no ordinance covering the situation, the officers reprimanded Clarke and departed the field in quiet defeat. Interestingly, the Goodyear blimp just happened to be in place to shoot some excellent footage of the entire scene.

A "Hollywood glamour boy" stunt pilot, along with Paul Mantz, Leo Nomis, and Frank Tomick, Clarke had a reputation for playing pranks. Arthur Kennedy recalled one incident in his biography *High Times*.

"Frank Clarke . . . was taking off in his souped-up Travelair Speedwing with clipped wings. Everyone went back to the party, but Clarke broke it up again by flying low and slow over the hangar and dumping a sack of ball bearings on the metal roof. When the crowd rushed outside to see what was going on, he jettisoned a load of garbage out of the cockpit and made a direct hit on a couple of dozen upturned faces. They were still hosing themselves off when Frank landed, laughing like hell. The ball bearing trick was a Clarke trademark." 4

To survive for any length of time as a stunt pilot required

exceptional presence of mind and quick reactions. A near fatal incident, still under discussion when Moye moved to Clover Field, exemplified Clarke's alert resourcefulness. Clarke had developed a specialty of landing out of a whipstall. He dove below the level of the telephone wires at the approach end of the field and pulled straight up until the ship ran completely out of speed. As the nose whipped down into a stall, he kicked the ship into a slip, leveled off and landed. This particular time, Clarke sensed a total absence of elevator control as the Canuck's nose whipped down. The ball and socket joint in the rocker assembly, or bell crank, had disengaged, leaving the aft end of the linkage rod to fall free. Heading straight for the ground, no time remained for him to extricate himself from the seemingly hopeless situation.

Almost instinctively, Clarke reached back past the side of his seat to seize the top of the right-hand rocker. By pulling forward, he raised the elevators and started bringing the nose up. In a crouched position, he couldn't see out of the ship to achieve effective control. He solved the dilemma by kicking a hole in the fabric on the right side of the cockpit and used up most of the field before landing. After that, he carried a short loop of clothesline that ran from the cockpit to the upper and lower ends of the right hand rocker when he flew a Jenny or Canuck. He also discontinued his habit of whip-stall landings.

Shortly after the war, Eddie Bellande fell victim to a similar ball and socket failure. His description of the crash was laconic. "I started the flight," he said, "with elevators, in a tidy rear cockpit. I ended the flight, without elevators, in the untidy bits and pieces of a front cockpit."

Spinning down to almost zero altitude brought Clarke considerable acclaim. Moye observed him make an abrupt recovery so close to the ground that his pull-out caused a good sized dust cloud on the field. When performing the stunt, Clarke didn't enter a true spin. He began the maneuver from an accelerated stall under partial power. His descent became a perpendicular, continuous snap roll. He told Moye that he held full rudder, easing forward on the stick until he felt the ship on the verge of popping out of rotation. Maintaining air speed above the normal stalling speed of the ship, he flipped the stick ahead and booted opposite rudder. When rotation stopped, Clarke centered the rudder and immediately started coming back on the stick to level out.

Ironically, Clarke would eventually die in an unintentional spin of his own doing. The accident occurred when Clarke flew his surplus BT-13 to Frank Tomick's cinnabar claim near Kernville, California. 5

"Clarke's ship . . . came diving down from the sky directly at the little mine shack. Tomick ran out to wave, then froze. The BT-13 had rolled inverted and was plunging out of control. Inside the ship Frank Clarke struggled fiercely to roll over but something had jammed behind the control column. A sack of manure. He'd meant to have Owen toss it out on top of Tomick's head as they buzzed him upside down. The gag cost two human lives." 6

When Tomick reached the wreckage, passenger Mark Owen and the friend with whom he survived thirty years of stunt flying were gone. Tomick never fully recovered from the devastating loss.

Stunt pilots, according to their public audience, seemed to be reckless show-offs and possessed little regard for life. Moye disagreed. Now a professional stunt pilot, he learned that stunting required a great deal of planning. Whether drawn with a stick on the ground, laid out on diagrams, or developed through dialogue, aerobatic maneuvers incorporated basic elements of safety and precision. Pilots assessed their skills and response time while, at the same time, paid close attention to the capabilities of their airplane. A momentary lapse of attention could be fatal. Every error discovered before evolving into a crash or fatality was shared with other pilots. These factors combined to make flying safer.

Moye profited from his own experience as well as that of others. As a novice, he established a continually expanding list of situations to avoid. He would not naively accept another's opinion on flying options; he would test out the parameters of a scene before becoming entangled in a potentially dangerous scenario; and, when exploring take-off areas, he would assess the danger inherent in each object encountered regardless of how harmless it might appear.

Witnessing a fatal or near-fatal accident on the home field,

A group of Clover Field pilots. Al Morgan is standing on the left; Dick Ranaldi is to the right; Bon MacDougall is kneeling front right. Photo courtesy of Katy Ranaldi.

particularly one that could easily have been avoided, made the consequences of foolish flying a disturbing reality for Moye and his fellow pilots. These accidents lessened their feelings of invincibility, believing that such things only happen to the other fellow. There seemed to be many of these life lessons.

One Sunday, in the summer of 1926, Moye's friend Ward Poulson arrived at Clover with Katie Lund, a Stanford coed. They hoped Moye would take Katie flying. Not having any commitments at the time, Moye began pre-flighting Leo's Jenny when word passed down the row of hangars of a pending take-off by Lieutenant Carlyle. Activity on the field came to a halt. Hangars emptied and, as everyone watched and waited, a silence settled over the scene.

Carlyle had purchased a decrepit Jenny from Al Wilson some weeks previous. A group of young men put up the money for the ship with plans to restore it in exchange for flying lessons.

Carlyle would be their instructor. Upon completion of the ship, Carlyle took it up for a test flight which, by minimum standards, bordered on disaster. He flew with the plane in nose-high attitude which never allowed the Jenny to pick up speed. The biplane seemed on the verge of a stall as it staggered around each turn. His landing was as poor as one could do without incurring significant damage to the aircraft. Wilson, feeling a degree of responsibility, diplomatically offered to donate a little dual to sharpen Carlyle's skills. Carlyle indignantly pointed out that he flew in the war and engaged none other than Baron Von Richtofen in a dog flight. Although shot down, he survived the crash without major injury. Al carefully concealed his lack of surprise at the outcome of that encounter while he persisted in his efforts to persuade the rusty pilot to accept his help but to no avail. Carlyle had planned, after a few minor adjustments to his flying and the ship, to schedule a flight with the first of his students.

That fateful day, Carlyle completed a test hop from the rear cockpit, one much more successful than the first. During the lesson, he occupied the front cockpit, a position which made it difficult for him to determine the attitude of the airplane. The additional weight of the student further handicapped Carlyle. Considering his sad performance on the test hop and the additional negative factors of the impending lesson, the consensus on the field was that he would never bring it off. Everyone hoped that somehow Carlyle could be made to listen to reason. Aside from the human aspect, crashes discouraged business. The efforts of additional pilots to persuade Carlyle to accept Wilson's offer of a refresher flight went unheard. With no competent authority to whom to appeal, they could only wait and hope some miracle might prove them wrong.

The stuttering of the Jenny's engine broke the eerie hush on the field. Carlyle's take-off repeated his first blundering roll. Failing to put the Jenny's nose down and gain speed, he managed to somehow negotiate the two turns leading to the back stretch. The ship floundered less than a hundred feet above the field, still in a nose-high attitude. By simply lowering the ship's nose to allow it to pick up the proper flying speed, Carlyle could have easily averted what seemed inevitable.

FLYING CARPETS, FLYING WINGS

As he approached Centinela Avenue, Carlyle pulled the nose up even higher to gain sufficient clearance over the low hill just past the road. The Jenny stalled, entered a spin, and plunged into the side of the hill. The student survived the crash; Carlyle died on the way to the hospital. Moye witnessed something more disturbing than the accident on the way to the crash scene. He saw an unknown bystander tear a strip of fabric from the plane's fuselage and dip it in a pool of blood as a souvenir. He wondered what could inspire morbid curiosity seekers to resort to such outlandish extremes. He knew a stunt man who habitually wore a blood-stained helmet of a friend who had met his demise in a fiery crash. This, however, belonged to the stock in trade of the stunt man to create an element of bravado.

In an era plagued by all too frequent accidents, pilots and aircraft mechanics rushed to the scene of a crash to assist possible survivors. They knew if the public arrived on the scene first, the victims inevitably suffered further injuries when removed from the wreckage by inexperienced do-gooders. Knowledge of aircraft construction was critical to the successful extrication and survival of the injured. The ignorance by cigarette-smoking spectators constituted an additional hazard. A discarded cigarette, carelessly tossed into a pool of leaking fuel, caused a number of fiery deaths. During the 1925 Stanford quarter preceding his appendectomy, Moye became involved in just such an incident. Only his knowledge and skill prevented a catastrophe.

Driving from Palo Alto to San Mateo, Moye and a fraternity brother, Gordon *Willie* Williams witnessed a Jenny crash near the Redwood City flying field. The pilot's foot, pinned between the rudder bar and a ruptured gas tank, prevented his immediate removal from the wreckage. The reek of raw gasoline permeated the immediate area encircled by an alarming number of spectators. Keeping them away from the scene became increasingly difficult. Moye and Willie managed to have the first individuals on the scene assist in preventing cigarette smokers from lighting up. Fully aware that the arbitrary flick of a cigarette could light up the entire area, Moye felt relieved when, through trial and error, they managed to pull the pilot from the wreckage and clear the fuel-soaked site.

CLOVER FIELD AND A *TOMMY*

Moye's summer had been filled with flying and the warm camaraderie of his fellow pilots. He had purchased an airplane, flown in the movies, and gained immeasurable experience. In all probability, his future held further opportunities for more flying jobs. As he prepared to return to Stanford in October, Moye looked forward to spending his vacations at Clover. The Christmas holiday gave him the chance to reunite with many of his friends. An unidentified newspaper clipping made note of Moye's participation in the opening of Adams Airport just west of Union Air Terminal. Previously known as Bob Lloyd Field, J. J. Adams now owned the 80 acre facility. Moye and Art Wedemeyer, flying their *Tommy*'s, joined a parade of planes to celebrate the occasion. T. C. Young, President of the Western Aero League arrived in his Kinner sport plane; Victor Fleming piloted his OX5 Travel Air; and Leo and Dick Ranaldi flew Leo's Jenny. Studios used the field to a limited degree but, not part of Los Angeles County's Master Plan of Airports, Adams disappeared during the 1940s. 7

Moye and Dick were inseparable on the airfield. Dick admired and respected his friend. Katy Ranaldi photo.

5

WACOS AND TRAVELAIRS

In June 1927, Moye arrived home after completing his third year at Stanford. That first week, he received an early morning phone call from J. B. Alexander offering him a job with Theodore J. Hull's American Aircraft Corporation. Hull couldn't have timed the creation of his company any better. Just weeks earlier, Lindbergh's historic Atlantic crossing set off a fervor within the United States for aviation. Though Hull began operations as a distributor for Wacos, he now offered services to the general public and needed flight instructors and pilots. Alexander, based at American's downtown Los Angeles office, called on businesses in southern California to convince their owners of the need and convenience of owning an aircraft. Before working for Hull, Alexander, a former automobile salesman, partnered with Claude Ryan in the operation of the Los Angeles-San Diego Airline. Later, from 1927-1929, he would become Chief of Aeronautics for Howard Hughes' *Hell's Angeles*. 1

Alexander, referred by Doc Whitney, explained the details of the American position to Moye. It included demonstration flights, passenger hops, and flight instruction at Clover Field. He needed to start immediately, that very morning – not an easy task for Moye. The previous evening he had attended the wedding of a fraternity brother where he indulged in far too many toasts. Having a remarkable tolerance for alcohol, Moye's consumption must have been considerable. Once, at the request of a friend, Moye pocketed a toothpick for every martini he drank. He counted seventeen toothpicks at the end of the evening – with no visible effects of inebriation.

Despite his miserable condition, Moye accepted J. B.'s offer and headed out to Clover. Every rut the Model T encountered on the fifteen mile trip made Moye acutely aware of the challenges that awaited him. The roar of the radial engine would be deafening; instructing a new student in an unfamiliar airplane would require deliberate attention and a patient disposition. The most potent remedy for his state of health would be the promising circumstances of full time employment as a pilot.

When he arrived at Clover, Moye found Doc Whitney inside the American Aircraft hangar. Doc shuffled paperwork while American's mechanic Cavanaugh studied a carburetor in need of rebuilding. After warm greetings and a brief discussion of Moye's daily duties, Doc introduced him to his first student and the Waco Nine parked on the flight line. Standing authoritatively in front of the engine, Doc began explaining in meticulous detail just exactly how to fly the airplane. His characteristic drawl seemed somehow oddly at variance with the preciseness of his directions. One item in particular intrigued Moye. "After starting, close the throttle to idle and wait until the bottom of the crankcase is warm to the touch before taking off."

To make this determination, Doc reached through a small access door in the side cowl and placed his hand at the bottom of the motor. In the absence of a panel mounted temperature gauge, Doc's 'touch' system proved a workable, yet distinctly inconvenient, substitute. Even in the middle of summer the crankcase oil pan took an inordinate amount of time to reach a temperature pleasing to him. Satisfied Moye and the student understood the procedure, Doc disappeared into the hangar. Moye reviewed the basics of flying with his student and then gingerly fit his bursting head into the tight leather helmet. At the conclusion of the fifteen minute flight, his first student left the airport anxious to return the next day for another lesson. The rest of the day turned out to be extremely busy as predicted by J. B. Moye's headache decreased with each and every flight. By nightfall, time and fresh air had enabled him to join the human race once again.

The Waco Nine's performance seemed the only part of Moye's new job that he found unfavorable. Combining improperly balanced stick forces with proportionately heavy ailerons relative to the rudder and elevator made consistently good three point landings impossible. As the Waco lost speed during approach, the airplane's sink rate rapidly increased and prevented the pilot from lowering the tail before the wheels touched down. The unprepared pilot discovered just how high a Waco could bounce on those occasions. To avoid this lack of control, pilots attempted intentional wheel landings. This procedure, however, made on unimproved fields with brakeless airplanes added another element of danger. Without the tail-skid contacting the ground and serving as a brake, the speeding airplane could strike an unseen rut or object and flip over on its back, or worse, impact an object.

American Aircraft hired Charles A. La Jotte a few days after Moye. With a deadpan expression, La Jotte habitually delivered gems of humor without prompting. His colorful wit compared to his rich flying experience that began in 1917 in the Air Corps. By 1919, he was operating government forest patrols in northern California and Oregon. In 1923, La Jotte established one of the first commercial air operations in Nome, Alaska flying his war surplus Jenny. He returned to the states after crashing the Jenny in 1924. [2]

With the addition of La Jotte, Doc Whitney initiated a schedule designed to make the most of daylight hours. He created two shifts, 5 a.m. to 12:30 p.m. and 12:30 p.m. to 8 p.m. At the beginning of each week, the pilots rotated the schedule. Midway through the first week, with Moye on the morning shift, Howard Hughes arrived to begin a course of flying instruction. Doc personally introduced Hughes to the Waco Nine although La Jotte would be his instructor. Following Doc's detailed lecture, La Jotte directed Hughes to hop into the rear cockpit and then proceeded to re-explain the starting routine, pulled the propeller through precisely four revolutions, and called for contact. With the engine running smoothly, he returned to stand alongside the rear cockpit. He pointed to the throttle and instructed, "Don't touch that." Hughes promptly reached up and shoved the throttle wide open. The Waco surged over the chocks onto its nose, splintering the propeller. La Jotte replaced the disabled airplane with another Waco and began Hughes' first lesson.

Some individuals pointed to the incident as an example of the willfulness of a young man spoiled by his great wealth. They contended that his action indicated rebellion against being given a direct order. Moye drew his own conclusion about the incident. Overly sensitive about a hearing loss, Hughes simply did not understand what Doc told him and was too proud to admit to the cause of the misunderstanding. Moye further suspected that Hughes' lack of hearing acuity may have been responsible for some of his eccentric behavior.

The week following the accident, Moye took over the afternoon shift. When Hughes arrived for his lesson, Doc informed him that Moye would now be his instructor. "I won't fly with him" Hughes responded. "He's too young!" (Hughes was one year older.)

Hughes also refused to shift his lessons to the morning which relegated Moye back to the morning shift. On the bright side, returning to the morning shift continued to leave his afternoons free to enjoy the company of Clovers' regulars - Leo, Dick, Al Morgan, Howard Batt, *Mac* McCallister, Slim Maves, and a cross-section of stunt pilots. From time to time, celebrities such as Victor Fleming, Howard Hawks, Reginald Denny and Wallace Berry showed up on the field to fly or spend some time 'hangar flying'.

The upcoming Dole Race, from Oakland to Honolulu, became the topic of conversation at the beginning of August 1927. The fifteen entrants included two from Clover Field, Frank Clarke and Art Goebel. Clover pilots naturally rooted for Clarke and Goebel. Goebel, slated to fly the *Woolaroc,* a Travelair monoplane, would likely beat out Clarke in his new Fisk International biplane. Army Reserve pilot Jack Frost, flying a Lockheed *Vega*, seemed to be Goebel's stiffest competition. The *Vega*, more advanced than anything else at the time, stood the best chance of winning.

When August 16 arrived, the starting date for competition,

only eight of the original fifteen entrants prepared to take off. Three ships crashed earlier with a loss of three lives. One ship did not qualify and three, including Clarke's, withdrew from the competition. Clarke's flight from Long Beach to San Francisco clocked a disappointing time. The Fisk's fuel capacity, combined with its slow cruise speed, made it impossible for the plane to cross the open ocean to Honolulu or qualify for the race with the mandated 15 per cent fuel reserve.

Only Frost's *Vega*, Martin Jensen's Breese monoplane, the *Aloha*, and Goebel's Travelair made successful starts. Two ships crashed on take-off. The pilots, Norman Goddard and Livingston Irving, survived. Three ships, including Augie Pedlar's Buhl Air Sedan, quickly returned with problems. Pedlar made some adjustments and made a second start. Goebel and his navigator, Bill Davis, won the race and collected the $25,000 prize. Jenson came in second. Frost and Pedlar never arrived. The exact fate of the

Vance Breese and his 'Aloha' flown by Martin Jensen in the Dole Race. Photo courtesy of Vance Breese.

Lockheed and Buhl is unknown. Some believed that Frost may have actually reached the islands but crashed in a virtually inaccessible slope of the 13,680 foot Mauna Loa. 3

Upon his return, Goebel told the Clover Field pilots that he attributed a large part of his success to his determination to climb above the stratus layer over the Pacific. He held his plane at its maximum rate of climb, just barely skimming over the tops of the cloud bank. He thought he saw another airplane on top, some distance ahead. He believed that it was probably Frost in the high performance *Vega*.

August 7, 1927, one week prior to the Dole Race, La Jotte soloed Howard Hughes who added this significant accomplishment to the successful completion of the ground work for his great air classic, *Hell's Angels*. Filming of the air sequences would begin in October of that year. When a scheduling conflict threatened to prevent him from witnessing one of his first aerial scenes, he hired Moye, through American Aircraft, to land one of their Waco Nines at Ross Field in Arcadia, pick him up from his country club in a taxi, and fly with him to the proposed scene of the crash in the San Fernando Valley. The sequence required Al Johnson to crash a Jenny altered to resemble a British Avro.

Hughes had chosen a vacant block in a newly subdivided tract as the landing site. An approach over power lines and a roll-out between two closely spaced oak trees required an experienced pilot, one that could clear the obstacles without damaging the aircraft. As Hughes circled the block to size up the layout, Moye concluded that the landing was beyond the capabilities of the recently soloed pilot and prepared to take the controls if necessary.

Hughes passed neatly over the high wires and began his descent but his speed was too fast. He needed to decrease his speed if he wanted to stop in the designated area. When Hughes showed no sign of doing so, Moye prepared to take over and execute a missed approach just as Hughes followed procedure and aborted the landing. Following a second unsuccessful attempt, Hughes climbed to a safe altitude, throttled back, and shouted, "You do it."

Moye came in over the wires in a steep, nose-high slip to the left from which he swung into an extreme fishtail to the right as he leveled off. Traveling sideways as they passed between the oak trees, he used all but 25 feet of the available landing area. The Waco came to a stop as Johnson's Avro approached to stage the scripted crash. He touched down right on target, hitting an invisible trip wire located mid-field. The Avro flipped onto its back as required. Johnson emerged unscathed.

The director left his position near one of the cameras and came running toward the Waco. "Did you see the crash, Mr. Hughes?" he inquired excitedly.

Hughes sounded unimpressed, "Yeah, sure." Turning toward Moye to emphasize his presence, Hughes replied with emphasis, "But did you see *that* landing?"

Johnson and Hughes' mechanics repaired the Avro for further scenes in the film, a role Johnson would not fulfill. On a routine take-off for a ferry flight, the Avro's motor failed. Johnson, a stunt man of limited piloting experience, allowed the plane to enter a spin. He died within minutes of being pulled from the burning wreckage. Moye found the deaths of former wing walkers and plane changers, a result of crashing an airplane, difficult to comprehend. From his perspective, he believed their former activities to be far more hazardous than flying.

The filming of *Hell's Angels* took over three years to complete and Moye believed it to be the happiest period of Howard Hughes' life. His association with pilots on the set provided Hughes with a camaraderie not possible in any other situation. A more carefree, irrepressible, irreverent, and engaging group would be next to impossible to duplicate. The pilots treated Hughes as one of their own and Hughes loved it. The stunt pilots tested their cavalier treatment of Hughes upon occasion. When one of the pilots twice failed to execute a take-off to Hughes' satisfaction, the exasperated producer declared that he would do it himself. Not deterred by the candidly expressed opinion of several pilots that he lacked the experience to fly a Thomas Morse Scout, Hughes took off in the *Tommy*. Seconds after becoming airborne, the plane made an abrupt turn to the right. The uncontrolled gyroscopic precession of the rotary motor caused the ship to dig a wing into the ground and cart wheel. According to Moye, members of his crew arrived on the scene just as Hughes emerged from the wreckage, nursing a broken nose. Several biographies on Hughes describe a different outcome of the crash, one which placed the director in the hospital with a coma, crushed cheekbone, and several lacerations. 4

The stunt pilots subjected the young tycoon to their special brand of impudence. Caddo Field, Hughes' base of operations for his fleet of *Hell's Angeles* airplanes, possessed a large latrine. A galvanized iron gutter slanted across one wall at a convenient elevation. Semi-circular troughs were attached to the gutter at evenly spaced intervals. The trough at the upper end measured approximately two inches wide and eight inches long. The other troughs in descending order became progressively smaller. The smallest, at the low end of the gutter, was about a half inch wide and an inch and a half long. A sign on the wall above the largest trough read, *Frank Clarke and all longhorn bucks rest it here.* The simple notation, *Howard Hughes*, hung above the bottom and smallest trough.

October 1927, Moye made one last flight in his *Tommy* before returning to Stanford. Having neglected the airplane while working for American, he briefly considered taking it with him but there were too many factors that made it an unrealistic decision. The *Tommy* was not considered a cross-country airplane. It lacked a compartment for baggage and its fuel capacity required at least two stops between Clover and Palo Alto. A worn out condenser caused the motor to run rough after an hour of continuous flight. And, as his father pointed out all too well, the *Tommy* might become a distraction to his studies.

For that last flight, Moye chose to fly to Riverside Airport managed by aviator Roman Warren, the "Cowboy Aviator". Warren received considerable notoriety in 1926 by flying his *Tommy* under the Mission Bridge which spanned the nearby Santa Ana River. Bert Rhine, a Stanford classmate and owner of a *Tommy*, accompanied Moye. Bert acquired his biplane in wrecked condition and talked a trade school into rebuilding it. He paid for the materials; the school supplied student labor. Considering the practice and knowledge the students gained restoring the *Tommy*, this proved a valuable exchange. When completed, Moye test flew the ship for Bert. Dick Ranaldi, sitting on Bert's lap, flew along side in Moye's airplane. Thirty minutes later, Moye declared Bert's *Tommy* airworthy.

The hour flight to Riverside took a near disastrous turn when the motor in Moye's *Tommy* quit abruptly. A newly planted vineyard, just south of the Riverside/Ontario highway, offered the only viable choice for an emergency landing. Moye managed to set the ship down in between two rows of the embryonic plants without unearthing any with his tail skid. Bert landed a few rows over. Too late to determine the cause of the Le Rhone's failure, Moye and Bert spent the night at the Stephens family ranch in La Verne. The next morning, Steve, a ranch hand, drove them back to the vineyard. Unable to effectively fix the motor, Moye decided to nurse it back to Clover. Steve, Moye, Bert, and the vineyard owner pushed the planes to the edge of the nearby highway. Once in place, they asked a passing motorcycle officer to expedite their take-off by stopping oncoming traffic. He took a position one half mile down the highway in the proposed direction of departure.

As Bert began his take-off roll, Moye noted that they had overlooked a white wooden fence separating the pavement and a deep ditch on the north side of the highway. The airplane's lower wing would hit the fence unless the plane became airborne before reaching it. Holding his breath, Moye watched the *Tommy*'s tail come up and the plane's flying speed increase but not soon enough. A burst of flying fence fragments accompanied the splintering crash. The impact twisted the ship to the left and forced it sideways into the ditch. Only the tail surfaces remained visible. Moye jumped onto the running boards of the ranch pickup as he and Steve raced to Bert's aid. Screeching to a stop opposite the airplane, they expected the worst. A string of emphatic profanities coming from the wreckage eased their anxiety. Though his prized *Tommy* suffered substantial damage, Bert escaped injury. After the dust settled and nerves calmed, Moye, Bert, and Steve decided to remove the *Tommy*'s wings and truck the fuselage and wings separately to a nearby field. The motorcycle officer discouraged Moye from another attempt at fool-hardiness. Moye concurred and had Steve tow his plane backwards to the field

The dirt field, a narrow strip of land between the Southern Pacific and Union Pacific Railroads, would provide an adequate take-off area. Some years earlier, pioneering aviator Waldo Waterman had leased the property from Union Pacific. Waterman originally intended to use the field for flight instruction but, instead, it became the terminal for scheduled flights to Big Bear Lake, a mountain resort approximately 60 miles to the north of Ontario. Two Boeing-C seaplanes purchased at auction for $200 each and converted for land use were scheduled to carry both passengers and cargo up to the resort. The second day of operations, Waterman and four passengers departed Big Bear in adverse weather conditions. Hot temperatures, strong eastern winds, and a complement of five passengers prevented the plane from climbing more than fifty feet off the ground. Before Waterman could clear the lake and return to the field, a severe downdraft slammed the plane into the turbulent water. Ontario's Mayor Ball, a newspaper editor, manager of the Ontario Hotel, and Waterman received only minor injuries. A San Bernardino businessman died, apparently from a heart attack, when the plane hit the icy waters. The accident was a major set-back for Waterman. In 1928, after four years of sporadic operations, he liquidated the airline and relocated the Boeing airplanes to Clover. 5

Moye, Bert, and Steve found the Ontario field deserted and the hangars closed. Pushing the two *Tommy*s into a partially empty hangar, the dejected pilots took one last look at their prized possessions and then boarded a Pacific Electric Railway *Red Reaper* home.

Before Moye departed for Stanford, Dick Ranaldi promised to repair the *Tommy*'s motor and fly the plane back to Clover. On his first trip to Ontario, he fired up the Le Rhone and concluded that the motor needed replacement parts. Returning with tools and parts, Dick discovered that a windstorm had collapsed a portion of the hangar roof. It had fallen on top of Moye's airplane and damaged one of its wings. The task of rescuing and repairing the airplane required money that Moye didn't have and an absence from school he couldn't take. When Dick found a buyer for the plane, in 'as is' condition, Moye consented to sell. During his lifetime, he would own five more airplanes; none would ever replace his beloved *Tommy*.

As Moye closed the hangar door on the *Tommy* in Ontario, he closed the door on a distinct epoch in his life. The landing in the vineyard marked the conclusion of his final flight in a WW I aircraft. He never returned to Clover Field as a tenant and future visits were infrequent. The colorful, ramshackle hangars gave way to uniform, austere structures of steel and concrete. Business men in suits operating flying schools, airplane sales, and charter services replaced rugged individualists. An era highlighted by spectacular stunting and amazing performances gradually disappeared. Ever increasing restrictions imposed by the United States Department of Commerce would soon relegate wing walkers and plane changers to descriptive commentaries in history books.

In 1926, the federal government created the Aeronautics Branch of the Department of Commerce. On January 1, 1927, they passed the Air Commerce Act which regulated air commerce involved in interstate activities. The responsibility for enforcing the act belonged to six offices located throughout the United States. Moye, resenting the bureaucratic intrusion into aviation, knew he must apply for a pilot's license if he wished to continue flying. Considered a forfeiture of his freedom, he stalled the inevitable as long as possible. During Christmas vacation 1927, he underwent the mandatory physical examination for the license. The following month, Moye reported to Department of Commerce Inspector Frank Jerdone at Angeles Mesa Drive Airport to take the tests for his transport rating, the highest of the three established classifications. American Aircraft Corporation established Angeles Mesa north of Rogers Airport's third location. Rogers had moved from Western Avenue a year earlier.

Following Moye's successful completion of his written exam, Jerdone asked his friend Lieutenant Jimmy Collins, with whom he was reminiscing about their cadet days, to give Moye his flight test. During the practical exam in a Waco Nine, Moye had the unnerving feeling that the Army Air Corps pilot delighted in subjecting him to a much more rigorous procedure than customary for a civilian rating. Despite the over-zealousness of the examiner, Moye became, quite possibly, the only civilian pilot to receive a civil pilot's license, number 1667, through military guidelines in a civil aircraft, by a military pilot without a civil rating.

Moye joined hundreds of other licensed pilots in Los Angeles County, a region which possessed more legal flyers than any other county in the United States. By 1928, with 58 airports and landing fields, 12 aircraft factories, and six aircraft engine factories, Los Angeles became a major hub of aviation. Production that year totaled $4 million dollars, estimated to be 32% of all aviation–related revenue in the country. Douglas, Lockheed, Kreutzer, Bach, Timm, and American Eagle belonged to a group of more prominent aircraft manufacturers. Companies turning out engines were Kinner, Menasco, Hallet, Axelson, Enesco, and MacClatchie. Some of the success and prosperity of aviation would find its way to Moye.

February 1928 marked the beginning of the most fulfilling period of Moye's college years. Norman A. Goddard established the Palo Alto School of Aviation on the northeast corner of the Stanford campus during Moye's junior year. Born in England and a member of the Royal Flying Corps during WWI, Goddard moved to Canada after the war and then to the United States. He became a naturalized citizen and subsequently joined the San Diego contingent of the United States Naval Reserve. In 1927, he crashed his airplane, the *El Encanto*, at the start of the Dole Race. Now thirty-two, Goddard believed that he possessed as much, or more, flying experience than the birds.

J. B. Alexander knew that Goddard needed a part-time flight instructor and advised Moye to apply. Moye did and Goddard scheduled him for three weekday afternoons and weekends which enabled a third Waco to earn its keep. In return, Moye received a modest income and, more importantly, wings. The school's complement of aircraft consisted of three Waco Tens purchased from American Aircraft and Goddard's *Gypsy*, previously the *El Encanto*. Harry Brown, a slender, quiet man, served as the school's full-time instructor. Brown saw combat with the Royal Canadian Air Corps during WWI but, in common with most combat pilots Moye met, seemed reluctant to discuss his experiences. He did, however, allow Moye to examine his logbook listing his combat missions.

Moye found the Waco Ten to be a much more satisfying airplane to fly than the Waco Nine. Shortly after he began instructing for Goddard, he lived through a demonstration which confirmed his belief. In a moment of unguarded innocence, Moye agreed to accompany Goddard on a stunt ride. Goddard performed a series of wingovers and half rolls then peeled off into a dive that seemed a prelude to a loop. As he pulled out of the dive, Moye fully expected to see the nose start to rise into the climb and carry them up and over the top. Instead, Goddard jerked the airplane into a vicious snap roll.

In Moye's estimation, having felt the wings bow under the stress imposed by the roll, Goddard attempted the maneuver at an excessive and unsafe speed. The frightening scene of an American Waco Nine losing its wings some months earlier flashed across Moye's mind. Before his emotions changed from concern to anxiety, the airplane safely emerged from the roll. Moye later reflected on Goddard's wild stunt. He liked the man. Goddard always treated him fairly and was obviously an able pilot, barring an overly optimistic estimation of an airplanes capabilities. Should the opportunity for another stunt flight with him arise, however, Moye would have urgent business elsewhere.

As Stanford's spring term came to a close, Charles Kingsford-Smith lifted off the tarmac at Oakland Airport in his heavily loaded Fokker F-7 named the *Southern Cross.* He intended to fly across the Pacific to Australia. His crew for the May 31, 1928 departure consisted of co-pilot Charles T. P. Ulm, navigator Harry W. Lyon, and radio operator James W. Warner. Financial worries had plagued the initial planning stages for Kingsford-Smith's flight. Only through the support of Captain G. Allan Hancock was the Australian able to realize his dream. Hancock revitalized the project by purchasing the Fokker and donating additional funds for the flight.

An oilman, real estate developer, philanthropist, and one of the most respected and influential men in southern California, Hancock owned the land where De Mille Field No. 2 and the original Rogers Airport had operated. His other properties included the La Brea Tar Pit location on Wilshire Boulevard and Hancock Park, all later donated to Los Angeles County. Despite his involvement in Kingsford-Smith's flight, Hancock had no interest in learning to fly until the *Southern Cross* arrived safely in Australia. So impressed with the flight's success, he presented the Fokker to Kingsford-Smith and Ulm in appreciation of their feat. The flight also inspired Hancock to take up flying as well as establish the Hancock College of

Moye explains the basics of flight to his new student Allan Hancock in front of the Travelair D-4000. Photo courtesy of John Underwood.

Aeronautics to enable student pilots to become experts in the science of aviation. 6

A client of the Stephens law firm, Hancock mentioned his desire to fly to Moye Sr. who naturally recommended his son. Moye welcomed the congenial Hancock as a student and found him very generous. Hancock loaned Moye the money to purchase a Travelair D-4000 in which to start Hancock's instruction. When not flying with the oilman, Moye used the airplane for other activities. Leo hired him to fly the Travelair in the 1928 Fox film *Air Circus* about three student pilots played by Arthur Lake, Sue Carol, and Dave Rollins. The title of the film reflects its content. "Flaming youth now becomes flying youth . . . and scales the heights of

Moye stands in front of the Hancock's Buhl Model CA-8 Senior Air Sedan. The identity of the other gentleman is unknown. Photo courtesy of the Museum of Flight.

entertainment in a romance of daring and danger among clouds of adventure to the roar of tempestuous laughter." 7

Moye doubled for Rollins during a scene in which he attempts to save Lake and Sue when their airplane loses a wheel on take-off. Leo, hidden from camera view, piloted their airplane. After Rollins leaps into a waiting Lincoln-Page, the filming stops to allow Moye to replace him. He then positions his plane next to Lake's, waving his arms and pointing excitedly toward the landing gear. Moye later wrote that he felt his dramatic performance of brilliantly conceived gestures would add immeasurably to Rollins' renown as an actor. Viewing the completed movie, he changed his mind. Only a few frames taken by the camera ship showed him pointing in the general direction of the Travelair's landing gear.

As the summer wore on, Hancock acquired additional airplanes. He purchased a Buhl Model CA-8 Senior Air Sedan powered by a 400 hp Pratt & Whitney Wasp and a Lockheed Vega with a 220 hp Wright Whirlwind J-5. Advanced aircraft for the time, they provided Moye his first opportunity to carry more than one passenger. He ferried the seven-place Buhl from Los Angeles to the factory in Marysville, Michigan for a thorough inspection – his longest cross-country to date. On board were the Air Sedan's designer Etienne Dormoy and two other gentlemen.

Navigating with Rand McNally Standard Indexed Maps with Air Trails and a compass, Moye made the 2,300 flight via the southern route through El Paso. The Davis-Monthan Aviation Field Register shows him landing on the field September 13, 1928. Back from the factory, the Air Sedan failed to pass inspection on November 7 because of landing gear spreading. Two months passed before the Department of Commerce approved the airplane to carry five passengers including the pilot. 8

In addition to Hancock, Moye instructed other individuals destined to become distinguished leaders of pivotal aviation companies. Eddie Bellande, who test flew the first Lockheed *Vega* and would fly Northrop's original flying wing in 1929, introduced Moye to Allan Lockheed and a number of his employees. Several became Moye's students - Jack Northrop, Jerry Vultee, and Cliff Garrett. Northrop ultimately soloed with Eddie Bellande but gave up piloting after approximately 50 hours of flying time.

When the time came to return to school, Moye passed the Hancock hat to Dick Ranaldi. Dick, referred to as the "boy pilot", appreciated the opportunity to fly the high powered aircraft. Moye valued his opportunities as well. With one semester left, he returned to Stanford in the Travelair and to his part-time job at the Palo Alto School of Aviation. He couldn't have asked for a better combination – school, a plane, and a flying job. Somewhat irritated that Moye arrived in an aircraft that he did not sell, coupled with

Moye's obvious and undoubtedly overbearing opinion on the Travelair's superior performance, Goddard challenged him to a race. The Travelair sped past Goddard's Waco as they raced at tree top level over a triangular course laid out on the Stanford campus. Disconcerted by the outcome, Goddard planned to replace the Waco's OX5 motor with an OX6, believing that the additional ten horsepower would enable him to out-perform Moye's plane. Unfortunately, fate denied Goddard that opportunity.

January 26, 1930, Goddard's luck ran out. Flying a Stanford Glider Club project, Goddard received a tow off Alameda Airport from Paul Mantz in a Fleet biplane. "At 3,000 feet, Goddard cut loose, flew in a big circle, and then dove for speed, intending to pull up through a powerful loop. The strain was too much; a wing snapped and the luckless pilot was killed." Moye was not surprised when he heard the news. Goddard had demonstrated little respect for an airplane's limitations on many occasions. Because of his blatant disregard for safety, his last flight ended tragically. 9

Having the Travelair at Stanford, Moye found time in his busy schedule of school, work, and sports, to take his friends aloft. He demonstrated his improved aerobatic expertise to Allie McReynolds, the young friend he flew four years earlier. Allie now attended Mills College across the bay in Oakland. Ward Poulson and Moye, together with other school mates from Los Angeles, often arranged dates with Allie and her equally charming friends, Jean Hall and Florence Hamberger. Most of those occasions involved the Travelair. Florence's father, D. A. Hamburger, owner of the Hamberger Department Store, played a minor role in Moye's aviation career. Hamberger served as Chairman of the 1910 Dominguez Air Meet Executive Committee.

Just before Moye flew home for the Christmas holidays, he took Lieutenant Charles S. Whitmore, the coach of the polo team, flying. Association with the regular Army officers assigned to the Stanford ROTC detachment proved satisfying for Moye. He felt more in tune with them than any other university staff and regarded the commanding officer, Lieutenant Colonel Edward Warner McCabe with great esteem. McCabe, a gentleman of the First Families of Virginia, led the company in strict military style but practiced fairness. He never called anyone out during inspections in a manner one might deem humiliating. Transgressions were dealt with privately in his office, a considerable improvement over the Stephens' practice of 'holding court' heedless of a family member's feelings or providing any privacy. Moye attributed the practice to his father's inability to leave 'his work at the office'.

January 1929, Moye graduated from Stanford with a Bachelor of Arts degree in Law. His first term of law school was under way when he received an urgent phone call from Eddie Bellande, now flying for Maddux Airlines. When he landed in Alameda on his regularly scheduled Maddux run later in the day, Bellande wanted to meet with Moye. He had an important matter to discuss. Moye agreed, if for no other reason than to see his good friend. 10

A Stanford graduate with a bachelor's degree in law, Moye was not destined to practice with his father. Photo courtesy of Steve LeFever.

6

MADDUX AIRLINES

Anxious to play a role in commercial aviation, the Ford Automobile Company began manufacturing airplanes in 1925 with the purchase of the Stout Metal Airplane Company. Bill Stout established his company in 1922 to design and construct all-metal aircraft. By 1926, his well-designed Ford trimotor became the backbone of an emerging airline business. Ford encouraged their larger automobile dealers to establish local passenger routes using the new trimotor. Jack Maddux, a Los Angeles Ford/Lincoln dealer, formed Maddux Airlines and planned to carry passengers between Los Angeles and San Diego. The airline began operations with two Ford trimotors and, by the end of 1928, operated a fleet of thirteen Ford trimotors, two Lockheed Vegas, and two Travelairs. The airline opened a route north to Alameda and a southern route extended to Agua Caliente just south of the Mexican border. Maddux became the first successful west coast passenger airline of true consequence. 1

Larry Fritz, former chief pilot for Stout, maintained this role for Maddux. Fritz began his flying career during WWI as a member

Commodore Larry Fritz. Jim Fritz photo.

of the 282nd Aero Squadron based in England. Before signing on with Stout to test his single-engine all-metal transport plane, Fritz barnstormed and test flew Northrop's sleek Alpha. He took delivery of Maddux's first tri-motor in July 27, 1927. Large crowds gathered to watch the airliner touch down at Rogers Airport. A full-time guard was hired to keep the curious spectators at a safe distance.

Realizing that he could not direct Maddux's expanding business alone, Fritz hired Eddie Bellande, a close friend and roommate, as his assistant. Eddie's relaxed manner contrasted sharply with Fritz's short fuse and propensity for profanity. The two experienced pilots commanded respect and established sound polices; they conducted business in a manner reflective of their personalities. Fritz reputedly began reprimands with "You SOB," although he had a "heart big as his head." 2

The Alameda landing strip, located on the tip of a slender peninsula, lay between an estuary and the eastern shore of the San Francisco Bay. Landing a large airplane at Alameda proved a challenge for any pilot. Not only did they have to stay centered on the narrow strip to avoid the bay but also to avoid contact with a row of hangars near its edge. Moye landed his Travelair just minutes before Eddie turned on final in a Maddux trimotor. Over dinner at his hotel, Eddie brought Moye up-to-date on recent airline developments. Rapidly expanding Maddux Airlines planned to move from Rogers to Glendale's Grand Central Airport where Maddux held the keystone position as the newly-built facility's first tenant. The move was scheduled for the end of February.

Eddie continued the conversation with information about a new airline. "There's a new outfit starting operations this summer, Transcontinental Air Transport. It's backed by Clement Keys' financial group and involves the Pennsylvania Railroad. The first transcontinental passenger airline will operate between New York and Los Angeles. Crossing the continent will take two days and two nights. At the start, airplanes will be used only on the two daylight

Above, Maddux Ford 4-AT with modified windshield parked in front of Grand Central's hangars. Photo courtesy of Katy Ranaldi. Below, Maddux Airlines fleet of trimotors at Grand Central Airport. Author's collection.

sections - Columbus, Ohio to Waynoka, Oklahoma, and Clovis, New Mexico to Los Angeles. Passengers will travel by rail over the two night segments - New York to Columbus and Waynoka to Clovis. [3]

"Larry Fritz is working on the deal right now. Three Maddux captains, Steve Shore, Johnny Guglielmetti, and me, will leave Maddux when TAT starts and are already slated to fly the leg between Los Angeles and Winslow, Arizona. That's where you come in. We will need four captains to handle our section. Your experience, topped off with time in Hancock's equipment, qualifies you for the job except for one thing. TAT wants captains with previous airline experience. If you quit school now, I can get you on at Maddux as a captain. When TAT starts, you, Steve, Johnny Gug, and I will hold down this end."

Bellande's blunt proposition and what it promised seemed truly exciting. Moye never discussed making flying a career with Bellande; in fact, he had never given serious consideration to the idea. He thought of leaving Stanford, but not to become a professional pilot. His law classes now demanded more time than he cared to invest. While his classmates debated trial cases on the steps outside the law building, Moye hurried past them on his way to the airfield. Becoming absorbed in the complexities of jurisprudence and the heated arguments they spurned no longer engaged his interest.

"There's one aspect of the plan that bothers me." Moye confided to Bellande. "Going to work for Maddux, knowing I would be leaving them in a few months, seems pretty shifty. I wouldn't feel too happy about putting them to the expense of checking me out and then having to repeat the procedure with my replacement."

"Wait till you see the bankrupting cost of a checkout." Bellande replied drolly. "But, even if it were an important amount, it wouldn't make any difference. If you're not available for the job, we plan on taking another Maddux captain. When he goes, they'll have to check out a pilot to take his place. The airline is saddled with a checkout either way. Believe me it won't work a great hardship on Maddux.

"The pay involved should be of interest to you. With Maddux, it's $250 a month base pay and five cents a mile for daytime flying, ten cents a mile nights. It generally works out to around $500 a month. On TAT, the pay will be a flat $500 a month. This could be an advantageous setup in view of what the weather in the Rockies might do to schedules. Think it over, but we can't wait too long. I'll have to make other arrangements if you decide not to go along. This is Tuesday. Tomorrow I return to Los Angeles. Thursday, I round trip to Caliente. I have Friday and Saturday off. I'll be back in Alameda Sunday. See if you can't come up with an answer by then. You might meet me here to let me know what you decide."

Over the next five days, Moye agonized over his future and weighed his options. He believed that his father looked forward to the day he would join the family law practice. He also believed that defecting from tradition would be a bitter disappointment for Moye Sr. With two more years remaining to obtain a J. D. (Juris Doctor), Moye questioned whether he possessed the stamina to complete the program, and further, did he have the character necessary to sit in a stuffy office? He knew he didn't. Having experienced the freedom of flight, a lawyer's job seemed stifling and constrained. Whatever he decided, Moye felt obligated to obtain his father's approval.

Moye compared the differences in compensation between the two careers. His first few years as a law clerk would net him approximately $75 a month. Promoted to lawyer status, his earnings would be less than that of an airline captain. The possibility of a greater, ultimate reward practicing law existed. Could that goal be reached by a less than dedicated lawyer? Once Moye realized the progression his passion for flying had taken, accepting an airline captain's position seemed a natural development. That being the case, what better opportunity could he hope for than the one Bellande tossed into his lap?

Never did he imagine, as he poured through those early aviation texts, that he would fly for an airline. Moye knew about early attempts to provide air transportation for the public. A mixture of endeavors included the Zeppelin in 1912 and a Benoist seaplane a year later. Other companies followed using Junkers and Fokkers. American Airways, United Aircraft and Transportation

Corporation, Pan American, and Western Air Express under the direction of C. C. Moseley were, by 1928, among the largest. Confident that airlines would evolve as an essential part of public transportation, Moye saw an opportunity to be part of a definitive epoch of aviation. He welcomed the responsibility the job entailed.

Moye applied for an indefinite leave of absence from Stanford, packed his belongings, said goodbye to Trow, now a freshman at Stanford, and flew home in the Travelair. He debated about giving the family advance notice of his visit but decided it best not to reveal his purpose ahead of time. He believed a face-to-face meeting would somehow lessen the impact of his decision. Countless rehearsals of how to respectfully inform his father consumed Moye during the flight south. By the time he touched down at Clover Field, he felt prepared to calmly argue his resolution. His reserve, however, failed him as he walked through the front door of his home. Seeing the looks of surprise on his parent's faces, Moye nervously blurted out, "I've been offered a full-time job as captain on an airline, Dad, and I want to take it." Attempting to disguise his mixed emotions, Moye Sr. replied, "Okay son. If you'll shave off that god damned mustache, I'll give your decision my blessing."

Rather than expressing excitement over his father's reply, Moye felt like crying - tears of joy, relief, and respect. The significance of earning a living doing what he loved most was prodigious. His father's approval validated his choice. In all probability, Moye's decision did not surprise Moye Sr. Eight years of animated conversations about flying and airplanes could not be dismissed. Moye, thankful for his father's insight, shaved his mustache off before dinner.

That Sunday, Moye met Bellande to accept his offer. Bellande appreciated the decision-making struggle Moye must have endured. He knew it had been an enormous task but was thankful for the outcome. He looked forward to mentoring his friend into the captain's seat of a trimotor. Bellande presented him with all the necessary paperwork and a start date of February 24.

Moye filled the next three weeks with instructing,

passenger hopping, and flying charters for Jim Webster at Rogers Airport. One charter involved a three ship fly-over for a graveside funeral ceremony. Friends of the diseased planned to drop flowers over the ceremony as they circled above. Clarence *Ace* Bragunier, former wing walker, stunt pilot, and flight instructor, led the formation in a Rogers' Travelair. Moye flew one of the wing positions.

An old pilot's superstition gave Moye some misgivings as he watched the flowers being loaded into the airplanes. Turning to Webster with feigned seriousness Moye asked, "Aren't you worried about your ship, Jim? After all, carrying flowers in an airplane is almost as unlucky as changing your helmet or being photographed before a flight." Webster replied that getting paid for the job trumped superstition.

February 22, 1929, Moye joined dozens of southern California pilots for the opening of Grand Central Air Terminal. The Hollywood crowd made their presence known. Howard Hughes, Jean Harlow, Dolores del Rio, and Gary Cooper circulated inside the

Century Pacific Airlines' trimotor parked on the ramp at Grand Central Airport. Al Morgan would work for Century when TAT downsized in the 1930s. Photo courtesy of Katy Ranaldi.

terminal with Los Angeles' financial leaders. Some celebrities arrived in their own airplanes. Wallace Beery, Hoot Gibson, and Ben Lyon with his lovely actress wife Bebe Daniels parked their aircraft in the area reserved for notables. Governor of California Clement C. Young, accompanied the flamboyant Roscoe Turner in his airplane. Over 125,000 spectators gathered for the official ceremonies and the unveiling of new private and commercial aircraft flown in for the occasion. Grand Central would remain Glendale's airport for thirty years, officially ending operations on July 15, 1959. 4

Bellande gave Moye the two required Maddux familiarization flights on his runs to Alameda and then the round-trip from San Diego to Agua Caliente. Seated in the cockpit's right seat, Moye took on the role of *mate*. Maddux did not use copilots. Mechanics went along as mates to repair or service the trimotor as required. Generally captains allowed mates to handle the controls. Eventually some acquired sufficient experience to become captains themselves.

Maddux's fleet consisted of two different Ford trimotor models, the 4–AT and the 5-AT. Powered by three Wright J-5 220 hp engines, the 4-AT could carry up to twelve passengers. The Model 4-AT was far from luxurious. Neatly fitted with canvas covers, the wicker seats were stiff and the noise level from the engines and vibrating metal could reach unbearable levels. With no heat available, the cabin temperatures reached freezing. On the positive side, large windows provided an excellent view; curtains facilitated naps.

Three 450 hp Pratt & Whitney engines gave the Model 5-AT considerable more power. In June 1929, Maddux added several to his inventory. Somewhat larger than the earlier model, the 5-AT carried a few more passengers and afforded a more comfortable ride. Sound-proofed, heated, and properly ventilated, passengers remarked at its luxury. Removable real leather seats replaced the wicker chairs and a compact lavatory added to the passengers' comfort. Nicknamed the *Tin Goose*, the trimotors provided thousands of individuals with their first airplane ride.

Following the San Diego-Agua Caliente trip, Howard *Pop* Fey who recently replaced Fritz as chief pilot, summoned Moye to his office. Moye found the former Army Air Service pilot studying his application as he entered the small office.

"I see you have Lockheed *Vega* experience but it's my duty to at least go through the motions of a check-out. I'm not quite sure how to go about it in a *Vega* with its single-place cockpit and one set of controls. I'm sure as hell not going to ride with you cooped up in the passenger compartment. I guess the flight line will make a moderately safe vantage point. I should be able to count your bounces from there. Come on. Time's a-wastin'."

Fey led Moye to one of the Maddux *Vegas* and directed him to make three landings. Completing them, Moye taxied back to the flight line for a critique of his performance. Fey had disappeared. The next day, Fey sent Moye on a chartered *Vega* flight to Palm Springs. Upon his return, Fey called Moye to his office and this time asked him if he had any experience in the trimotor. Moye said that he had flown with Bellande but did not take off or make any landings. Fey, indicating that now was as good a time as any to do a check-out, escorted Moye to the cockpit of a 4-AT and placed him in the left seat. Fey took the right seat. Moye took off, made a circuit of the field, and then landed.   After three additional landings, relying on the mental notes taken when flying with Bellande, Moye believed his demonstration ended successfully. Maneuvering the airplane with a control wheel rather than the standard stick was initially awkward but not at all unnatural. The same could be said for the plane's unique braking system.   Pulling a lever located between the two seats applied pressure evenly to the two brakes.

The next time Moye boarded a Ford trimotor, he did so as a captain. Assigned the regularly scheduled run to San Diego and Agua Caliente, he departed Grand Central with a mate in the right seat and trusting souls in the passenger compartment. He now understood Bellande's lack of concern about Maddux's check-out procedures. The airline's published practices told a different story.

"Every pilot who is employed must undergo very severe tests before he is permitted to take command of one of the big trimotored Fords which this company operates. Included in these tests are several landings under difficulties. In the first of these, the chief pilot or operating vice president takes the candidate for employment in an otherwise empty transport to a height of 1,000 feet and there, without warning, the switches are suddenly cut on one of the wing motors. The pilot must make a good landing in a field selected by the official who is making the test. In the second of these, the prospective employee is taken to a slightly greater altitude and required to land the ship with only the nose motor. In other tests, the pilot is called upon to land the ship from varying altitudes and from varying positions with all possible combinations of motors." 5

Moye assumed that Maddux subjected all fifteen of their airline pilots to check-outs similar to his. If any of them possessed previous multi-engine flying time, their numbers were few and their time limited. Astonishingly, no accidents resulted from the casual check-outs. Maddux Airlines suffered two crashes, neither a result of poor piloting skills. Investigators declared one to be weather-related. A mid-air collision caused the second.

Maddux scheduled two trips a day to San Diego and Agua Caliente. The first departed Grand Central at 10:30 a.m., stopped in Long Beach and San Diego, and remained in Caliente until 4:00 p.m. before returning to Glendale via San Diego. The second flight departed Grand Central at 4:00 p.m., stopped in San Diego, unloaded its passengers in Caliente, and landed at San Diego's Ryan Field for the night. Next morning, the pilot picked up passengers in Caliente at 9:00 a.m., cleared customs in San Diego, and arrived back at Grand Central via Long Beach.

Extending the airline route across the border to Agua Caliente located northeast of Tijuana, proved very profitable for Maddux. With the Prohibition Act in place and virtually every form of gambling outlawed in the United States, Agua Caliente became an entertainment mecca. Thoroughbred horse owners traveled to Caliente's racetrack from as far away as Europe to compete in purses comparable only to those of the English Derby. Handicap purses ranged from $85,000 to $100,000. Winning thoroughbreds included Sir Harry, Crystal Pennant, and Phar Lap. In 1938, the great Seabiscuit won the last Agua Caliente Handicap Purse of the era. 6

The Agua Caliente Hotel, a sumptuous resort complex designed by Wayne McAllister, opened in 1928. Guests enjoyed cozy bungalows with all the amenities, steaming Turkish baths, a casino, and championship golf and tennis facilities. Talavera tile decorated courtyards hidden behind arcaded portals; the landscape was lush and exotic; and massive doors opened into an interior that included high-beamed ceilings and an abundance of beautiful floor and wall tile. The elegant bar and gambling casino were irresistible attractions to the international set and California's high society which included politicians, actors, and pilots. The Marx Brothers, Joe E. Brown, Charlie Chaplin, Jean Harlow, Clark Gable, Howard Hughes, and Gary Cooper were just a few of the celebrities indulging themselves at the Agua Caliente Resort. 7

With a full load of passengers for Caliente, a cloudless blue sky greeted the newly appointed Captain Stephens as he departed Grand Central on his first flight. The crisp, clean air resonated in tune with his effervescent spirits. As he flew south, his thoughts went back to the day Gil Budwig flashed past the Rogers Airport hangar in his vintage Fokker D-VII. The spectacle inspired wistful memories for him. At the time, he wondered how many eons

The 85 foot campanile stood at the entrance to the elegant Agua Caliente Resorts and served as a beacon for the airfield. Note the trimotor circling overhead. Vintage postcard part of the author's collection.

would pass before he, too, would be permitted the thrill of flying a high performance airplane. Now, here he sat, at the controls of an airliner, a member of a select group entrusted to fly passengers and being paid for it!

The route to Caliente took place over flat terrain or the Pacific Ocean which allowed Moye to concentrate on familiarizing himself with the trimotor's capabilities. If he encountered adverse weather, he could follow the Los Angeles River to Long Beach and then hug the shoreline to San Diego without fear of running into any mountains. Dense fog was the only weather condition that resulted in Maddux canceling a flight.

During his first layover in Caliente, Moye wandered through the fashionable hotel. His posture reflected the smartness of his new navy blue uniform with gold wings, gold stripes, and brass buttons. As he strolled into the lobby, his sense of pride reached a pinnacle, far higher than his six feet. Passing the front desk, a guest in the middle of a hurried check out, stopped him

"Young man, that's my wife standing over there with the suitcases by the potted palm. Would you please carry the bags out to our car? She'll show you where it's parked."

So much for Moye's swelling pride. He mumbled something about not wishing to interfere with the bellman's union and continued on to the casino.

Though Maddux pilots abstained from drinking while on their runs, gambling was permitted. Moye observed the games of roulette, baccarat, and faro; learned the rules and methods of playing; and decided they were all games of chance with little skill required. Having just begun a new career, he believed opening a savings account preferable to squandering his money at the table. He would continue to observe, leaving his earnings in his wallet.

On his third run to Caliente, a problematic situation confronted Moye. An unusually heavy passenger booking required the scheduler to add a second flight. Captain Henry G. *Andy* Andrews commanded the first run. Moye flew the second. Thirty minutes before his 4:00 return flight, a stratus formation drifted in from the Pacific at about 500 feet. A telephone call to Ryan Field indicated that the ceiling held at that level. In a brief consultation before Andy's take-off, he and Moye agreed to proceed, flying under the clouds to San Diego and on to Grand Central.

Andy took off ten minutes before Moye. When Moye departed, it appeared that the ceiling would hold but as he approached the southern end of San Diego Bay, the ceiling dropped to less than 200 feet. Half way up the bay, he held steady at fifty feet over the water, aware that the mast tops of naval vessels anchored in the bay loomed higher than his altitude. An abrupt turn would be impossible if the ceiling lowered further. But where was Andy? If he turned back, Moye would certainly have seen him. If Moye turned around and Andy flew through the weather, how would it reflect on his competence as an airline pilot? Focusing on his primary responsibility, Moye made a 180 degree turn toward Mexico. A reprimand by the chief pilot seemed far better than testing his competence and ending up in the hereafter along with his passengers.

Moye made a smooth landing in Caliente and, while taking care of some routine paper work, the door of the passenger compartment slammed open. A very drunk and irritated gentleman stood there, flushed and breathing heavily. "What in hell do you mean by cancelling the flight?" he ranted. "I have a nine o'clock appointment tomorrow morning in Los Angeles with a very important client faced with serious legal difficulties. I've got to get back. I demand that you take me to Los Angeles."

Moye, attempting to relax from the tensions of the flight and worried about Andy, responded to the gentleman in a rather curt manner. "Look, you're a lawyer. Your demand indicates you know little about flying. Even though I have an A.B. degree in law, I wouldn't presume to walk into your office and tell you how to run your business. What do you think qualifies you to tell me how to run mine? Would you rather be up the line with your ass wrapped around the mast of a battleship or back here in Caliente where you can down some gin on a bar stool?"

The next morning the disgruntled passenger came up to the cockpit, sober and in a contrite mood. He and Moye exchanged apologies.

When he cleared customs in San Diego, Moye learned that Andy managed to get through to Grand Central. Minimal conditions held just long enough for him to complete the route. On Moye's return, Captain D. W. Tomlinson, former leader of the Navy's crack stunt team, the Three Sea Hawks, and now Maddux's Director of Operations, summoned Moye and Andy to his office. "I'm sure there's a logical explanation, but when two of my ships take off ten minutes apart on the same route and one gets through and the other doesn't, I naturally have to find out what happened. Andy, you completed the flight. What was your weather?"

The situation did not bode well for Moye, the newest Maddux pilot.

Andy spoke abruptly. "I believe I know what you're thinking, Tommy. If I'm right, you're wrong. If I could have turned around over San Diego Bay, I would have. Before I realized it, I was in so deep and was flying so low, I was afraid to try. The ceiling lifted before I got to Dutch Flats. I had no trouble from there on." 8

Tomlinson asked Moye about the weather when he entered the bay. After listening to his description of the deteriorating conditions, Tomlinson agreed that Moye made the right decision. Moye breathed a sigh of relief. From that day forth, he held his supervisor in exceptionally high esteem.

By April, Moye had amassed an entire month's experience as an airline pilot with no major dents in his self-confidence. Practical knowledge, largely gained through trial and error, eventually placed Moye at the head of the class. His lessons ranged from amusing to tragic. A minor, but memorable, flying situation occurred on a flight to San Diego. His passenger list included two handcuffed convicts in the custody of a deputy sheriff. Not feeling comfortable with only one deputy guarding the convicts, Doc Whitney made his way to the cockpit and loaned Moye his .45 caliber Colt for added protection - just in case!

April 21, Captain Maurice Murphy and mate Louis Pratt departed Grand Central on the new Los Angeles-San Diego-Phoenix run. Murphy had renounced the nickname of *Loop* when he began his employment with Maddux. His associates now knew him as *Murph*. He and Pratt departed for Phoenix just before Moye landed at Ryan Field en route to Agua Caliente. Immediately after Moye shut down his engines, Jimmy Polk, a Maddux traffic man, informed him that Murph had crashed in Mission Valley. Shaken, Moye continued his run to Agua Caliente. Not knowing the particular circumstance of the crash intensified his distress. His friendship with *Murph* dated from his first days at the original Rogers Airport. Moye's anxiety persisted until his return trip to Ryan Field where other pilots confirmed the accident – a midair collision with no survivors. How ironic that *Murph* should survive for years as a stunt pilot only to lose his life shortly after settling down in a responsible career.

Climbing out over Mission Valley, an Army pursuit plane crashed into the trimotor. Murph's three passengers included the girl friend of the Army pilot, a Lieutenant Keeler. In an apparent effort to impress the girl, Keeler attempted to loop around the airliner. Approaching head-on, he dove below the trimotor and pulled straight up behind it in the start of a loop. The hair-brained stunt misfired. Coming off his back at the top of the loop, he dove vertically into the trimotor's nose engine. The impact severed the engine from its mount, crippled the right outboard engine, and seriously damaged the right wing. The propeller of the pursuit plane sliced through the cockpit, completely decapitating Louis and tearing away a piece of *Murph*'s skull.

From eyewitness accounts, it appeared that *Murph* remained conscious to within a few hundred feet of the ground. Intermittent bursts of power from the remaining engine indicated an attempt to maintain control of the airplane. At the point at which Murph either lost consciousness or died, the ship rolled inverted and crashed. Keeler survived the collision but attempting to parachute from his plane, he pulled his ripcord too soon. His parachute became entangled in the plane's tail and he was carried to his death.

Just nine days after Murph's fatal accident, another trimotor crash occurred that stunned all of the Maddux pilots. On March 17, Lou Foote, flying a Colonial Western Airways Ford 4-AT, took off from Newark Airport on a local flight with a full load of Sunday sightseers. The ship approached an altitude of 500 feet when its left wing engine failed. In an attempt to maintain flight, Foote no sooner leveled off when the center engine failed. The ship was unable to stay airborne with only one of its three engines functioning. The trimotor crashed into a Newark marsh. Foote remained the sole survivor of the worst United States airplane disaster in the history of aviation. [9]

The magnitude of the disaster inspired debate among the pilots regarding emergency procedures for the 4-AT. Those who had experienced the loss of one engine shared how they compensated with the two remaining engines. Creating scenarios for the loss of two engines in flight, they concluded that the 4-AT, fully loaded, would result in a catastrophic situation. With a gross weight of 10,000 pounds, one Wright 220 hp J-5 lacked the power to keep the airplane aloft as Foote discovered.

April 30, Moye lost his right outboard engine during the take-off from San Diego. With no runway left to abort the take-off, Moye calculated the altitude required to clear the high tension lines just past the end of the runway. The loss of power and the drag from the wind milling propeller left little room for error. He held the trimotor in a steeper nose-high attitude than usual and just skimmed over the wires. Much relieved, Moye began investigating the cause of the engine failure. Checking the right fuel valve, he discovered it to be in the 'on' position. Moving the handle, he heard a click into detent and the motor purred to life. Moye's new mate had turned the valve but not far enough. In that position, the engine consumed all available fuel during the low rpm period before take-off.

Having remedied the right engine, the center engine swallowed a valve twenty minutes later. Though performance was marginal, the Ford handled well enough to return to Grand Central. Only four of the seven passengers, all very intoxicated Hollywood notables, decided to try again for Caliente. Moye took the company's Lockheed *Vega* on the second attempt to reach the south-of-the-border town. An absence of lights in the airplane and on the Caliente strip necessitated an immediate departure even though the dispatcher pointed out that the almanac gave him plenty of time to reach his destination before nightfall.

Preparing the *Vega* for departure took longer than anticipated yet Moye still believed he could land before all daylight disappeared.   Forty miles out, he started having misgivings. Whether the sun set prematurely behind the heavy cloud build-up out to sea or the dispatcher embellished on the time of sunset, darkness set in before Moye reached Oceanside. He navigated by following a faint white ribbon of foam marking the coastline as he passed over the sleepy seaside community.   Then, without the slightest warning, the *Vega*'s engine quit.   Moye, hoping for a low tide, quickly began looking for a sufficient width of beach on which to land.   Fortunately, just before touching down, the engine sputtered to life. Having unpleasant visions of sinking into the soft sand and flipping the plane onto its back, Moye was greatly relieved.

Moye considered landing at Ryan Field but he knew the difficulty of finding the unlit field on a dark night.   Too many unknown obstacles existed once he passed over outlying high tension lines. A landing at the Naval Air Station San Diego, in an aircraft not equipped for night flight and carrying four inebriated passengers, meant the inevitable scrutinizing of Maddux operations and the revoking of Moye's pilot license for an unconscionable period. Moye continued south.

Perched on the brink of a steep bluff, Agua Caliente's narrow strip overlooked the resort to the north.   A deep gully crossed each end of the runway making the point of contact on landing critical. Moye located the strip by referencing the lights of the hotel, the headlights of cars on the adjacent highway, and most importantly, the eighty-five foot campanile that served three purposes. It was a bell tower, the beacon for the airstrip, and the lighted sign entrance from the road leading to the hotel.

The dispatcher had promised to aim his car's headlights down the strip but as Moye circled over the area, he saw no headlights in the vicinity of the field. His eyes strained on final approach to determine the location of the gully in the darkness ahead. He did not spot it until he was practically on top of it, his wheels just inches from touchdown. Holding the plane off the tarmac for a few extra seconds, he set down clear of the gully but he was not out of danger yet. He had the gully at the opposite end with which to deal. He applied maximum brakes and planned a ground-loop as soon as the *Vega* slowed down enough to complete the maneuver safely. When he started the ground-loop, his landing light gave him a quick glimpse of the gully. Less than a foot lay between the *Vega*'s tail wheel and the gully.

Moye's last month of employment with Maddux Airlines proved uneventful. The airline promoted him to the San Francisco route and Bellande hired Dick Ranaldi as Moye's replacement for the Agua Caliente route. Dick was extremely happy to have his two familiarization flights with Moye. Always competent and at ease in the cockpit, Dick handled the Ford well. Entries in his logbook began with his Maddux employment. A persistent doodler and note-taker, Dick filled his logbook with humorous drawings, notations concerning flights, and important events such as a daughter's birthday and Leo Nomis' unexpected death in 1932.

May 25, 1928, Moye made his final run in a Maddux trimotor. Before signing on with Transcontinental Air Transport (TAT), the Professional Pilots Association elected Moye as president. Following WWI, a group of twenty pilots, including Waldo Waterman, formed the organization. They elected Gilbert Budwig as their first president. Moye, a staunch supporter of the organization, shared its concern for a pilot's safety in the air and their fair treatment by management. He encouraged open communication between the organization's members and their employers. Sharing experiences relating to all aspects of flying, improved the safety of crew and passengers. 10

That same year, Moye helped found the Los Angeles Hangar of the Quiet Birdmen. Conceived in France on Armistice Day, former WWI pilots founded the organization in 1921 to "keep flying alive" after the war. "QB Hangars" gradually became established throughout the United States. The organization's rules were strict and included the following prohibitions - "a constitution, by-laws, dues, assessments, agendas, officers, speeches, big shots, head tables, attempts to sell anything, conduct business of any kind, or "Kee-Wees" (non-aviators) and women as members. The only women allowed at the meetings were professional entertainers. QB meetings continue to maintain their informality but are far from quiet. 11

Clement M. Keys, founder of Transcontinental Air Transport, appointed Paul Collins, WWI veteran and airmail pilot; John Collings, former chief pilot at Ford; and Colonel Charles Lindbergh, Chairman of the Technical Committee of TAT, to select the pilots. Two distinct groups resulted. The first group consisted of pilots recruited from the airmail lines, aircraft manufacturing companies, and the military services. They averaged 3,000 flight hours, 500 of which were in trimotors. Graduates of the Army Training Center at Kelly Field, Texas made up the second group. All pilots were assigned to the particular part of the country with which they were familiar.

TAT issued orders for the pilots to report for duty on June 1 in St. Louis. The four captains assigned to the Glendale-Winslow division boarded the Santa Fe Chief for the trip east. Bellande, Steve Shore, Johnny Guglielmetti, and Moye thoroughly enjoyed their leisure time together. It was almost like those carefree days at Clover or Rogers when they participated in easy conversation in front of someone's hangar. They discussed their past, present, and future, pooling their cumulated experience to prepare themselves for flying at high altitudes, through winter blizzards and summer thunder storms, and the regulations of TAT.

Prior to employment by Maddux, Steve Shore served as chief petty officer in the Navy. While Moye worked at Rogers, Steve belonged to a three ship contingency of Navy DH-4Bs that flew in formation over the field before landing. Engrossed in thumbing his nose at the other two planes, Steve flew into a huge haystack at the northwest corner of the field. He still bore scars on the bridge of his nose from the mishap.

Johnny *Glug* soloed in Santa Rosa in 1922, two years prior to Moye doing so. Before hiring on with Maddux, he flew the mail for Varney Airlines. He spent two years flying the Rocky Mountain run from Elko, Nevada to Pasco, Washington. At the age of twenty, he became the youngest pilot approved by the post office to fly the U.S. mail at the time. When asked how they could draw on this experience to help them tackle the new route, his answer made sense. "What the hell. Every run is different. We'll have to learn to fly this one in the only way possible - simply by doing it."

Maddux Airlines advertised on holidays to acquire additional revenue from passenger hops. Author's photo.

7

TRANSCONTINENTAL
AIR TRANSPORT

Transcontinental Air Transport began preparations for a rail-air passenger service in May 1928. Routes and airports needed to be selected. Hangars, passenger stations, beacon lights, and radio towers were essential for superior airline operations and passenger safety. In some cases, an entire airfield had to be built. When Colonel Charles Lindbergh selected Kingman, Arizona as a refueling and passenger stop, an area in the Wallapai (Hualapai) Valley north of town was transformed into Port Kingman, the first dedicated airport in northern Arizona. Kingman would serve the airline well. Known as a crossroads for travel since 1859 when the United States experimental Camel Corps passed through the area, the town was now a major railroad and highway junction. 1

January 18, 1929, bids went out for construction of a hangar large enough to hold four trimotors, a passenger depot, and radio station. Leveling and grading land for the runway began in March. All structures, a radio tower, 30,000,000 beam candle power flood light, and infrastructures were completed or installed by mid June. Dedication of the new TAT facility took place June 25, 1929. That Tuesday, every business in Kingman closed to allow their employees

TAT original pilots. Left to right - (Row 1) Paul F. Collins (General Supt.), H. H. 'Pat' Gallup, Carl W. Rach, Harry E. Campbell, Vernon R. Lucas, Wm .M. Campbell, Clifford W. Abbott, Fred Richardson, Eddie Bellande, Wesley Philippi, Howard E. Hall, John A. Collings (Supt. Eastern Division). (Center Row) Morley F. Slaght, H. J. Zimmerman, Ambrose Banks, T. B. Hoy, Moye W. Stephens, Joseph S. Bartles, Stephen R. Shore, Otis F. Bryan, Earl F. Fleet. (Back Row) J. B. Stowe, D. W. Burford, T. R. Howe, Edwin A. Dietel, N. A. Laurenzana, Nobel G. Hueter, Paul Scott, Lester D. Munger, J. A. Guglielmetti. Missing from the photo are Ben O. Howard, Harry W. McGee, St. Clair D. Welsh, F. V. Tompkins, and George C. Price. Author's photo.

to join their fellow Arizonians to watch the proceedings. Some hoped for a glimpse of Lindbergh but he was not on the field that historic day. He would, however, make the inaugural TAT flight to Kingman in the *City of Los Angeles* on July 12, 1929. 2

The indoctrination of the new TAT pilots in St. Louis gave the thirty-three pilots an opportunity to become acquainted. They came from the four corners of the country, possessed a variety of experience and stood united by one common certainty. The lives of their passengers and the survival of the airline depended upon their competence and good fortune.

The TAT training prepared the pilots for a second class radio telephone operator's license test and a proficiency test operating the low frequency radio communication sets on board the TAT trimotors. Assistant pilots or mates were responsible for winding in the antenna before landing, a task often overlooked and one responsible for the loss of several antennas. The company also required an instrument flight check which consisted of taking a load of pilots aloft in a 5-AT and giving each a turn at the controls in a hooded left front seat. They demonstrated flying straight and level and initiating simple turns using an earth inductor compass, a stable heading indicator as was the directional gyro that later replaced them. Moye never used the compass which incorporated a wind-driven generator. Meant to reduce wear and tear, a locking pin, normally inserted in its drive shaft, kept the generator inoperative. If the pilot wanted to use the compass, he simply had to remove the pin. It could only be relocked on the ground by a mechanic. This indicated to Moye that the compass acted as an emergency device, something he never needed. 4

When a pilot achieved the requisite skills for flying on instruments, his instructor sent him to check pilot Dean W. Burford. Burford's proficient instrument skills saved his life as a mail pilot for TWA in the late 1930s. On a flight from Newark to Columbus, he encountered a dangerous sleet storm over the Alleghenies. Climbing above the cloud layer, he found warm air but became disorientated after four hours. Burford's ability to rely on his instruments and the plane's radiophone (very high frequency receiver/transmitter) enabled him to regain his bearings. 5

Following the training in St. Louis, Moye ferried a 5-AT to the Ford factory in Dearborn to have skins on the top wing surfaces replaced. Flying alone in small airplanes was common place. Accompanied by 15 empty seats induced a feeling of loneliness bordering on the eerie. On June 18, he delivered the ship to Clovis, New Mexico, TAT's eastern station for their western division. Scheduled flights, albeit empty, started the next morning. For one week, the pilots familiarized themselves with the route, weather, and procedures. Moye rode in the passenger compartment from Clovis and then took over the controls from Winslow to Glendale, his permanent assignment. Wesley Philippi, congenial and anxious to help as best he could, served as his mate. The two made the first scheduled flight with passengers from Winslow to Glendale in the

City of Washington.

Moye's first trips carrying passengers went smoothly. Passengers presented no complaints and fair weather persisted until his fourteenth flight. South of Flagstaff, a towering, unbroken line of thunderheads stretched from north to south. The storm was easily visible from Winslow, 45 miles to the east. Weather reports gave no hint of its magnitude. As he approached the storm at an altitude of 7,500 feet, Moye encountered sufficient turbulence to require everyone to tighten their seat belts. His co-pilot, Noble G. *Bass* Hueter, advised the courier, the TAT designation for steward, to check on the passengers. 6

TAT trimotor flying over a heavy cloud layer. Photo courtesy of Katy Ranaldi.

Realizing that the most threatening weather he had ever encountered lay ahead, Moye quickly began assessing whether to proceed or turn back. Before he could make a decision, a giant, ominous-looking cloud loomed directly in front of him. Deluging rain, intense lightning, and dangerously low visibility flanked the massive shape on either side. A constant barrage of flashing thunderbolts emanated from the graying sky. Circling down to an altitude of 1,000 feet above the ground, Moye discovered a faint glimmer of light at the far end of a tunnel-like passage at the cloud's base. Although the weather remained foreboding above him, he believed he could make it through as long as the beacon light at the end of the passage stayed visible. Flying at near ground level offered the best chance of avoiding the wrath of the storm and resulting in the loss of the ship and all aboard.

As Moye was congratulating himself on his remarkable weather wisdom, the storm abruptly seized the trimotor and propelled it upward with an unrelenting, rocket-like thrust. He instinctively nosed the plane down into a steep dive, frantically striving to maintain visual contact with the all important patch of light. The futility of the maneuver became apparent. Airspeed and rpm indicators red-lined. The rate-of-climb indicator pegged at maximum ascent. The viciousness of the turbulence caused the ship to pitch and roll wildly. Moye reduced airspeed and relied on instruments to maintain control of the ship. He felt ill-prepared to cope with the predicament in which he found himself. Mixed emotions of fear and exhilaration consumed him. Time ceased to exist.

At 18,000 feet, the thunder cloud tossed the airplane out into bright sunlight. Moye had escaped a disastrous encounter with destructive weather in a worthy aircraft. Had TAT decided to use the Fokker F-10 tri-motor, the only other United States airliner at the time, instead of the Ford tri-motor, the outcome of his flight might have been similar to the following incident. Eight on board a Fokker F-10, flown by Bob Fry and Jesse Mathias, perished along with the famed Notre Dame football coach Knute Rockne when the load from heavy icing snapped the plywood spars and caused the wing to separate from the fuselage. Had Rockne not bullied Fry into taking off that day, their lives would have been spared. Jimmy Dole lost both wings on his F-10 in weather over the San Bernardino Mountains. Ralph Montee, an original Western Air Express captain from Texas, lost the ailerons on his F-10 near Albuquerque. There were no survivors in any of these crashes. 7

Taxing up to the terminal at Grand Central, Moye realized how exhausted he was. Laboring with the trimotor's heavy controls through the tempestuous storm, battling strong head winds into the Los Angeles basin, and harboring a constant and genuine concern for his passengers had taken their toll. A flight in normal conditions in the all-metal trimotor was a challenge; it must have been horrendous as the storm tossed the plane about like a toy. Moye and his mate normally helped the passengers out of the airplane after shutting down the engines. This time, crew and passengers remained in their seats to absorb the moment. Eventually stepping onto the tarmac, the passengers looked pale and worn. Some thanked Moye for his skills; others just looked stunned as they headed silently toward the terminal.

Moye felt obliged to share his experience with his fellow pilots as a means of alerting them to the particular weather phenomenon but was met with disbelief. Not one of them could

Maddux-TAT Ford trimotor departs from the Kingman airfield. Photo courtesy of Mohave Museum of History and Arts.

comprehend the forces that Moye had encountered. In fact, he received a good dose of their ribbing for quite some time. "Man!" Captain Steve Shore commented. "It sure is a good thing you were able to come down out of that cloud! Why, we might have had to break out the biscuit gun. Starvation is a nasty way to go."

"Say," he began another of his absurd suggestions, "I heard a feller back in Oshkosh just invented an upside down parachute.

Maybe you ought to look into it."

Not too long after, Eddie Bellande, dean of pilots, returned from a run with an account of his own experience which duplicated Moye's almost exactly. He reported that at the onset of the rocket ride, he momentarily put the ship into an absolutely vertical dive with wide open throttles but to no avail. Bellande's encounter reaffirmed Moye's account. With two reports of the same weather and subsequent consequences, the other pilots paid more attention and eventually achieved a respect for Mother Nature. They learned alternative approaches that led to safer flying as they accumulated more air time.

TAT issued memos regarding weather from Paul Collins, General Superintendent. The pilot, field manager, and weather observer were required to consult as a team in the case of uncertain weather conditions. In the case of differing opinions, the pilot's judgment was final. "He has the responsibility in the air where adverse conditions are met . . . Naturally, he will be guided by all information submitted on the ground and through radio in the air. We wish to reiterate, and strongly emphasize that no pilot shall *take a chance* on getting through." The company recommended pilots fly at a minimum altitude of 1,000 feet but gave them the discretion of flying lower if weather warranted it. With a ceiling of less than 500 feet and one mile visibility, a pilot with a load of passengers was to land, either by returning or by landing on an emergency field. 8

In addition, Collins cautioned TAT pilots about discussing weather with the passengers. "Please do not discuss weather conditions within the hearing of any of our passengers as it only results in these remarks being magnified as they are passed on, and eventually, it reacts badly upon them. If a passenger in any way anticipates rough weather, you can readily appreciate how it will prey upon his piece of mind." 9

On September 3, 1929, Moye completed his eastbound run to Winslow fifteen minutes behind schedule due to bad weather. The station manager and the relief crew for westbound pilots expressed alarm over the failure of their plane to arrive. Captain J. B. Stowe, co-pilot Edward A. Dietel, courier C. T. Canfield, and five passengers were over an hour and a half late. Dietel radioed the plane's last position report fifteen minutes past Albuquerque.

Eastern division superintendent John Collings called a meeting of the three crews and the station manager to discuss the apparent emergency. J. B.'s next position report should have followed the last within fifteen minutes. Static interference could not be ruled out as an explanation for the missing communications. Radio failure posed another possibility. At the conclusion of the meeting, the pilots regularly scheduled for the eastbound run, Captain Lester D. Munger and co-pilot Morley F. Slaght, took off to complete the flight to Clovis. The crew awaiting the westbound ship, Johnny Glug and Bill Campbell, stood by to continue the flight in the event J. B. showed up. Collings, Heuter, and Moye took off in the reserve ship and flew a serpentine search course over the area between Winslow and Albuquerque. Persistent foul weather and eventual darkness greatly reduced their chances of finding the missing ship.

That night in Albuquerque, Collings took steps to organize a search that ended up lasting ten days. TAT abandoned all regular airline functions and transferred its entire fleet of airplanes to Albuquerque and Winslow to take part in the search. The Army and Navy contributed additional planes. The promise by TAT of a $10,000 reward for the discovery of the missing ship enticed a number of private planes to participate. Ironically, in spite of the large number of planes and pilots participating in the search, an airline crew on a routine flight discovered the wreckage. 10

On the tenth day of the search, George Rice, flying a Fokker F-10 trimotor for Western Air Express, deviated north of his course to scout the southern slopes of 11,301 foot Mount Taylor, 57 miles west of Albuquerque. As his steward scanned the mountainside, he caught a glint among the trees and notified his captain. The flash of light turned out to be J. B.'s trimotor, the *City of San Francisco*. George, his steward, and co-pilot collected the $10,000 reward. Moye and other pilots had flown over the crash site a number of times but conditions did not allow for a sighting through the dense forest. The wind apparently blew J. B., flying on instruments at the time, off course and into the mountain. The nearby town of Grants reported an eighty mile an hour wind out of the south at the approximate time of the crash.

Paul *Dog* Collins, now Chief of Operations, enlisted the aid of forest rangers to lead a rescue party composed of himself, a few pilots, and a large contingent of cowpunchers to the crash. A pack of reporters and a photographer tailed behind. Arriving at the crash, they discovered a ghastly site of badly mangled victims in a state of decomposition. Nevertheless, the photographer made the rounds, taking meticulous close-ups of the gruesome remains.

Collins watched quietly until the photographer had exposed all his plates and, after confiscating the lot, smashed them on a rock. The reporters lashed out at Collins. They shouted that he had violated their right of free speech by destroying the photographic evidence. "The holy right of the people to know has been viciously profaned!" Just as the enraged newspapermen began to rush Collins, the rangers and cowpunchers stepped in and rudely chased the swarm off the mountain.

Results of any tragic accident are predictable. The number of deaths made airline news in a time when much of the public considered airline travel to be frivolous and dangerous. The accident proved their point. Any airplane crash after that, big or small, related somehow to the example of the "TAT Mount Taylor Crash". For months, TAT's ticket sales dwindled. Many scheduled trips flew without a single passenger. The pilots amused themselves by chasing herds of antelope on Mormon Mesa, southeast of Flagstaff. They raced past Santa Fe passenger trains at ground level hoping to impress their passengers with their superior speed. Moye noticed that the trimotor executed nice wing-overs and half rolls.

To stimulate business, TAT decided to lower fares to the level of train fares. This produced a few passengers. By further reducing them to match bus fares, an additional handful of brave souls purchased tickets. A reduction to less than bus fare filled every flight to capacity. The airline could not hope to survive on these meager sales, however. When they reinstated the original tariff, the passenger rate dropped to its former deplorable figure. Passengers or no passengers, the schedule needed to be maintained if the airline hoped to qualify for a prospective air mail contract. With the passage of time, the public would gain more confidence in flying which increased ticket sales.

TAT hired new pilots for the Clovis-Winslow route following the Taylor crash. Frederick G. *Ritchie* Richardson transferred from the eastern division to take Stowe's place. Al Morgan landed the copilot spot. Piloting Wallace Beery's Travel Air Model A-6000, with a 425 hp Pratt & Whitney Wasp engine, significantly enhanced Al's flight experience. Moye and Dick Ranaldi happily reunited with Al. Despite the different directions each took, they maintained the close friendship that began at Clover Field. Within ten years, all three would become part of another phase of aviation.

On November 16, 1929, TAT and Maddux Airlines merged in order to eliminate duplication of services and avoidable expenses. Employees of both airlines received an official memo from TAT Vice President J. Magee, on November 5, 1929.

In order to promote greater efficiency, the Executive Committee of TAT has ruled that the TAT and Maddux organizations be combined effective November 16, 1929. The present Western Division of TAT, from Clovis to Los Angeles, will be operated by Mr. J. L. Maddux, vice president and director of TAT. The combined organizations will be known as TAT-Maddux and will extend from Columbus to Los Angeles and from Agua Caliente to San Francisco. I take this opportunity to thank you for the whole-hearted and efficient assistance you have given me and I sincerely request every employee to cooperate with Mr. Maddux to the fullest extent. 11.

Former Maddux flight operations manager D. W. Tomlinson served as vice president in charge of operations for the combined airlines. Equalizing the salary for TAT and Maddux pilots became his first priority. Base pay started at $150 supplemented by mileage at the rate of five cents per mile for day flying and ten cents per mile for night flying determined by one half hour after sunset. A pilot earned ten dollars a day for ground duty. The airline provided the

Maddux-TAT Captains J. B. Stowe, T. B. Hoye, and Moye with a group of local Kingman residents outside the terminal building. Photo courtesy of the Mohave Museum of History and Arts.

pilots with leather fleece-lined boots and a life insurance policy valued at $10,000. Pilots paid for their uniforms — suit, cap, ties, and shirts — totaling $44.35 which was deducted from their paycheck. Optional items, such as leather gloves and company overcoats, were also paid for by the pilots. Although Maddux provided the pilots with free lunches - typically a fruit cocktail, fried chicken and rolls - TAT cancelled this practice. A number of the pilots, including Moye, were deliberately accused of making a trip more turbulent so at least one passenger became too ill to eat his box lunch. "After all, at the age of 22 or 23," Moye grinned during an interview for the Airport Owners and Pilots Association (AOPA) magazine, "a fellow had quite an appetite." 12

Tomlinson appointed Bellande as superintendent of the Glendale to Winslow "Section A" route; Tex Marley supervised "Section B" from Winslow to Clovis. Maddux mates became co-pilots after obtaining a pilot license. The responsibility for the Glendale-Clovis route went to former TAT copilots, obligated to complete the entire run without an overnight stop in Winslow. The two day round-trip took eighteen hours followed by two days off.

The change required Al to shift his base from Clovis to Glendale which enabled him to fly with Moye on many of his runs.

Moye considered some TAT management practices unfair. The treatment of the pilots composed part of his grievance. The majority, however, focused on the airline's tendency to burden pilots with unwarranted responsibilities for mechanical difficulties which, through maintenance, could be avoided. Once, the left outboard engine of his trimotor ran slightly rougher than normal. Readjustment of the carburetor mixture provided no change. A magneto check revealed nothing. Upon landing in Winslow, he noted the roughness on the flight report. He also discussed the puzzling nature with Ritchie Richardson, the captain who, with Al Morgan as copilot, would complete the flight to Clovis.

The next day Les Munger and Al flew the ship on its return flight. As Les handed the next leg to Moye, he commented, "Oh, by the way, the left outboard is running rough." Moye stated he previously squawked the rough engine and inquired if mechanics inspected the motor in Clovis. Les didn't know.

Leveling off at 12,000 feet, Moye varied the rpm on the suspect engine. Higher rpms increased the irregularity; lower rpms produced less. Just south of Bill Williams Mountain, he shut the engine down with positive results. On the tarmac at Kingman, with the left engine nacelle cowling removed, the motor mount displayed cracks in three places. The supporting straps for the oil tank were broken; only the oil lines held the tank. Glendale learned of the incident by teletype. Dick Ranaldi was immediately dispatched in a 5-AT with a welder and welding outfit to repair the motor mount. Upon Dick's arrival, his copilot and Moye loaded the passengers into his ship and completed the run to Glendale. Dick stayed over with Al to ferry the repaired trimotor to Grand Central.

Just off the ground on the return trip, Al shouted above the roar of the wide open engines, "Dick, it's running rougher than before!"

Dick made a quick circuit of the field, landed, and removed the cowling with the assistance of a mechanic. The motor mount was cracked again, in two places this time. Dick leaned against the propeller to see behind the engine and into the naked nacelle

A TAT team that achieved some notoriety as the 'Chinese Crew' - Moye, Hoy, and Lee. Left to right, Courier Charley Lee, Copilot Ben Hoy, and Captain Moye Stephens. Museum of Flight photo.

structure. The driver of the gasoline truck, standing behind Dick, told him to lean forward again. As Dick pressed against the blade, a crack of startling proportions in the hub opened up. If the crack progressed in the air, a separated propeller could cause irreparable damage to the airplane, if not result in an unfortunate crash. When Al and Dick returned to Glendale, complete with a new propeller, the bulletin board in the pilots' room displayed an official reprimand of Captains Stephens, Richardson, and Munger for flying the ship in an 'unsafe' manner. Moye wondered what the consequences would have been had he grounded the ship 'on a hunch'.

When Major R. W. "Shorty" Schroeder, aviation engineer

and Ford factory executive, lost a blade, the complete engine assembly shook loose from the wing. The assembly, composed of the engine, nacelle, and main landing gear strut, then dropped down and, swinging on the hinge fittings of the landing gear brace struts, passed under the fuselage. Gaining momentum, the assembly traveled to the opposite side of the plane and became entangled with the propeller of the other outboard engine. The engine's nacelle promptly shook loose, swung down, and then both engine nacelle-landing gear assemblies tore loose and fell earthward. Schroeder immediately found himself in command of a single engine 4-AT. Even minus the weight and drag of the missing assemblies, the question remained as to how long the ship could stay airborne with one 220 hp J-5. Not wanting to risk his life finding out, Schroeder made a belly landing in a convenient cornfield.

Moye, Dick, and Al, in addition to enjoying each other's company as airline captains, spent their leisure hours together. They met for drinks at recently divorced Leo Nomis' bachelor quarters followed by dinner at Loren McHuron's Grill on Hollywood Boulevard. They always ordered the specialty of the house, *Toad in the Hole.* The entree consisted of an entire steak inserted in the cleft of an enormous baked Idaho potato garnished with sour cream and chives. Dick, known for his off-colorful escapades, supplied most of the entertainment. During one dinner, he shared a story.

Amelia Earhart, Assistant to the General Traffic Manager of TAT at the time, asked Dick to retrieve her Lockheed *Vega* from Kansas City. En route to the west coast, foul weather forced her to land at the city's Fairfax Airport. Aware of his reputation for downing a few drinks before and during a flight, she cornered him and asked with apprehension, "I know you won't take a single drink on this flight, will you, Dick?"

Dick, eyes growing round in innocent amazement, provided an affirmation of sorts. "God no, Amelia. It's at least a two quart job." The remark left Amelia speechless.

Dick also shared his first encounter with a Rocky Mountain thunderstorm on a TAT run. After departing Albuquerque for Clovis, Dick and Al Morgan had just cleared the Manzano Range when a line of threatening thunderstorms, extending from north to south, loomed directly in front of their trimotor. Flashes of lightning emanated from the black clouds, spearing the ground as far as the eye could see. Some strikes terminated in a ball of fire that bounced and rolled along the earth. The two pilots had never seen anything like it.

Threading his way below the thick clouds and lightning, Dick ran into severe turbulence. The airplane pitched and rolled about relentlessly. Saint Elmo's fire ringed the propellers. After a seemingly endless time, the plane emerged on the eastern side of the storm into welcome twilight with clear sailing ahead. Greatly relieved, Dick took a deep breath and settled back in his seat. Glancing over his shoulder into the passenger cabin, he exclaimed, "Whew! I bet those people back there were scared pissless!"

Moye, Al, and Dick frequented the Caliente Bar on Olvera Street, a favorite of Paul Mantz's. Most often accompanied by a cute little blond, Paul entertained the customers with amusing tales. Once a week, the three joined the non-stop festivities at the San Marino home of Florence Lowe *Pancho* Barnes. Moye met Pancho at Clover Field in the fall of 1928 soon after she received her student pilot license. Though not conventionally attractive, her magnetism, warmth, and infectious smile rendered her lack of physical beauty truly unperceivable.

Pancho flew high in the sky during the day and high in the bars at night. Author's photo.

Moye genuinely cared about Pancho. "She was a straight-up gal that told it like it was yet she possessed a heart of gold. Her last dollar belonged to anyone who needed it." She knew a lot of people both within and beyond her social class. Her brief experience writing scenarios for Eric Von Stroheim, the famed Hollywood director, resulted in numerous friendships with members in the film industry. She knew practically everyone in aviation. From time to time, Pancho impishly mixed representatives of the infinitely wealthy Four Hundred, the Hollywood set, the flying fraternity and her collection of bootleggers in a single gala affair. The chemistry of these events generated intriguing potential. Bootleggers and pilots claimed the honor of bringing down the house on most occasions.

Dick took the responsibility for one such finale. The scene took place on Pancho's patio where her guests listened to Ramon Navarro, the popular motion picture star, performing *Pagan Love Song*. As the final strains faded into silence, Lawrence Tibbet, the celebrated operatic baritone, strolled in from the garden with a lovely young woman on his arm. Dick, inspired by Ramon's less than perfect singing and Pancho's liquor, boldly asked Tibbet to join him in *The Bastard King of England,* a piece filled with deliciously ribald lyrics. Tibbet declined to participate on the pretense that he did not know the song. Dick briefed the orchestra and then proceeded with a solo performance.

His theatrics, besides the lewd content of the song, silenced the audience. The elite, shocked and confused, slowly exited during the aria with the motion picture crowd following close behind. By the time Dick concluded, only the pilots and bootleggers remained. As the evening wore on, Moye, Al, and Frank Clarke shared a space at the end of Pancho's bar. Clarke surveyed the room as he drank his Scotch. Several moments of contemplation passed before he delivered his studied conclusion of the event. "You know. We have more fun than the people." No one came forward to dispute his premise.

Pancho excelled as a pilot, song writer, and equestrian. One of her ranch hands summed up her horsemanship. "There ain't no outlaw bronco too ornery for Pancho to handle." In 1930, Pancho purchased a sleek Travelair Model R from Walter Beech and broke Earhart's speed record in August of that year. Howard Hughes hired her to create the airplane sounds for *Hell's Angels* by putting the Travelair through every maneuver possible flying around a balloon with a mike in it suspended a thousand feet over Caddo Field.

Following WW II, Pancho exhibited an unexpected talent. Acting as her own attorney, she succeeded, through three separate legal suits, to force the United States government to substantially increase the payment for her Rancho Oro Verde property adjacent to Edwards Air Force Base. The ranch, known informally as the Happy Bottom Riding Club, had been condemned to enable a base expansion and Pancho was not going to give up easily.

Believing that the love of her life, Duncan Renaldo, had fallen victim to a legal travesty, Pancho spent a small fortune in a futile attempt to prevent him from being incarcerated. She protected her bootlegger, Frank Bell, from the police. Returning from a flying lesson in Long Beach one evening, his competition pulled alongside his car and opened fire with a Thompson submachine gun. Bell curled up and fell to the floor. His rivals drove off, leaving him for dead. None of the .45 caliber slugs, however, had penetrated any vital spots. Somehow, Bell found his way to Pancho's, the scene of a well attended pilot bash. When Frank Clarke and Moye answered the door bell, they saw Bell half-collapsed with blood flowing from several bullet holes. Pancho directed them to carry him upstairs while she called a doctor not inclined to report the gunshot wounds to the authorities. Pancho harbored Bell until he recovered. Several years later, the state of Illinois executed him for killing a few of his competitors.

Over the years, Moye and Pancho kept in touch through written correspondence and visits. Moye and his wife visited Pancho at her Happy Bottom Riding Club, her place in Cantil, and later in Boron. She visited them at the Stephens' La Verne ranch. On one memorable trip, Moye recalled that she casually opened up her shirt to display her breastless chest, the result of a double mastectomy. As Moye stated, 'She had some kinks."

Moye's spotless flying record ended in 1930. Leo Nomis, flying in Frank Hawks' *Dawn Patrol*, invited Al Morgan and Moye to fly to the shooting location to watch him perform. Situated at the bottom of Pico Canyon near Saugus, the dirt landing strip required landing uphill regardless of the wind. Well into his final leg, a strong tailwind created a risky situation for Moye. Excessive speed and altitude made him consider a missed approach. He dismissed that idea when he realized the terrain at the end of the strip rose too quickly. With little space remaining, the airplane would impact somewhere below the canyon rim. Any hope of avoiding a complete disaster depended on making the shortest landing possible.

Moye kicked the ship into a steep slip to kill off his excess altitude and reduce airspeed. Just short of the field's perimeter fence, he pulled out of the slip, fishtailed as he passed over fence, and stalled in for about as short a landing as technologically possible. Excessive braking slowed the airplane but not enough to come to a complete stop. Faced with an impending crash into an out building, Moye ground looped the ship, hoping he had lost enough speed to complete the maneuver without disastrous results. He hadn't. The Travelair swerved, forcing the lower wing tip into the ground, and flipped over on its back. Dangling from his seatbelt, Moye felt more helpless than during his frenzied attempt to prevent an accident. Leo and Hawks arrived in seconds to assist Moye and Al from the airplane. The two suffered no injuries but the plane seemed a total loss.

Frank Hawks, known for his fair treatment of his employees in a cut-throat industry, didn't view the accident as a major intrusion as another director might have been inclined to do. He simply instructed his crew to carefully move the Travelair out of camera range and, when shooting ended for the day, personally drove Al and Moye back to Metropolitan Airport to retrieve their cars. He left the two with a friendly comment, "I wish you'd let me know what you were going to do, Moye. If we had been able to shoot your landing, we could have paid you for it." His comments did little to ease Moye's embarrassment.

The accident brought no joy to TAT. In reporting the incident, the papers did not overlook the fact that the two occupants of the airplane were TAT captains. Still sensitive about how the press handled the Mt. Taylor crash, TAT reprimanded Moye. Tomlinson pointed out, that at the very least, he might have accomplished the foul deed on his own without involving another of the company's pilots. Further, he suggested that their joint piloting efforts should be confined to scheduled operations.

Shortly after the TAT-Maddux merger, two of the original Maddux pilots resigned. Larry Fritz became vice president of operations for Earl Halliburton's airline Southwest Air Fast Express Airlines (SAFEway) based in Tulsa. By the time Fritz retired, his career included leading roles with TWA and American and a distinguished record with the U.S. Army Air Force. Johnny Gug left TAT-Maddux to fly for Boeing Air Transport, a precursor to United Airlines. With no replacement for him, Bellande, Shore, and Moye continued flying the route with only one day off between round trips instead of the usual two. This made at least one of them available to test Jack Northrop's beautiful *Alpha*. As the airplane neared completion, Northrop contacted Bellande to handle the test program and find three additional pilots. Bellande recommended Steve Shore, Al Morgan, and Moye. 13

Powered by a single 420 hp Pratt & Whitney Wasp engine, Northrop's first, all-metal monoplane performed exceptionally well. Bellande flew the *Alpha* several times before Moye took a turn at the controls. The day following his flight, Steve Shore flew the plane on a test run. In the course of the flight, he lost an aileron. The control surface smashed into the horizontal stabilizer which caused the ship to pitch over into a bunt or dive. The momentum threw Steve against the slack in his seat belt, partially ejecting him from the cockpit. The slipstream tore off his goggles. Gasoline expelled by centrifugal force from a gasoline breather cap blinded him. Managing to free himself, Shore pulled the ripcord on his parachute, and hoped for the best. Landing in a cactus patch in the Hollywood Hills, Steve spent six days in the hospital receiving treatment for his eyes and removal of precariously-placed cactus spines. 14

After Steve's accident, TAT put an immediate stop to all 'moon lighting' for the three Northrop test pilots. Moye regretted not being given the opportunity to take part in the completion of the test program but followed the progress of Northrop's innovative design. Although a sweet airplane to fly, not all experiences in the *Alpha* satisfied the pilot. Hal George, occasionally a co-pilot for Moye, lost his life in an *Alpha*. Just before departing for a flight designated as a mail-only trip due to foul weather, a doctor pleaded with George to allow a patient to board the aircraft. Initially refusing, George outfitted the patient with a parachute and a promise to jump if told to do so. When visibility reached zero and fuel reserves indicated empty, George prepared his passenger for the impending jump. She refused. Because he couldn't jump and leave her behind, George attempted to land. It proved fatal for him and his passenger. Cliff Abbott, piloting *Alpha*s for TWA at the time, informed Moye of the details some years later. 15

Other incidents involving the *Alpha* did little to promote its reputation. Most were weather related. George Rice flew one into the mountains near the Newhall pass, north of Los Angeles. He survived the crash but suffered severe burns. Harry Campbell, known as *Bull-of-the-Woods* by his associates, lost a propeller blade and bailed out of the tumbling ship. He landed in the Mississippi River and was known thereafter simply as the *Mississippi Lion*. Ernie Smith, an early Maddux pilot and first civilian pilot to fly to the Hawaiian Islands, cracked up his *Alpha* in the dry Los Angeles River near Grand Central Air Terminal. His engine quit on final approach and his glide didn't quite make the runway. Despite the poor publicity these accidents created, the *Alpha* became a notable transport plane for the United States Army and air mail carrier for TWA. 16

With the passage of the Kelly Airmail Act in 1925, private airlines received mail routes throughout the United States. The act provided for the transfer of air mail operations from the post office sponsored United States Aerial Mail Service to private operators. By 1926, the government began awarding contracts. Boeing Air Transport received the western division; National Air Transport took over the eastern sector. Many small airlines sought to acquire mail contracts to provide service not supplied by the large carriers. Later, they all began carrying passengers and cargo to supplement their incomes.

Contracts of this kind implied political entanglements. Post Master General W.F. Brown manipulated the intent of the acts to ensure airlines of his choice received lucrative contracts. He manipulated a merger between TAT-Maddux and Western Air Express in October 1930. The union resulted in a new designation for the airline, Transcontinental and Western Air or T & WA. The airlines did not become a single entity until 1934 but continued as separate companies operating the route jointly under a common name. Moye, along with the other pilots from Western and the TAT-Maddux Airlines, became the original pilots for T & WA, the future Trans World Airways.

Many of the first Maddux captains stayed on through the airline's changes, retiring many years later after an incredible career with TWA; others found careers with different airlines or in the private sector. Moye might have chosen another career path had he not received an unexpected phone call one mild winter morning in Los Angeles.

After pulling a double shift, Moye woke from a good night's sleep, looking forward to a hearty breakfast and a well-deserved day off. Understandably, he hesitated to answer the ringing telephone. At that hour, he expected the dispatcher needed him for a short flight. Moye took a chance and picked up the receiver. The gentleman on the other end of the line blurted out, "Would you fly me around the world," and then hung up. To say Moye was mystified would be an understatement. Sometime later, Moye received another call from the same individual. This time he introduced himself as Richard Halliburton and continued with, "I'm contemplating a vagabond journey around the world by air and I want you to be my pilot."

8

GRAND CENTRAL TO MEMPHIS

Richard Halliburton's call left Moye stunned. Newspapers heralded Richard has the most read author of the day. His celebrity status matched that of Lindbergh, Earhart, and Howard Hughes. Both intrigued and skeptical, Moye agreed to meet Richard at the Hollywood Roosevelt Hotel the next day. The historic Spanish-style hotel, currently Richard's residence, opened in 1927 financed in part by Douglas Fairbanks, Mary Pickford, and Louis B. Mayer. Constructed to house east coast film-makers and their actors, the hotel soon became a rendezvous for stars, socialites, and politicians.

Stepping down into the tastefully decorated lobby, Moye was immediately put at ease by Richard's gracious reception. Moye listened cautiously from his over-stuffed leather chair as Richard touched on the places, people, and adventures awaiting them. When Moye offered his opinion on the world flight, Richard gave him his undivided attention. With a subtle tilting of his head, he focused his ingenuous blue eyes directly on Moye who found these particular mannerisms of Richard very flattering. Richard impressed Moye as an energetic speaker and engaging raconteur. His cultivated voice contained no trace of his southern origin.

Moye later wrote "My first impression of Halliburton was one of surprise at his slight build and medium height of the boyishly handsome, vibrant young man." Yet, he thought, "His lack of a robust physique was compensated by a remarkable fund of nervous energy and dogged determination." 1

Following the 1929 publishing of his book, *New Worlds to Conquer*, Richard occupied himself with lectures, a possible movie contract, and a quest for a fresh adventure. In a decade when newspaper headlines featured sensational attempts to fly the oceans and travel across continents, a journey by air seemed a pressing choice. Commander Byrd navigated over the North and South Poles; Lindbergh conquered the Atlantic; and the *Graf Zeppelin* became the first airship to circumnavigate the earth. Richard Halliburton, the pilot, planned to tour the world by air and write another best seller. His naivety quickly made him a target for scam artists interested in his money or attempts to gain fame by association. Richard seldom, if ever, questioned the expressed intentions or stated abilities of individuals with whom he came in contact. A preoccupation with a romantic view of life or his generous disposition may have contributed to this flawed trait.

Captain Pat McCarthy, a professed former Royal Air Force pilot with all the attractive features of a movie star, approached Richard in February 1930 inviting him to participate in a transatlantic flight. The idea captivated Richard. He advanced McCarthy $500 to set the project in motion. That would be the last time he ever saw McCarthy or the money. Resolute on an adventure by air, Richard confirmed to the press two months later that he planned a round-the-world flight. He just needed to learn how to fly! 2

Newly-opened United Airport in Burbank, the United States' first million dollar airport, offered flying lessons and Richard lost no time signing up as a student. He spent two days trying to grasp the mechanics of flight but came to the conclusion that he possessed no aptitude for the science. Not to be deterred by his lack of piloting skills, he chose to hire an experienced pilot. He thought he found his man when Harry Halley contacted him with a most persuasive resume. Halley's Marine captain's uniform, with its pilot wings and many ribbons, gave credence to his credentials. Richard hired him on the spot and assigned him the task of acquiring an airplane. 3

Knowing little about the advantages and disadvantages of

aircraft, Richard placed himself in the hands of this self-evident high priest of aviation. Richard's sole stipulation for the purchase of an airplane related to cost, a reasonable request considering Richard's economic state mirrored that of the United States. When asked what type of aircraft would be suitable for the flight, Halley seemed neither confident nor specific on the criteria for selecting one but soon found a single-wing Velie Monocoupe in southern California. Widely advertised as "the ultimate plane for the private flyer", the Velie possessed attractive features for a world flight - an enclosed cabin, the capability to install pontoons, and a reasonable price tag. Disadvantages were its diminutive size and lack of power - 30 feet in length, a wingspan of 32 feet, and a small engine with 62 hp. Navigating through adverse elements would present a challenge. 4

Richard purchased the Velie on Halley's suggestion and began the process of obtaining insurance. Although Halley assured him that it wasn't necessary, Richard disagreed. Presented with the pilot's qualification questionnaire, Halley refused, feigning insult. Richard apologized and assured him that he did not intend to disparage his flying abilities. Halley grudgingly completed the form.

Haley's comments gave Richard some concern. Realizing that he should talk to someone who possessed professional experience in the field of aviation, Richard approached Major C. C. Moseley, WWI ace, former commanding officer of the Army Air Service at Clover Field, and highly respected in the aviation community. Moseley, familiar with Halliburton from a previous meeting, agreed to have lunch with him and Halley. Following the meeting, Mosley contacted Richard by phone.

"Mr. Halliburton, ordinarily I wouldn't meddle in affairs not strictly my concern, but those of us in the aviation game who love it and have worked hard to advance its best interests, hate to see anything happen that might work to its disadvantage. So, knowing that you've had very little experience in the field, I thought someone should point out to you that while Captain Halley has all those medals, to be sure, quite a few of them are incorrectly attached to his uniform." 5

Richard's insurance agent dropped by the Roosevelt the next day. When reviewing the captain's questionnaire, a curious fact emerged. During a stay in Mexico, the captain accumulated 600 hours of flying in a Curtiss Robin a year before the first Robin prototype flew. The results of a more thorough investigation revealed that the captain never joined the Marine Corps nor possessed any solo flight time. Richard confronted Halley who confessed that the facts spoke for themselves. He did not know how to fly. Because he liked the fellow and, perhaps he didn't want to admit to being duped twice, Richard offered to pay for his flying lessons at a San Diego flight school, a well-intended offer but not a practical one. After two weeks, the flight school refused to let him fly their airplanes. He was a danger to himself and everyone else.

Frustrated by the turn of events, Richard realized the futility of his current predicament. He owned an airplane but no one to fly it. His experience with McCarthy and Halley convinced him he couldn't trust himself to select a qualified pilot. Consulting with Moseley and Jimmy Knoll, a Department of Commerce Inspector, seemed the best solution. Richard met with them and discussed his requirements for a pilot.

"I don't want an out-of-work pilot. I don't want one that's working at just any old flying job. I want a pilot that's holding down a top flight position." [6]

Knoll suggested airline captain Moye Stephens. He related a few facts concerning Moye's personal background which he thought would appeal to the author. Although only 24 years old, Moye had flown for eight years, four of which he held a commercial license. No need to investigate further, Richard telephoned Moye with his startling offer.

During their meeting at the Roosevelt Hotel, Richard thought Moye seemed competent and exercised sound judgment, a good balance to his impulsivity. He discussed the trip as though Moye had already agreed to be his pilot. With adolescent zeal, he described his projected itinerary. Moye knew that, if he were to agree to accompany Richard, he would have his work cut out for him. Impetuosity and flying tended to combine in rather spectacular ways. Richard's comment made this clear. "We'll fly until we find a place that excites us, stay until we get tired of it, and move on to the next." [7]

Moye and Richard soon became partners in an adventure that would take them around the world in a Stearman C-3B. Photo courtesy of Moye F. Stephens.

The prospect of flying over so much of the world, visiting exotic places, and enjoying unique experiences seemed to be an incredible opportunity and one to be considered seriously. Richard offered to pay Moye a salary which he declined. Awkward situations in connection with invitations, both social and "state", might occur were he considered an employee of Richard's. Perceived as a traveling companion experienced in flying, such embarrassments could be avoided. Richard would provide Moye with an unlimited expense account in lieu of a salary. Richard also requested that Moye keep the expense records during the trip. Moye presented Richard with additional prerequisites. Richard would arrange for separate hotel rooms and not obligate Moye to attend the writer's social functions nor request him to make a public speech, an activity that horrified him.

"I had an unlimited expense account and we lived like kings. Dick was getting $400 a talk on his lecture tours and, in those days, airplanes were a great novelty so we were wined and dined by leading personalities at almost every stop. This friendship was partially due to the *Flying Carpet* but also because of Dick's worldwide reputation as a writer," Moye recalled in a later interview. 8

Moye felt comfortable with the arrangements agreed upon for the trip. The choice of an airplane presented some challenges. Informed that Richard had purchased a Velie, Moye realized Halliburton possessed little, if any, understanding of aircraft. Examination of the plane, its engine, and log books confirmed this fact. The Velie, once splattered over a hillside somewhere, appeared to have its pieces gathered up and stuck back together with spit. A fancy paint job carefully disguised the travesty. Halley replaced the original motor, completely demolished in the crash, with an experimental engine. Performing a thorough inspection, Moye realized the danger in which Richard had placed himself.

"A projected flight of great length to any number of outlandish places, many with marginal landing possibilities," stated Moye, "over stretches of hazardous terrain - with someone who never completed a successful landing - in a cracked up junk of an airplane powered by an engine practically guaranteed to fail - for which spare parts existed nowhere - not even at the factory was bizarre." 9

Any consideration on Moye's part to accompany Richard rested on replacing the Velie. He initially considered an *American Eagle* A-129 built in 1929 and powered by a 100 hp Kinner engine. The open cockpit airplane designed by Giuseppe Bellanca possessed a reputation as a stable and relatively easy airplane to fly. After studying the reliability of Kinner engines, Moye concluded that it proved less than dependable. The versatile Stearman C-3B designed by Lloyd Stearman was eminently suited for landing and taking off from small unimproved areas. A three-place, open cockpit biplane, the Stearman provided plenty of room for two passengers and their cargo. The forward cockpit could hold 3.3 cubic feet of storage space. Powered by a 220 hp Curtiss-Wright J-5, the airplane possessed an inherent stability, ruggedness, and a reputation for excellent and consistent performance. The biplane's ceiling of 18,000 feet provided a safety margin for navigating over mountainous country. 10

Confronting Tommy Tomlinson at T & WA about a leave of absence seemed to be Moye's most formidable task. Tomlinson agreed to give Moye a leave for one year without the loss of seniority. He stated, however, that it would be unfair to pilots lower in seniority if the leave exceeded that length of time. The trip as planned required approximately two years. If Moye wanted to go, he would have to resign. He struggled with the difficult decision. He considered it an honor, greatly prized, to be selected as a captain with the first transcontinental passenger air service. In fact, all pilots flying in the same capacity shared a proprietary pride in their contribution to the historic achievement. To resign meant he would become an outsider, relegated to the side line to watch his former teammates continue in a position he'd had a part in developing. His associates in the Professional Pilots Association considered him crazy to consider Halliburton's offer.

On the other hand, Moye sensed the disturbing developments on the part of management. Their attitudes seemed arbitrary. Somewhere along the way, the sense of pilot camaraderie became lost on those that no longer flew but delegated. Captain Doc Whitney, the oldest TWA pilot, was demoted and then let go when he could not pass the instrument flight proficiency test. Moye understood the need to be competent flying on instruments but felt that TWA could have had the decency to provide Doc with an alternate job.

Government's relentless control over aviation became more obtrusive with each new directive. As the size and complexity of the industry increased, restrictive rules and regulations kept pace. Rumors circulated about the organization of a pilot's union. Moye recognized the need for a collective stance on the part of pilots to negotiate with management. Resolving the issue by affiliating with a labor union did not seem the appropriate direction to take. Inevitably, indifference and business-like attitudes would replace the love of the game.

Moye's decision to resign from the airline did not come easily. Accepting Richard's proposal meant the end of another distinct epoch in his life. At the conclusion of the round-the-world flight, Moye planned to return to aviation. He could not predict the role that he would play in the advancing science, however; he only knew that he would be a part of its evolution. To some degree,

Richard's adventure would compensate for the passing of a time when pilots soared the skies without constraint, a time when those who dared called the blue expanse home.

While Moye deliberated over his career with the airlines, Richard went in search of a Stearman C-3B. He hoped someone would donate an airplane in return for publicity the trip would generate. Everyone he approached showed doubt for a successful outcome. They thought his chances of returning in one piece were less than fifty per cent. Richard tried to sell his plan in Wichita, Chicago, and St. Louis. He learned of a 500 hp Stearman for sale by Cliff Durant in Detroit. Durant offered the airplane to Richard for free provided he use Durant's personal pilot for the trip. Richard turned him down. The larger engine burned twice as much as the smaller engine and he already had a pilot. His cousin, Erle Putnam Halliburton, offered Richard his Lockheed *Vega.* When he formed SAFEway Airlines in April 1929, Erle initially used *Vega*s to provide service to St. Louis, Tulsa, Oklahoma City, and Fort Worth. His pilots, based at the Tulsa Municipal Airport, next flew Ford trimotors. In June 1929, SAFEway added Los Angeles and New York City to their route. Although the airline lasted less than a year, Erle established the concept of profitable passenger operations. A beautiful airplane, the *Vega*'s closed cockpit would provide more comfort and carry a larger load than the Stearman. The comfort did not outweigh the cost to operate the engine. 11

Richard also considered using a Pitcairn autogiro for the trip. A telegram dated November 1, 1930 indicates his interest in Harold Pitcairn's design and his efforts to persuade the company to loan him one.

"The [Ladies Home] Journal has a circulation of three million and goes into three million high class American homes . . . My three previous books have been in turn read in ten other countries . . . [the] Autogiro ship would fix the attention on my flight, and cause a sensation wherever it landed. This flight is by no means just an ambition, but already a fact financed equipped, piloted, publicized, waiting only for an extra gas tank to be installed . . . I can pilot my *Flying Carpet* with far greater safety into many more outlandish places . . . It would promote your new ship and my new book to the utmost."12

When Pitcarin declined Richard's proposal, Richard sent a letter on November 4.

"Mr. Erle Halliburton and I are very grateful to you for your telegram in reply to ours. I am terribly disappointed that you feel the autogiro is not yet ready for a round-the-world trip. I can fully understand what difficulties might arise if I were in need of spare parts, with no service station near. However, might it not be possible to ship ahead several sets of gyro blades along with the spare parts for my engine, which AI will have to send anyway? Also, would it not be possible for my very expert and experienced pilot to come to your factory along with me and take a thorough schooling in the servicing and operation of your new device? We could then be our own service station.

"The more I consider the possibilities of a trip around the world, with the new Pitcairn, the less interested I am in flying any other plane. Naturally, it would not rebound to your profit if anything went wrong with the ship – especially as there will be a concentrated searchlight of publicity turned upon my expedition should I use the gyro. On the other hand, as I am in no hurry whatsoever, and plan to travel leisurely and cautiously, there would be ample opportunity to wait for proper weather, and to give the ship and engine the sharpest attention.

"The pilot who is to accompany me (my own flying ability is not sufficient for a round-the-world flight) has had a vast experience and I should hate to substitute any other pilot for him, but I would be entirely willing, if you so recommended, to take with me, one of your own Pitcairn test pilots, provided we could find one who might be interested in accompanying me. Safety, both for my name and for my neck, is to be my first commandment. Nor is it my purpose to take longer hops than the ship is well equipped for. I plan to dismantle it several times and not try to fly any long water stretches.

"Tomorrow night – Wednesday, November 5th, I am accompanying Erle Halliburton to Tulsa, Oklahoma in my Lockheed, and would be obliged to you if you would communicate with me there . . . I shall be there three or four days. If the conditions I have set forth in this letter have put a different light on the situation, and have been convincing arguments in favor of my using a Pitcairn gyro after all for my *Flying Carpet*, and if you would be willing to confer with me at your own factory, I would gladly fly from Tulsa on to Philadelphia immediately upon your advice.

"This combination of your ship and my flight has such dramatic possibilities and such potential profit for us both that I am exceedingly reluctant to abandon the idea so long as there is the slightest hope of bringing it to pass . . ." 13

Why Richard continued to pursue other avenues to acquire an airplane for his air adventure is unknown. His letter to Pitcairn emphasizes his lack of insight about airplane development; it also reflects his persuasive persistence.   The suggestion that Erle Halliburton was involved in the world flight was most likely meant to impress Pitcairn.

The Pitcairn autogyro attracted a great deal of attention but remained in design and construction stages in 1930. This eliminated the rotary wing as a plausible choice for Richard's world journey. Had it been available, the prototype Pitcairn's high price and fuel inefficiency would have rendered it impractical. Pitcairn designed his second model, the PCA2, to sell in quantity but did not go into production until May 1931.   Amelia Earhart borrowed a factory PCA2 in April of that year and set an altitude record of 18,415 feet. The following month, she flew the airplane across the United States in an effort to set another record.   Upon landing in Oakland, California, she discovered that John M. Miller completed the transcontinental flight just nine days earlier. Not to be outdone, Earhart headed back east in hopes of setting a round-trip record but, after three crashes, abandoned her efforts. 14

With Monocoups, Vegas, Electras, and Pitcairns ruled out, the Stearman continued to stand out as the best choice. Richard located a reasonably priced model at United Airport. Previously a test bed for an experimental McClatchie engine, the unflown Stearman was offered for sale when the engine was unable to meet expected standards. November 13, Richard purchased the biplane from the Aero Brokerage Service Company owned by Ed Erickson and Lieutenant Walter Hawkins. Moreland Aircraft sold Richard a Curtiss-Wright J-5 engine, serial number B9925, manufactured at the Wright factory in Patterson, New Jersey. The engine had a total of 1,080 hours. Pacific Airmotive, based at Union Air Terminal, disassembled the J-5 for a complete inspection. The following was taken from the engine logbook. 15

All valves ground. Mags overhauled. 2 valve springs replaced. 10 rocker arm bushings replaced. carb checked. All cylinders repainted. New set of B. G. plugs installed. Motor run on test block 3 hours at 600 rpm rechecked. Turned 1600 on block with test prop. 60 lbs oil pressure. 140° oil temperature. New mag couplings installed.

Pacific completed the work on November 21 and Fred H. Mathews signed it off as airworthy. 16

To increase the range of the Stearman, two 8.5 gallon tanks were installed outboard of the main 40 gallon wing tank; an additional 20 gallon tank in the fuselage gave the plane a cruising range of 700 miles. A secret compartment under the floorboards in the front cockpit was added to hide handguns and plenty of ammunition. Oversized tires replaced the stock ones. The Department of Commerce gave the airplane a restricted license due to the modifications, NR-882N. The factory tool kit and Moye's early training as a 'grease monkey' would prove vital in the months ahead. 17

Moye's family invited Richard to their home for Thanksgiving dinner to celebrate the holiday and impending flight. They welcomed Richard with the familiarity awarded a respected relative. He wrote the following in a letter to his parents. "Mrs. Stephens, who is a most wise and charming woman, wanted us to stay for Thanksgiving Day, that she might give us a farewell party. I had hoped to be home for Thanksgiving myself, but couldn't make it, and to be with the Stephens family, to whom I have become truly devoted is the next best thing. They have not the slightest uneasiness over the hazards of our expedition; they have seen Moye flying almost daily for eight years and think no more of it than they do over his driving their motor car." 18

The Stephens' optimism for the world flight delighted Richard but did nothing to placate his growing exasperation with the necessary but tedious preparations for the trip. Following the holidays, he asked Pancho Barnes to fly him and five friends to Ensenada on the west coast of Baja, California. Pancho couldn't refuse her friend. They borrowed cousin Erle's *Vega* hangared at the Riverside Airport and booked rooms at the recently opened Hotel Playa Ensenada and Casino. Much of the Hollywood set attended the inaugural event on October 31, 1930 which featured the music of Xavier Cugat and his band. Heavyweight boxing champion Jack Dempsey, listed as an investor, used his name to attract large crowds to the hotel. More of a resort than a hotel, guests could gamble, socialize, or simply take in the magnificent panorama of the Pacific Ocean from the grand lobby with its Persian rugs, Spanish chandeliers, and imported mosaics. 19

Jimmy Angel, Richard Halliburton, Pancho Barnes, and Moye pose in front of the newly unveiled Flying Carpet. Photo courtesy Moye F. Stephens.

The beginning of December saw the auspicious unveiling of the *Flying Carpet*. Sunlight glistened on its lacquered surfaces when it was rolled out of its Grand Central hangar. Richard had chosen the paint scheme –black cowling, struts and trim; silver wings with scarlet leading edge trim; and a brilliant scarlet fuselage. The name of the airplane, scripted in black over a gold stripe, ran down each side of the fuselage. American flags decorated both sides of the rudder. The *Flying Carpet*'s debut sparked an excitement not yet experienced for the impending journey. Moye was proud to be its captain.

By the third week of December, Moye and Richard put the final touches on the endless parade of last minute preparations for the flight. Richard had passed his training on how to prop the engine. Rounds of inoculations, fittings for warm flying suits, purchasing supplies, and arranging the shipment of a spare cylinder to New York were completed. Rand McNally Standard Indexed Maps with Air Trails for each state en route to New York were in hand. The maps contained an airport directory, aids to navigation, and practical air navigations such as following compass courses and corrections for wind. Comprehensive aeronautical charts, designed by Elvry Jeppesen, did not appear until 1934. [20]

Moye consulted with Ross Hadley who made a tour of Europe from April to December 1929. Flying the same type Stearman, Hadley's experience in England, France, Italy and Austria provided Moye with useful information on airport procedures and permits. Hadley, owner of Charles R. Hadley Book Bindery and a partner in Pacific Airmotive Corporation., embarked on another tour in November 1930. After crossing the Atlantic on the *Ile de France,* Hadley and co-pilot John Pratt flew from LeHavre, France to Singapore. The purpose of the tour was to demonstrate the feasibility of making a sight-seeing tour by air. Hadley returned home in May 1931. [21]

The day before the planned departure, reporters interviewed Moye and Richard; staff photographers snapped a number of images. More importantly, Pancho Barnes arranged for her friend George Hurrell, photographer to the stars, to accompany her to the airport. Using the *Flying Carpet* as a focal point, Hurrell

Pancho congratulates Richard on the impending adventure while Moye looks on from the cockpit of The Flying Carpet. Photo courtesy of Moye F. Stephens.

captured classic impressions of the two adventurers posing with Pancho and Ramon Novarro. Richard had met Novarro and Pancho at one of her parties. Moye provided the introduction to Pancho.

Just before daybreak on December 22, Moye and Richard arrived at Grand Central Airport. With their supplies stowed on board, fuel tanks full, and a promising weather forecast, the two anticipated a smooth flight to Richard's hometown of Memphis. They planned to arrive on Christmas Day if all went well. A modest group of family, friends, and supporters gathered to wish them well. H. C. Lippiatt, west coast distributor of Travelairs, flew alongside the *Flying Carpet* with members of the Stephens family; Leo Nomis and Al Morgan took a position on the opposite side of the Stearman.

Richard, with the stature of an experienced ace, propped the engine and hopped into the front cockpit. Moye pushed the throttle to the fire-wall. The *Flying Carpet* roared down the runway, carrying its crew to the greatest adventure of their lives. Moye had second thoughts just before departing. They had more to do with

A classic Hurrell photo of Richard, Moye, and Ramon Novarro taken the day before the Flying Carpet departed Grand Central. Photo courtesy of Moye F. Stephens.

the length of his separation from his family than the actual flight. As a young man, firm on his feet, his ability to communicate and enjoy his parents was unequivocal. Over the past few years, his appreciation for his family had matured. He valued their insight and support for his choices, particularly the *Flying Carpet* trip. Once in the air, however, Moye's doubts evaporated as he turned his attention to the flight ahead.

"I am awfully sorry that I haven't gotten around to writing to you before," Moye wrote from Memphis on January 2, "but I have been so darned busy that this is really the first opportunity I have had. Of course, on the way, flying all day and dead tired at night, I couldn't do it. Since we have been here in Memphis, it has been one continual round of gaiety interspersed with periods of work on the motor which has been behaving badly. But I will begin at the beginning and tell you the whole story.

"First of all, I almost gave up and called the trip off when it came to actually leaving. I certainly wanted to stay home just about that time. It was really quite thrilling to have such an escort on the take-off. It felt very chummy to have the family following along in Lips' plane. I wonder how our formation looked from your ship. Leo and Al left us shortly after you did. It was quite a lonely feeling when we continued on our way. Shortly after passing through Cajon Pass, the first signs of motor trouble appeared. It manifested itself in a sort of skipping or irregular pulsation in the power, but as it got no worse after a certain point, I continued on to Kingman where we stayed the night. Our late start and head winds made it inadvisable to continue."

The next morning, Moye and Richard departed Kingman for Winslow. Temperatures in northern Arizona were recorded in the twenties – record lows for that part of the state. Despite the freezing air, Moye and Richard managed to keep warm in their flying suits but became concerned when the Stearman's engine began skipping after 45 minutes. Increasing power to 1,700 rpm, the skipping lessened considerably. Curious to determine how the airplane performed at altitude, Moye took it up to 11,000 feet. The skipping continued. In Winslow, Moye asked TAT mechanic Al Wolters to take a look at the motor. Al checked it thoroughly and, decided that the B. G. spark plugs weren't correct for cold weather flying. By the time Moye installed another brand of plugs, the sun had set. He and Richard found rooms at the El Garces Hotel where TAT pilots stayed on layovers. Much to Moye's delight, Dick Ranaldi was a guest there. During dinner Moye learned that Dick hadn't flown an airplane in three weeks. The Depression was taking its toll on the airline. Dick, dismal over prospects of continuing his job as a captain, had submitted a bid to dig ditches for the gas mains.

At 5:00 a.m. the following morning, Dick rode out to the field to see his pal and Richard off. Forty-five minutes after becoming airborne, the Stearman's engine once again began skipping. Mechanics in Albuquerque checked the irksome motor while Moye and Richard ate lunch. Discovering the intake manifolds to be loose, they tightened them and declared the problem cured. Moye and Richard, optimistic over the mechanic's decree, took off for Amarillo. They experienced forty-minutes of smooth flying before the engine reverted to its previous intermittent operation. Discouraged by the time they arrived in Amarillo, Moye prevailed upon Jack English, the airport manager and expert mechanic, to fly with him and listen to the motor. Of course, it ran like a clock. Upon landing, Moye directed Jack to have the oil changed and the valve clearances and magneto points checked. Christmas Eve day, Moye and Richard left Amarillo just before dawn.

Moye paid closer attention to the engine during this leg. He wanted to know exactly how much time elapsed before it stopped operating smoothly. From the time he reached level flight until the engine began running rough was as predicted - 45 minutes. Airborne after refueling in Oklahoma City, the motor failed completely. Moye managed to return and land safely. Determined to resolve whatever issues the engine might have, he put blocks under the wheels and ran the motor up for the mechanics' benefit. It performed efficiently. Moye, aware that this might happen, requested the mechanic investigate further. He took the carburetor apart, checked the mags, cleaned out the gas lines, checked the vents in the gas caps, changed back to the B. G. plugs, and finally decided a sticking valve was the culprit. After applying penetrating oil on the valve stems, Moye took the airplane up. The engine ran well. Although anxious to continue on to Memphis, it was nearly dark by the time Moye finished testing the engine. They would take off at dawn only to discover that, after one hour, the motor began skipping worse than before

At Fort Smith, Arkansas, Moye explained the problem to the mechanic. He swore an air lock in the gas line caused the problem. Watching the mechanic fuss with the gas line for an hour, Moye gave up and departed for Memphis, going by way of Little Rock to stay over flat country. Thirty minutes out, heavy rain and a lowering ceiling forced them to return to Fort Smith to spend a quiet Christmas. December 26, the *Flying Carpet* touched down in Memphis at 11:00 a.m. Richard's parents, anxiously awaiting their son's arrival, drove onto the airport just as the airplane taxied up to the hangar ramp. Moye received a warm welcome from the Halliburtons, equal to, but more subdued than that for their son.

While Richard unloaded the suitcases, Moye went in search of an experienced mechanic. He found an elderly fellow named Sewart who had been in the game since year one. He held the opinion that the float level in the carburetor needed adjusting. Upon checking, however, he discovered the device in perfect working order. His next experiment involved the oil lines and oil tank. Wrapping them with asbestos would increase the motor's temperature and cause the skipping to cease. Moye flew the usual 45 minutes but the trouble remained. Sewart returned to the carburetor, wrapped insulation around it, and fabricated a piece of cowling to further protect it from cold air but to no avail. Changing carburetors and enlarging the opening on the exhaust pipe made the problem worse. Sewart scratched his head and, with the greatest assuredness, told Moye that the size of jets in the carburetor must be causing the problem.

Moye's frustration grew as Sewart continued his hit and miss experimentation. Invited to attend a celebration that evening, Moye left Sewart to trouble shoot. After five days of what had become an annoying quest to solve the engine's erratic firing, Moye needed to relax. He looked forward to a few martinis in the company of Richard's family and guests.

9

MEMPHIS TO THE MEDITERRANEAN

"Beginning with the night we arrived," Moye wrote from Memphis, "we have been to one and sometimes two parties every night and also quite a few in the afternoons. Needless to say, Dick is a very large big shot in his home town - their fair-haired boy. I find myself something of a big shot also by reason of my association with him on this trip. The people here are very hospitable and have shown us a marvelous time. Mr. and Mrs. Halliburton have treated me wonderfully, almost if I were their own son.

"While out at the field testing the plane I have met a number of local aviators, one of whom is Dick's cousin John Halliburton, an instructor for the Curtiss Wright Flying Service. He is a peach of a boy and gave a party for Dick and myself, inviting the local aeronautical celebrities. Today, he let me fly one of their Curtiss Fledglings and it certainly was a kick. I believe old Amos could fly one.

"The Halliburtons both assured me that they felt a thousand times better about the trip after having gotten to know me. I think they felt that Dick might want to take chances and after talking to me, must have felt greatly relieved. Mrs. Halliburton said I was the oldest young man that she had ever met. As mothers usually judge other children by theirs, I wonder how old that makes thirty-year-old Dick."

In between what seemed a whirlwind of social activities, Moye checked on Sewart's progress. He had installed larger jets in the Curtiss Wright which resulted in a modicum of success. The airplane performed well below 4,000 feet but that precluded the Stearman from flying over higher terrain. The only option left for Moye was to wire ahead to the Wright factory in Patterson, New Jersey and arrange for their mechanics to examine the engine.

With a celebratory send-off by the Halliburtons and Memphis residents, Moye and Richard departed the first week of January for the east coast. A persistent cloud cover slowed their progress. To avoid the overcast, they hopped from one small town to the next at near ground level. In St. Louis, their first overnight destination, they intended to speak with Jimmy Doolittle, a representative for the Shell Oil Company. Doolittle, approached by Moye in Los Angeles, told him he would help them anyway he could. Richard hoped Shell would provide oil and gas for the trip in exchange for the publicity generated by it. Two hours before their arrival, however, Doolittle had flown to Miami. In his absence, Doolittle's assistant, a Princeton classmate of Richard's, hosted them during their overnight stay. Moye visited with a group of original TAT pilots - Milo Campbell, Andy Anderson, Ernie Smith, "the little general" Richie Richardson, Pat Gallup, and Benny Howard – all on a layover from Amarillo.

The flight east to Indianapolis from St. Louis proved uneventful until Moye climbed to 7,000 feet. Once again, the motor repeated its previous and continually occurring roughness. Landing for fuel in Columbus, Indiana, Moye decided to install still larger jets thinking that he might be able to get more altitude without the motor misfiring. The larger jets resulted in the engine running worse than before. He replaced them with the medium-sized jets in Wheeling, West Virginia

In Indianapolis, Moye lunched with Johnny Collings and Richie Richardson who came through St. Louis the day before. Richard met with his friend and editor, David Chambers of Bobbs-Merrill. When Moye joined them, he discovered that Chambers had flown hundreds of miles with him in a trimotor. The three spent the evening discussing Halliburton's plans for his air adventure.

The next morning, Moye navigated under an overcast sky toward Washington with smoke and haze further obscuring visibility. Following the railroad track north of their planned course to stay clear of mountainous terrain, Moye refueled in Pittsburg. Still plagued with poor visibility, Moye checked the weather reports and consulted with a pilot on the field. He marked a highway on Moye's map that would take him all the way to Washington. Once airborne, Moye became disoriented and followed the wrong route. He landed at the nearest field when it became apparent he was off course. The sign on the snow-covered field indicated they were in Ebensburg, 50 miles north of the designated road to Washington. Exhausted and too late to continue, they pried open the frozen doors on the field's sole hangar and pushed in the airplane. Most likely, they found someone to drive them to the nearest lodging.

Over breakfast, Moye and Richard changed their itinerary. They originally planned to continue on to Washington, but because it was Saturday, the Department of Commerce in Washington would be closed. This meant waiting two days before they could obtain the documents for their flight. Instead, they would fly to Philadelphia to meet with Loring Shuler, an editor for the *Ladies Home Journal*. Clear skies greeted them as they took off from Ebensburg. Passing over rolling hills and forests dusted with snow,

the 250 mile flight provided them with the most pleasant experience since leaving Burbank. That Sunday, January 11, Richard met with Shuler to discuss possible stories for the magazine. Not entirely convinced of the trip's merits, Shuler told Richard that he would print whatever Richard sent him.

Monday morning, the *Flying Carpet* touched down on the tarmac at Washington-Hoover Airport. Gil Budwig, now Director of Air Regulations, reviewed Moye and Richard's plans and explained the red tape involved in obtaining the required permits. Satisfied that he had all the information, Richard went off to celebrate a belated birthday with friends. Moye and Budwig reminisced about flying at Clover and Rogers Airports. Tuesday, Moye and Richard made the rounds of government offices.

"Buddy sent us over to the State Department with a great recommendation and we went through the necessary red tape there." Moye later wrote. "We were assured that the State Department would get us the necessary permissions to carry our firearms with us. Buddy also gave us a special letter from the Department of Commerce requesting cooperation from the foreign governments."

Fair weather held for the *Flying Carpet*'s flight to New York from Washington via Philadelphia. Moye landed at Roosevelt Field on Long Island, one of America's busiest civilian airports in the 1930s. Pilots came from all over the world to be a part of its progressive aviation community. Located at the eastern edge of the United States, Roosevelt Field launched several trans-Atlantic flights. Lindbergh's was most memorable; *America*, *Old Glory*, and *The American Girl* were least notable. Some of aviation's greats – Harriet Quimby, Charles Lindbergh, Elinor Smith, and Alexander de Seversky - called the field home at one time or another. Although the *Flying Carpet* would not be flying across the Atlantic, Roosevelt seemed the premier field on which to land. The airport attracted the press, newsreel cameramen, and aviation buffs. As always, Richard wired ahead to alert Roosevelt of his arrival.

June 21, 1931, the *Flying Carpet* caused quite a sensation as it touched down on Roosevelt's runway. Halliburton's reputation attracted more than the usual crowd. The public, along with field residents, gathered to see the famous author and airplane that would be the subject of his next book. Richard, occupied with entertaining his fans, left Moye no choice but to tie down the plane, unload the bags, and locate a ride to the modest but cosmopolitan Duane Hotel by himself. The following day, he flew the Stearman to the Wright factory in Patterson, New Jersey where mechanics would meticulously examine the motor to determine the cause of its malfunction.

For the next two weeks, Moye and Richard enjoyed teas, dinners, and social events, the majority of which were attended by them separately. Richard needed to raise more money for the trip as his finances dwindled. He sold some of his stocks, worth about one-fifth of their original value due to the Depression. Not one to neglect his social obligations, he dined with friend and film star Mary Pickford on more than one occasion and whiled away many hours with American novelists Charles and Kathleen Norris, Fannie Hurst, Edna Ferber, newspaper columnist O. O. McIntyre, and Ruth and Maxwell Aley, respected literary agents. A noteworthy group, Hurst's *Imitation of Life* and Ferber's *So Big* novels became successful films; McIntyre penned his syndicated column, *New York Day by Day*, for a quarter of a century; and Kathleen Norris was considered the highest-paid female writer of her time. 1

In New York, Moye renewed acquaintances with pilot and record holder Lee Schoenhair. He met with Ben Hoy, a member of the Moye, Hoy, and Lee Chinese team from TAT. Ben caught Moye up on all the latest new from the airlines.

". . . Upon receiving Ben Hoy's letter, I called him up and he came over to New York to show me the town," wrote Moye. "We have spent three evenings together and had a very enjoyable time. He is doing very well with Paul Collins' New York to Washington Ludington Line flying Stinson trimotors. He tells me there is quite a bit of agitation for the forming of a pilots' association, not a labor union, something more dignified but by means of which the pilots can set up certain standards such as the number of hours required for all different types of commercial flying, the maximum number of hours to be flown per month, minimum wages for different types of flying, etc. He points out that the doctors have their medical association, the lawyers their bar etc. I have said right along pilots needed something of the sort and I hope it develops into something."

Some years before, Moye predicted the move. T&WA, initially paying its pilots based on mileage, changed to an hourly rate. Fearing that management would reduce their pay further by averaging the duration of flight times, T&WA and United pilots formed the Airline Pilots Association (APA). In July 1931, the organization would become official. David Behncke, former Army pilot, barnstormer, and airline captain, served as the APA's president until 1951. 2

Stanford classmate Rich Hobson reunited with Moye during his stay in New York. Rich, the son of Admiral Richard Hobson and a successful New York real estate broker, introduced Moye to all the tea rooms and parlors in the city. One Saturday night, the two attended a dance accompanied by two young New York heiresses. Rich escorted Doris Duke, the daughter of the American Tobacco Company magnate; the other, Lita Morse, touted as the most popular debutante in New York, was escorted by Moye. Another evening, Moye attended a Quiet Birdman meeting followed by the movie *Beau Ideal* "to absorb a little atmosphere" for the trip. The 1931 film, starring Loretta Young and Ralph Forbes, relates the story of a young American man who joins the Foreign Legion in hopes of finding his captured childhood friend and returning him to his beautiful lady in waiting. An appropriate choice considering the amount of time he and Richard would soon spend with the French Foreign Legion in northern Africa.

On Wednesday, January 27, Curtiss-Wright completed work on the *Flying Carpet*'s engine. They attributed the motor's skipping to someone using shellac on the valve tappet guides in bolting them to the crank case. When the motor heated up, the shellac melted, ran into the guide, and gummed up the tappets which, in turn, retarded the valves from closing completely. It took the shellac approximately forty minutes to reach melting temperature. The mechanics thoroughly cleaned the engine of shellac, reassembled it, and pushed it out of the hangar for a test flight. After an hour Moye concluded, beyond a doubt, that the radial engine now operated perfectly. He flew the Stearman to Roosevelt Field where he had a fuel gauge installed, the propeller checked, and the compass compensated. He planned to ferry the plane to Newark Airport next to the docks that same day but the mechanics needed the rest of the afternoon to complete the work. Moye stayed at the field hotel to get an early start in the morning. At Newark, he supervised the workers who dismantled the *Flying Carpet* Friday morning and loaded it onto the steamship *Majestic* for the Atlantic crossing.

"We worked all day getting the ship to the dock," Moye wrote from Southampton. "The shipping people decided to put it on board the minute we arrived so it was about eleven o'clock by the time I got back to the hotel with no dinner. I thought we had lost the poor old Stearman during the process of loading. The man on the winch became very nervous and started to lower it too abruptly. When he checked it, the tail swung down and the ship started to career about in a most alarming manner, just missing stanchions, ventilators, and what not. Then he decided to pull it up which he did too quickly and there was the poor Stearman swinging around amongst the ship's masts and rigging. Then he lowered away again, making matters worse than ever. After this kept up for a period of what seemed years, the crew finally leaped in, seized the airplane, and dragged it to safety. How it escaped being bent double around a stanchion is one of the most miraculous things I have ever seen."

A remarkable history surrounded the ocean liner *Majestic*. Construction of the ship began in 1914 in a German shipyard. Known as the *Bismarck* at that time, it was to be the world's largest flagship. With the advent of WWI, however, it sat unfinished until the Treaty of Versailles ordered Germany to finish the ship and turn it over to the British. The White Star Company took delivery in April 1922 and renamed it the *R.M.S. Majestic*. In 1935, the *Normandie,* a 75,000 ton ship, took the *Majestic*'s title as the largest liner afloat. 3

Richard paid $450 for the *Flying Carpet*, considered personal baggage by White Star, and $270 apiece for his and Moye's tickets for the ocean crossing. Moye's connections with Earl Cocke, a member of TWA's traffic department, allowed a last minute upgrade from their modest accommodations to bridal suites.

The R. M. S. Majestic was the largest liner afloat when Moye and Richard boarded her in 1931. Author's vintage postcard.

Cocke's father, a top executive with White Star, facilitated the change. A luxurious steamship, the *Majestic* contained a magnificent restaurant for evening dining, well-appointed card and smoking rooms, an interior marble pool of impressive dimensions, a dance floor larger than either the Biltmore or Ambassador Hotels, and a theater capable of presenting full productions. "You couldn't possibly imagine a swanker layout," remarked Moye.

The day of departure, the press came aboard the *Majestic* to interview Richard. Posed theatrically atop the crated Stearman, he wore a black homburg, chesterfield coat, pearl grey gloves, and spats. He used his silver-topped cane to underscore his answers to the newsmen's questions.

He told the newsmen he would cross the Sahara to Timbuctoo "Why Timbuctoo, Mr. Halliburton"?

"Well, everybody talks about the place - 'from here to Timbuctoo' people say - but nobody goes there."

When asked why he was going by airplane, he replied, "An adventure not in the air," replied Halliburton impetuously, "is obsolete!" 4

February 5, 1931, with the *Flying Carpet* stowed on deck, the *Majestic* sailed for England. Richard believed his air venture was the modern way to see the world. What lay ahead would be far from an expedition of convenience. Traveling by air allowed them into otherwise inaccessible areas but necessitated additional preparation. The airplane engine had to be in superior condition, information about indigenous tribes gathered from area residents, and reports regarding terrain variations and contingencies for an emergency obtained from local pilots. Richard quickly realized the impossibility of simply hopping into the front cockpit and taking off during the flight from Burbank to Memphis. The Stearman needed refueling, the oil checked, control surfaces inspected, flying charts examined, and weather reports scanned. Although he became exasperated and impatient with Moye during the trip, Richard never wavered in his trust of his pilot.

"The experiences we had . . . from Memphis – fog, rain, mountains, strange country – have been a good test for Moye," Richard wrote from Philadelphia, "and he continues to give me a feeling of utmost confidence. His ability and steadiness as a flyer continue to amaze and delight me." 5

As the *Majestic* steamed across the Atlantic, Moye reflected on the challenges ahead. Most significantly, he realized the important role he played in Halliburton's saga. The outcome of the round-the-world flight rested solely on his shoulders. The journey was a tremendous undertaking but one which Moye felt he could handle. He looked forward to navigating over unfamiliar geography in changing weather conditions using the experience the airlines provided him. He believed that the successful completion of the epic flight would have historic significance but not as the first flight to circumnavigate the world. Two U.S. Army Air Corps Douglas Cruisers completed the first round-the-world flight in 1924. The crew attributed their success to meticulous planning. Although Richard's itinerary would change during his flight, Moye's commitment to detail and safety could never be faulted.

Dealing with Richard's eccentricities and mood swings would be far more difficult for Moye than flying, navigating, or repairing the airplane. As a celebrity, Richard thrived on public adulation. Other than stops in major cities, few opportunities existed to fulfill this need. The absence of attention would leave

Richard frustrated at times. Combining that with lack luster responses from his editors, he became very difficult to be around. Moye responded by leaving him alone. Upon occasion Moye traveled by air while Richard went overland.

"When Dick got a writing seizure," Moye told Ann Frank, "it could be likened to giving birth to a baby. He locked himself in a room, sometimes he kept at it for a week, unscrambling notes in solitary confinement." [6]

Richard's homosexuality might have become problematic for another pilot but it hardly concerned Moye. In his notes, letters, and information shared with his son and others, Moye made no mention of Richard's sexual preference. It bore no relevance to a friendship based on mutual respect. Not until prompted in a later interview with Michael Blankenship did Moye comment on Richard's sexuality.

". . . Halliburton appeared to have letters of introduction to gays located at major points along our projected route and possibly picked up other letters en route. In Tehran, Dick took me to a dinner party which turned out to be made up, with my exception, of five gay men. I had but two or three drinks and excused myself shortly after dinner. I had hardly reached the hotel when I was overtaken by the granddaddy of all headaches (any headache for me was a very unusual occurrence). It lasted almost the entire night, and nothing I tried could alleviate it. I have always suspected the dinner party host had slipped me a Mickey Finn to get me out of the way so the festivities could commence . . . Homosexual friends to whom Dick introduced me seemed to find it difficult to believe that a square could get along so well with one of their number." [7]

Two of Richard's friends, Ken Littauer and Max Aley, boarded the *Majestic* along with the *Flying Carpet* crew. Littauer, a fiction editor for Colliers magazine, enlisted in France's "Service Aeronautic" in 1916. By the end of the WWI, he retired from the military as Chief of Air Service, 3rd Army Corps and returned to his previous occupation as a magazine writer for Street and Smith. He next took the job with Colliers. Moye and Littauer passed many evenings together discussing flying and its future during the Atlantic crossing. [8]

The *Majestic* docked at Southampton on February 5. Richard left for London the next morning to see about permits and other necessary paperwork. Moye stayed to supervise the unloading and transport of the Stearman to the Avro plant in nearby Hamble. Assisting with the assembly of the airplane, he quickly made friends with the mechanics and pilots on the field and became an honorary member of the Hampshire Flying Club. Founded in 1926 to promote British aviation, the club's original members came from all over the world. Record-setting British aviatrix Amy Johnson, Spanish autogyro designer Juan de la Cierva, and pioneer Australian aviator Bert Hinkler were three early members. When Moye took the Stearman up for a test flight on February 9, a large number of pilots from the club gathered to watch the American plane put through its required maneuvers. The British pilots immensely enjoyed the stunting which Moye couldn't refuse them. The Stearman, with its 220 hp Wright J-5, out-performed their 85-100 hp de Havilland *Moths* and Avro *Avians*. 9

Moye encountered sunny skies when he departed Hamble for London's Croydon Airport, the first since arriving in England. He welcomed the warm sunshine as he passed over England' green countryside. He delighted in the rich colors and textures, so different than the desert terrain along his TAT route. With excellent directions from the fellows at Avro's plant, he located Croydon easily. London's principal commercial airport, it compared to Roosevelt Field on Long Island as the jumping off point for many record setting flights.

Before meeting Richard at the Flemings Hotel, their residence while in London, Moye secured the *Flying Carpet* in an available hangar. That same day, the two went to see the Shell Oil people in an attempt to obtain free gas and oil, an opportunity missed in St. Louis. Shell told Richard and Moye that they had sworn off providing fuel for spectacular flights. Too many ended tragically and that did nothing to promote the use of their fuel. They did, however, arrange for Richard and Moye to sign company chits for gas and oil. Shell would periodically forward the receipts to Richard's banker in New York for payment. This greatly simplified obtaining fuel and the necessity for carrying large amounts of cash or making payments in local currency. Shell also assisted the flight by sharing their phenomenal knowledge of worldwide aviation facilities. With their help, Moye mapped out their general route; side trips would be arranged en route as local sources of information became available.

After plotting a tentative route, Moye and Richard called upon Edward Stanford Ltd., cartographers to the king, just off Trafalgar Square. Stanford, London's most accurate map maker since the mid-1800s, created maps that were extremely convenient for viewing while seated in the open cockpit of the Stearman. Referred to as Stanford Air Route maps, the folding maps were mounted on cards approximately 10" tall by 5.5" wide. When fully opened, the maps ranged in width from less than four feet to almost six feet. Some were single-sided; others were double-sided. The accordion style allowed the pilot to view one section at a time.

All the maps were treated using a "Lutra" process. The process not only waterproofed and rendered them more durable, it also allowed the surface to be written on and wiped clean an indefinite number of times. Stanford made available a sliding map carrier designed to fit into the recess over the instrument facia board in the cockpit. Whether the *Flying Carpet* used one of these is not known. Moye marked their maps by indicating airports with red triangles; his route was in red ink; distances and headings were printed alongside the route. Because of the volume of maps, Stanford shipped them in increments to the *Flying Carpet*'s larger, overnight stops. Additional maps obtained in London were Michelin Maps of Europe and Curves of Equal Magnetic Variation, compiled by the Royal Observatory in Greenwich. Total charges for the Stanford maps were approximately 50 pounds.

Maneuvering through the various consulates and embassies to obtain travel permits turned out to be more involved than either Richard or Moye could have imagined. The most problematic issue they encountered was the fact that the United States did not recognize the French occupation of Morocco which made it difficult to receive the proper visas. Eventually they were granted.

". . . Everyday we've made the rounds of map-makers, insurance agents, consuls, flying offices - endless red tape and silly

Richard bought Stanford maps in London to use on the round-the-world flight. They were supplemented by local maps. Maps courtesy of Moye F. Stephens.

regulations," Richard described in his *Flying Carpet* book. "Our books and baggage have been shipped ahead, our insurance is settled, our maps glitter before us (to Morocco and back to Paris and over the Alps to Italy) - they are perfect and we can't possibly get lost. We have a stack of official papers a foot thick. Moye has continued to test the airplane. Our parachutes have been repacked; our complicated contracts with the Shell Oil Company made satisfactorily. This maze of custom deposits and military restrictions, etc., is all being ironed out here at the beginning, and once we're under way and get into our stride, we'll shed these worries and burdens." 10

Waiting for their permits, Richard and Moye flew to Heston Air Park just west of London on the recommendation of the Hampshire Flying Club pilots. They would get much better service there. 11

"It's true Heston has given us wonderful service," Moye wrote home, "but for that matter, we are treated like kings everywhere we go. The hotel attendants are all agog over our presence. We have been kept busy signing pictures that they have cut out of the newspapers.

"I have been having a great time and have suffered no qualms of home-sickness as yet; not that I haven't missed you all at home, but that is only natural. I think the reason that I have been so happy is that everyone is taking such a lively interest in us, showing us such good times, and then, of course, I have the airplane. Incidentally, it is due to these good times that my letters have been so few and far between. I really have damned little time to myself what with working all day and being entertained all night."

Moye spent his birthday, February 21, with Heston pilots who insisted that they properly celebrate the occasion. Swapping airplanes for short hops culminated at the local pub with numerous rowdy toasts to the American flyer who invited the British pilots to look him up if they ever came to California. Moye felt fortunate to be in his position. He relished the close camaraderie given him on the home field; experiencing equal solidarity on foreign soil proved incredibly satisfying.

A dinner party hosted by Richard's English publisher,

Geoffrey Bless, followed Moye's birthday celebration. The host and other guests thought Moye and Richard's black tie dress seemed an admirable gesture considering the limitations imposed by travel in a small airplane. Both men packed two suits each, one informal and one formal, as proper attire needed for the social events they would attend during the trip.

The next day, with permits in hand, Moye prepared to depart for Paris. The *Flying Carpet* looked regal as the sun's rays danced on its scarlet fuselage. The engine purred on start-up. Moye circled the English Station at Lympne as requested until he received a light to proceed across the English Channel. Lympne then cabled the French Station at St. Inglevert that the *Flying Carpet* was on its way. If overdue, speedboats would be sent out quickly to look for the biplane. Moye expected the Channel to be wider and have fewer boats traversing the waterway. So many floated below him that, if his engine quit, he could put the plane down almost anywhere and be picked up immediately.

Landing at Paris' Le Bourget Airport, their first non-English speaking destination, the ease of passing through customs surprised Richard and Moye. After two years of college French, Moye thought he would be able to remember something of the language. Neither he nor Richard could manage a sentence adequately. At the first opportunity, Moye bought a Frazer and Square grammar book to refresh his memory. Considerable practice allowed him to carry on a decent conversation without much difficulty. Monsieur Simonot, the watchman for their hangar at Le Bourget, commented that Moye showed *fantastique* progress. Moye thought the comment exaggerated, yet encouraging.

One of the English pilots had given Moye and Richard a letter of introduction to Vicomte Jacques de Sibour and his wife Vicomtess Violette who had made their own world flight. In 1928, they departed France in a De Havilland Moth called the Safari II. Ten months and 33,000 miles later, they returned home. Violette, an American raised in England, was the daughter of H. Gordon Selfridge, founder of the famous Selfridge Department Store of London. She published a book about their trip called the *Flying Gypsies*. Moye was anxious to meet them and learn about their journey. Having checked into the Hotel Wagram on the Rue de Rivoli, just a short walk from the Arc de Triomphe, Moye phoned the Vicomte. He told Jacques about their proposed trip and expressed the hope that he would be kind enough to give them whatever advice he could. 12

"Jacques showed up at our hotel in less than half an hour and promptly invited us to dinner at their home," Moye related in his notes. "We have since visited with them often and have formed what I wish could develop into a lasting friendship. It seems a forlorn hope, I'm afraid, in view of the distances involved. They are a couple after my own heart, completely unaffected, living simply, and wrapped up in aviation and big game hunting. If I could find another girl like Violette and have the great good fortune to have her consider me a kindred soul, I would be sitting on top of the world. She is very pretty, most gracious, and though utterly feminine, flies her own plane and loves it! She accompanies Jacques on all his big game safaris. She has shot lions, tigers, rhinos, elephants, and all the rest. Jacques tells me that I will have opportunities to do some big game shooting on our trip, so don't be surprised if you receive a stuffed elephant one of these days!"

Jacques held a top position within the French aviation administration. He gave Moye and Richard a tour of the Air Ministry and all its departments. Introducing them to the right people simplified the amount of red tape required in obtaining flight authorizations. Moye accompanied the Viscomte on a tour of the Farman airplane factory, usually off limits to a foreigner. He met Henri Farman, one of the truly great pioneers of aviation, who was building a custom cabin monoplane for Jacques. Similar in size to the Lockheed *Vega*, Jacques and Violette planned to take it on a month's tour in Africa. They would meet Richard and Moye in Morocco if the plane was completed in time. As a polite gesture for the de Sibour's hospitality, Richard and Moye took them to dinner and the theater. Moye also invited them to be his guests at the Stephens' estate when they attended the 1932 Olympic Games in Los Angeles.

Despite de Sibour's help with bureaucratic channels, Washington's neglect to include Spain in its flying permit requests delayed the *Flying Carpet*'s departure from Paris. It seems Madrid officials took their time returning the proper forms. By March 12, Moye and Richard's passports were in order. Only one problem remained. The Stearman's motor began to vibrate. Moye noticed it when crossing the Channel. Doc Maidment, the Wright expert in Europe, came to their rescue. The master mechanic found that the propeller hadn't been properly installed during reassembly in Southampton. Remounting the propeller, he assured them that the motor was in A-1 shape and would carry them to the ends of the earth.

The day after Doc pronounced the motor fit, Moye and Richard packed up and departed Paris for Perpignan on the Spanish border. The date was March 23. Powerful head winds forced the *Flying Carpet* down at Lyon for fuel. Moye, aware that they could not make Perpignan by nightfall, changed their overnight stop to Nimes. With the wind, still against them and increasing in intensity, he settled for Avignon, 50 miles northwest of Nimes.

"The trip down from Dijon was beautiful," Moye told his parents. "We had the Saone River off our right wing tip then, below Lyon, the great Rhone River. On our left, we could see the gleaming snow covered Alps; below us, the fascinating green, succulence of France's country side. Though we heartedly resented the near gale, it probably helped clear the atmosphere and contributed to the vivid high relief of each sparkling detail visible within the entire breathtaking panorama. Whatever the elements that combined to create the phenomenal clarity, I can thank them for one of my more memorable flights."

Moye had visited Avignon during his 1922 school trip. Remembering the beautiful gothic architecture, he suggested to Richard that they take a walking tour in the morning. He wanted Richard to see the Pope's Palace and visit the Villeneuve les Avignon, a small area containing the homes of popes and cardinals. Richard enjoyed strolling the town's narrow streets, peeking into shops and eating at a quaint outdoor cafe as much as Moye. Lifting off for Barcelona, Moye couldn't resist skimming over the countryside to the famous Roman aqueduct, Pont du Gard. He equated the *Flying Carpet* to a sky chariot drawn by 220 thundering horses reminding the French of their ancient heritage.

From the Pont, they turned south toward Nimes and then skirted the Mediterranean coast until reaching Perpignan. They lost three hours going through customs and attempting to locate the local Shell representative. The man eventually strolled onto the airport, gave Moye access to the fuel, and then watched the *Flying Carpet* thunder down the grass strip toward Barcelona. With severe storms over the Pyrenees, Moye circled north to pick up the coast where the weather remained beautiful all the way to Barcelona, the capitol of Catalan. The smoky chimneys of the city were visible for miles out. Upon landing at the military field, the resident commandant who was preparing to take off in one of the Spanish observation planes, an antiquated 80 hp Avro, enthusiastically greeted Moye and Richard. He had never seen an airplane with as much power as the Stearman. The more he studied the plane, the more suspicious he became of the two American. How was it that two foreign civilians could fly about the country in such an aircraft when most European private planes flew with less than a hundred horsepower?

Anxious to take advantage of the good weather, Moye planned to take off early in the morning. Getting ready just after dawn, he asked a mechanic to bring the wheel blocks. Moye then went about the business of starting the motor. He cracked the throttle and turned the switch to 'contact'. Climbing out on the wing to give the crank a twist, Moye felt the plane moving. He panicked as it rolled across the field. Somehow he managed to get back to the cockpit and close the throttle before the plane ran into something. The mechanic fetched the blocks all right but very carefully set them down alongside the wheels instead of in front of them.

The *Flying Carpet* reached Los Alcazares, 400 miles down the coast, about noon. Two French Cauldron biplanes landed just after the Stearman. With introductions all around, they went in search of a place to eat. Los Alcazares, just a tiny little burg right on the Mediterranean, seemed deserted. They eventually located a huge old house situated on the ocean's edge where they consumed a meal of at least 20 different courses. Thoroughly stuffed, Moye,

Richard, the two French pilots, and their mechanic had just enough time to return back to the airfield, gas up, and make Malaga by day's end. The Cauldrons took off first, followed by the *Flying Carpet*. Cutting across the numerous bays along the coast, Moye passed the French planes twenty-five minutes later.

As the sun approached the inland mountain tops, Moye set the Stearman down on the narrow strip at Malaga. The airfield was a little gem. An elegant carpet of fresh green grass and wild flowers covered the landing area. A quaint little tumble-down hangar surrounded by shade trees was the sole structure on the field. With the exception of an ancient caretaker, Moye and Richard had the whole place to themselves. Agreeing to wait for the French pilots, they stretched out on the clean smelling grass amid perfect surroundings. The whole affair was a genuinely sensuous delight. The sun hung low in the sky; the air felt crisp and refreshing. The experience was a fitting way to end a perfect flight. The French pilots had warned Moye of the horrendous air currents that swept off the coastal mountains but they had been absent that day.

When the Cauldrons arrived and were secured next to the Stearman, the five men proceeded to town to spend the evening with friends of one of the pilots, Jean and Annabelle Murat. Both popular French film stars, they proved to be a very entertaining couple. Beautiful Annabella would divorce Jean and marry Tyrone Power in the late 1930s. The next morning, engine trouble prevented the French from accompanying the *Flying Carpet* to Morocco. Moye offered his assistance but their mechanic seemed to have the situation well in hand. Before departing, he and Richard promised to look for them in Rabat.

With the Mediterranean on their left, mountains almost hugging the shoreline, and picturesque villages nestled in between, Moye and Richard found the coastal trip the most breath-taking so far. Richard swore that he would return to make the trip by automobile some day, stopping as often and as long as he wanted. Passing over Gibraltar's fortress, the two said farewell to Europe and started across the straits on a course providing the shortest distance across the Mediterranean to Morocco. Their first stop on the African continent would be Tangiers, Morocco's point of entry.

Richard and Moye looked forward to arriving in the Sahara and learning about the French Foreign Legion. The setting above is most likely in Colomb Bechar. Moye F. Stephens photo.

10

TIMBUCTOO AND THE FOREIGN LEGION

"As you know," Moye recalled, "it has been my plan to teach Dick to fly en route. In training planes instructors occupy the front cockpits so that they can direct the students by means of hand signals. In the *Carpet*, it has been imperative for me to man the rear cockpit as it contains all the essential controls and instruments. The front cockpit has only a stick, rudder pedals, and a throttle. It is completely devoid of instruments and provides no brakes or means of controlling the adjustable stabilizer to trim the ship. As a result, there have not been too many occasions when I could turn the controls over to Dick without having him stray from the course.

"Opportunities have been confined to times when the course paralleled an easily distinguished feature such as a river or shore line similar to the one we were following en route to Rabat. Previous sessions had not been too encouraging but I hoped that, with additional instruction, he would start to get the hang of air work. When ready for landings and take-offs, I would be able to fly in the front cockpit as long as our activities were confined to the immediate area of a suitable landing field. Shortly after leaving Tangier I shook the stick, signaling Dick to take over. Things progressed reasonably well for a short while until my aspiring student spied something on the seacoast that demanded his utter absorption. As the left wing slowly dropped, I leaned to the right in a fruitless but nonetheless automatic effort to bring the wing up by means of body English. As the wing continued to drop, the nose followed suit, and before the diving spiral entered the screaming stage, I took control of the stick, put the ship back on course, and again handed it over to Dick. After the third such maneuver, he turned to me indicating he wished to converse. I closed the throttle to lull the roar of the motor so I could hear his shouted message. 'It's black magic, Moye. From here on you do the flying and I'll stick to the writing.'"

Two hours and ten minutes after departing Malaga, the *Flying Carpet* circled over the town of Rabat, the capital of French Morocco. Landing at the French military airdrome, Moye taxied toward the civilian side of the airport, the normal procedure for a non-military pilot. Clearing the runway, he noticed a uniformed troop frantically waving a flag in front of the army hangars. Deciding the frenzied action was intended for him, being the only moving aircraft in sight, Moye changed directions.

Virtually the entire post turned out to welcome the two Americans and examine the beautiful *Flying Carpet*. Satisfied that they had counted every cylinder and scrutinized all structural details, several mechanics and pilots helped push the plane into an empty hangar. One enthusiastic officer, paying attention to the American's necessities, found accommodations for Moye and Richard, notified the Shell representative of their arrival, and asked what work, if any, their mechanic could perform on the ship. This degree of hospitality caught Moye and Richard by surprise. Although greatly appreciated, they had not experienced a similar welcome anywhere in France. This included the Commandant's personal escort to the officer's private bar. Moye and Richard spent the rest of the afternoon drinking rounds of beer until they could hardly stand up. By the time the Shell representative arrived, they readily accepted his invitation to drive them to their hotel and call it a day.

Rising early, the first item on Moye's agenda was to purchase a revolver. French customs confiscated the two pistols Moye stowed aboard the airplane before departing Burbank. If Richard had remained silent when officials asked if they had any weapons, they would still be in the airplane! Wandering the market place, Moye found a fairly new Colt Super .38 revolver which, for the remainder of the trip, he wore in a holster under his jacket. The weapon was a necessity if the airplane went down in hostile territory. Just as important was the permission Moye and Richard received from the French Resident General to carry an unsealed camera and land on any military airport in French-occupied territory. Officials in Paris had denied them these privileges. The military airfield concession would prove essential in the absence of any other type of viable landing strip. The Resident General also presented Moye and Richard with valuable letters of introduction for Fez and more extensive maps of the Sahara. The Stanford maps stopped three hundred miles south of the Algerian and Moroccan borders.

The hospitality of the military continued as Moye and Richard prepared their plane for take-off. Mechanics changed the oil and fueled the *Flying Carpet*; a young pilot proudly presented photographs of their plane taken upon their arrival; and Lieutenant Edgar *Ham* Hamilton, the only American officer in the French Foreign Legion, made arrangements with them for dinner the following evening in Meknes. March 27, with the entire post present to bid them adieu, Moye and Richard thanked them for their generosity and headed for Fez.

"We had headwinds so it took us an hour and twenty minutes to cover the roughly one hundred miles of the trip." Moye wrote in his letters. "We crossed over the Rif Mountains, a series of low plateaus, followed down the length of another range, and found Fez nestled in a fertile valley cradled by hills on all sides save the south. We circled the native village before landing and were instantly captivated by the exotic charm of its irregular complex of white-roofed buildings punctuated here and there by the towers of mosques. You couldn't possibly imagine anything more distinctively Moorish. It is the capital of Northern Morocco and is the area's most important center in all respects. It dates from the seventh century and its present population numbers approximately 100,000.

"Our reception at the flying field was no less cordial than at Rabat. Having been notified by his Rabat counterpart of our arrival, the ubiquitous Shell representative was on hand to take us into town. Before we left the field, an officer told me they had received a letter for me but had sent it by army airplane to Meknes thinking we would stop there first. Three hours later at the hotel, an army pilot knocked on my door and handed me the letter. They had sent it back from Meknes by army plane. He invited me to join a group of his fellow officers downstairs in the bar so I located Dick in his room and we all had cocktails and a very pleasant dinner together. The friendliness of these French pilots and their concern for our welfare is overwhelming."

As promised in Rabat, Moye and Richard flew to Mecknes, 40 miles southwest of Fez, to have dinner with Lieutenant. Hamilton. Hamilton enlisted in France's Service Aeronautique during WWI. He received his *brevet militaire* or pilot license in 1917. Fluent in French and well-versed in aviation science, he became a flight instructor and technical advisor for Americans who joined the war effort. With the signing of the Armistice, Hamilton returned to school, earned an engineering degree from Carnegie-Melon, and then joined the French Foreign Legion. He would spend 30 years in Algeria and Morocco building roads, tunnels, and bridges. [1]

Hamilton gave Moye and Richard a tour of the regimental barracks and drove them around Meknes. They saw miles and miles of huge mud walls and tremendous palaces. Sultan Moulay Ismail, inspired by stories of the great Versailles, attempted to reproduce the elaborate French structure in Morocco. Although built in the early 1700s, his efforts were surprisingly impressive. That evening, Hamilton treated his new friends to a delicious Moroccan feast before delivering them to the Hotel Transatlantique. He joined them for breakfast in the morning after which Moye and Richard made the short flight back to Fez.

Moye was honored when local pilots asked him to participate in Fez's first air meet. He put on an unforgettable aerobatic show in the *Flying Carpet*. Other pilots participating in the inaugural event were Rene Fonck, top Allied ace of WWI with 75 victories, and Michel Detroyat, a leading French aerobatic pilot, most likely flying his 230 hp Morane Saulnier. The contest between man and machine attracted thousands of spectators and provided a pleasurable diversion for Moye.

"I couldn't compare with Detroyat," Stephens told Ron Gilliam, "But they had to have another pilot to have an air meet. I noticed his plane – a high-wing monoplane – didn't perform well on its back so I did some slow rolls . . . loops, rolled the plane on its back, let the engine quit and glided down for a while, then rolled out. That made a great impression . . . !" 2

While Moye took part in the air meet, Richard searched for a house to lease. They needed a place to store their winter clothes and a comfortable residence upon their return from the Sahara. Richard located a typical Moorish-style house that would serve both purposes. Were he not so excited about reaching Timbuctoo, Richard certainly would have lingered indefinitely in Fez. Its exotic atmosphere mesmerized him.

Preparations for the flight to Timbuctoo took up the remainder of Moye and Richard's brief stay in Fez. Ready to depart on March 30, a message arrived from the Commandant delaying their take-off. A fresh outbreak of fighting had erupted along their planned route. He advised that if they still wanted to go, they would need to divert north to Oran, Algeria and from there, follow the railroad to Colomb Bechar, a 238 mile flight. The suggested route added nearly three hundred miles to the original Fez-Colomb Bechar flight. Having no choice in the matter, they went as directed.

The two hour flight to Oran, a large port city, took place over terrain quite similar to that of northern Arizona. The panorama evoked memories of Moye's time as an airline captain. Although only five months had passed since he left T & WA, it seemed much longer. Absorbed with all that was required for a safe journey, time passed quickly. Moye had little time to think about friends and family. His days were simply filled with too many activities which often left him exhausted. Flying through blue skies over familiar terrain allowed him isolated moments of nostalgia.

Moye and Richard's reception at Oran's joint military-civilian field lacked the warm welcome they received in Rabat and Fez. Civilian officials immediately demanded their papers. Moye couldn't find them. He had presented them to the Commandant at Fez and thought he must have overlooked retrieving them.

The Algerian authorities locked the Stearman in a hangar and started sending wires in all directions. The first day passed and nothing happened. During the second, Moye discovered the authorizations in the airplane logbook. The Commandant must have placed them there without making mention of the fact. Sadly, presenting the documents accomplished nothing. They bore no official attributes - no sealing wax, ribbons, or stamps. Moye and Richard started sending a few cables of their own. The following day, officials informed Moye and Richard that they were free to proceed and apologized for delaying their flight. That night, Monsieur Meziah, the Shell representative for Oran, told Moye and Richard that the Prefect of Oran had received a cable from Paris signed by Aristide Briand, Foreign Minister and former Premier of France. Briand wanted to know why the two Americans were being delayed. They attributed their good fortune to Jacques de Sibour.

Preparing to leave the next day, a telegram from Colomb Bechar arrived. An immense sandstorm was wrecking havoc across the entire desert portion of their route. They were advised to postpone their flight until the storm subsided. The succeeding three days brought repetitions of the same dismal tidings. With no other options available, Richard and Moye languished in Oran until Monsieur Meziah came to their rescue. He and his wife organized a hiking expedition to an ancient citadel, Fort Santa Cruz, perched at the 1,312 foot summit of the Aidur. Built by the Spanish following their capture of the city in 1509, the fort provided a magnificent view of the Mediterranean and a pleasant diversion for Moye and Richard.

On April 6, a favorable weather report arrived from Colomb Bechar. Moye and Richard dashed out to the field for an immediate departure only to find one of the plane's tires had been punctured by a huge thorn. Frantic pleading and cajoling managed to get it fixed by noon. Moye took off without further delay, flying south over the northern Atlas and Sidi Bel Abbes, the central training installation for the French Foreign Legion. Located in a deep valley, it would be the site for Legion's centennial celebration scheduled to take place in three weeks. Richard and Moye hoped to return in time to participate.

An hour out of Oran, a storm dramatically changed the flying conditions. Gale force winds and blowing sand made navigation challenging. Rather than relying solely on his compass, Moye flew east to pick up the Algerian State Railways narrow-gauge track which terminated at Colomb Bechar. Clearing an area of high plateaus, they found themselves flying over a vast expanse of sand and barren mountain rock. The better part of the next four hours produced little change. Toward the fourth hour, they saw a few small oases and, at long last, made out their destination. The large oasis and military strip, right on the edge of the Sahara proper, were a welcome sight. Upon landing, it took Moye, Richard, and several army pilots to maneuver the plane into a hangar as the wind turned into a gale. Removing their suitcases from the airplane, Moye noticed that the cushion tire had ripped away from the hub of the tail wheel. He wrapped the rim in heavy cording rather than wait for a new tire from London. 3

Lieutenant Bodin, a French army pilot, drove Richard and Moye into town. With every Christian for a hundred miles visiting for Easter, the hotel was completely booked. The proprietor offered them a couple of mattresses, some blankets, and the dining room floor as a bedroom. Too tired to care, they accepted with pleasure. Bodin then invited Moye and Richard to his house for dinner. He and three other pilots had set up housekeeping in a typical residence made of mud with a wrinkled old Arab for a cook and a German Legionnaire for a maid. They found the food very tasty. A staple of couscous combined with various vegetables and meats served with flatbread seemed to be the usual fare. They ate at Bodin's home so often they felt embarrassed and began bringing bottles of champagne which were quickly consumed by their hosts.

"Columb Bechar is as yet unspoiled by civilization," Moye wrote, wanting to describe his first oasis experience for his parents, "There are no electric lights, no baths, only one or two autos, and absolutely no sanitation. The number of flies is terrific. Ditto for the odors. Yesterday, Dick and I left the village which is on the desert side of the oasis and went for a four to five hour hike through the palm trees along the *wadis* or river channels. It was beautiful beyond description. The river channels appeared to be a series of lakes with just enough current to keep the water clear. Walking along the edge of the water one could easily imagine that he was in the South Sea Islands. The huge date palms lean out over the water with a luxuriant tangle of vegetation underneath. The Arabs have cultivated small patches of land all along the river and each little patch is surrounded by a picturesque mud wall. We saw many Arabs at work irrigating their plots by the primitive method of lifting bucketful after bucketful of water from the lakes and pouring them into elevated irrigation ditches which directed water to their land. Towards the bottom of the oasis, the stream was alive with Arab women washing clothes in pools of water and drying them on the rocks. We sat for half an hour or so in the shade smoking cigarettes and watching the women work. All in all, the oasis is as lovely a spot as I have ever seen. I wish as much could be said for the village."

The village of Colomb Bechar swarmed with Legionnaires. Very near the site of the war, soldiers came and went all day long. Every morning, army planes took off to bomb the rebels. When they returned in the afternoon, many of the planes were riddled with bullets. A red heart-shaped patch placed over each bullet hole by a mechanic made some of the airplanes look as though they had measles. Moye did not concern himself about being shot down; the French government refused him permission to fly over enemy territory considered too dangerous.

The Moroccan Rif Berbers, indigenous tribes of northern Africa, had battled with other Berber tribes, Arabs, and foreign invaders for centuries. When France and Spain subjugated Morocco and Algeria in the early 1900s, the Berbers, led by Abd-el-Rim, began a barbarous attack against the Europeans. Abd-el-Rim defeated the Spanish in 1925. When he turned his attention to French Morocco, Marshal Petain, Inspector General of the French Army, launched a full scale offensive. The French Foreign Legion, fighting the Berbers since 1923, assisted in forcing the Berber chief to surrender in 1926. The conflict should have ended but France erred when they decreed that all the Berber tribes would be subject to French law. As a result, the Berber rebellion continued. Their long tradition of fierce fighting skills and marksmanship made them a treacherous enemy. 4

Sporadic fighting in the desolate Rif Mountains, combined with poor weather, kept the *Flying Carpet* grounded for nearly two weeks. Richard pursued his research on the Foreign Legion, jotting notes on his café receipts. Most of the information he and Moye learned was contentious and not documented in history books. *Le Caffard* was one. It came as no surprise that Legionnaires stationed in Colomb Bechar for years suffered with *Le Caffard*, a state of delirium in which they believe that cockroaches crawl inside their heads. They would do anything to rid themselves of the horrid pests. The month before the *Flying Carpet*'s arrival, a delusional Legionnaire shot and killed his two comrades believing them to be responsible for the cockroaches.

The status of Legionnaire prisoners suggested another controversial issue. Colomb Bechar held the distinction of being the penal center for the Legion. Prisoners lived in a grim, foreboding looking fortress between the village and the aviation field. Nobody but the French army men were allowed near it. The place seemed shrouded in mystery. Ask any of the Legionnaires about it and they glance furtively around and say, "No, I have never been in it and I don't want to be!" Late one evening, a Lieutenant of the Legion and member of the Disciplinary Committee related a few unknown facts about the prisoners to Moye.

Imprisoned Legionnaires were never allowed to speak to one another and must do everything on the count of the officer. At meal times, they line up at the table with their hands folded in their laps. The sergeant blows a whistle and starts the count. One, they seize their spoons; two, they raise their spoons; three, they commence to eat frantically because they have to finish before the sergeant blows his whistle again. On the blasts of the whistle they all stop. Their whole life is regulated the same way as is their status. The classes - normal, transition, and repression – define the men. Those in the normal division are treated decently. Men in transition are required to work very hard. When Moye asked how those in repression were treated, the Lieutenant shrugged his shoulders and said, "Comme les moutons. One does not speak about it."

April 17, twelve days after arriving in Colomb Bechar, Moye and Richard received official permission to continue their flight to Timbuctoo in the French Sudan. The local Commandant also gave them the key to the precious fuel dumps in the Sahara. Circling over the airfield, Moye rocked the airplane's wings as a farewell salute to the large crowd of Legionnaires gathered for their send off. He would follow the Tanezrouft track to Gao on the Niger River. If he experienced any difficulty, military planes or mail trucks would spot the Stearman within a week. Every fifteen days, specialized postal vehicles made the trip from northern Algeria to the banks of the Niger. Military pilots flew the track weekly, carrying five or six day's worth of food and water for emergencies. Moye and Richard had enough for ten men for twenty days!

On take-off from Colomb Bechar, Moye and Richard were able to take a look inside the foreboding Legionnaire prison - a hollow, roofless square. Tents stood in the open area which they assumed were for the prisoners. A few small buildings most likely served as officers' quarters. Strange, fantastic-looking paintings covered all four interior walls.

The next leg of the *Flying Carpet* flight would be the most challenging. From Columb Bechar to Timbuctoo, a distance of 1,300 miles, they would encounter vast expanses of inhospitable terrain. Moye felt prepared. He gathered as much information as possible from the local pilots - jotting down his notes on the edges of his maps. Military fields, geographic markers, and fuel dumps were aptly noted along with headings and distances. The only element that Moye could not control was the weather. Flying from Oran to Bechar had given him a sense of the unpredictable southern winds that blew across the desert. When air currents became choms -

strong, hot, sand-laden winds – his navigating skills and his resolve would be tested. Without precise navigation and considerable skill, the mission could turn deadly. The *Flying Carpet* would provide no magical ride over the harsh, forbidding Sahara.

Expecting the worst, Richard and Moye were pleasantly surprised as they headed for Adrar, 325 miles south of Colomb Bechar. The sky was cloudless; its color defined sky blue; the visibility was immeasurable. They passed over oasis after oasis situated on the extreme western edge of a huge sea of mountainous sand dunes of various shades of red, orange, and yellow. No words could capture the beauty of the oases - thick clusters of green palms, patches of cultivated land, and tiny lakes of water, all nestled against the rolling dunes. Maintaining a heading of 154°, Moye easily located the oasis of Adrar. After refueling, Moye left a chit or receipt in the designated box to indicate how many gallons he took. It seemed an efficient system in the absence of any personnel in the vicinity.

Approximately one hundred miles later, the *Flying Carpet* landed in Reganne, the last in a long line of date palm oases. Flying over the field, it looked completely deserted. With no visible indication of transportation, Moye buzzed the Bordj Estienne, a Compagnie Transahariene Hotel on the outskirts of Reganne. Moye and Richard finished securing the Stearman between two sets of crisscrossed walls which served as windbreaks just as a chauffeur arrived from the hotel. That evening, they dined with the manager, Raymond Bauret, a young Parisian "resplendent in his flowing black silks and bright-colored sandals" and also the local director of the Trans-Saharan. They most likely enjoyed a few drinks at the well-stocked bar, "with brass rails, high stools, and mirrors" which gave the impression of a New York speakeasy. 5

Journalist William Seabrook, traveling the same route as the *Flying Carpet* and at approximately the same time, wrote the following about Bordj Estienne in his book *Air Journey*. "All the servants, including the bartender, were Arabs. We had whiskies and soda with him (Bauret) at the bar, American cigarettes, a French table-d'hôtel, illustrated French and English magazines less than ten days old in the lounge library, bedrooms with electric lights, modern-art curtains and counterpanes." Like Seabrook, Moye and Richard found it odd to find such comfort in the middle of the desert. 6

At sun-up, Moye and Richard topped off the fuel tanks and planned to make Gao by evening. Flying nearly 800 miles in one day, assuming calm winds, seemed optimistic.

The terrain changed dramatically as Moye flew further into the Sahara. Miles of sand, hard-packed and flat as a billiard table, stretched to the horizon. An airplane could land anywhere but the prudent pilot would stay near the main route to enable search planes to find him. Although the Stearman had a range of 600 miles, Moye planned to make fuel stops more frequently. Carrying extra fuel served as a safety precaution in the advent of excessive headwinds. Between Reganne and Gao, he marked the refueling stop of Bidon Cinq, which, according to Moye's map, was located 30 miles west of the road. His map also indicated Quallene or Tarit approximately half way to Bidon Cinq as an emergency refueling depot.

The leg from Reganne to Bidon Cinq introduced Moye and Richard to the harshness of the Sahara. The intense heat, reaching well over one hundred degrees, was suffocating. The strain of following the track that disappeared and then reappeared left them worn and emotionally debilitated. Moye often had to circle back to pick up the track. Nearing where he calculated Bidon Cinq should be, Moye strained from the cockpit at 500 feet to locate the fuel dump but saw nothing. Everything seemed to blend together – the sky, the sand, the mirage in between. Descending to 100 feet, 50 feet, and then dropping to 10 feet, he spotted what looked like gas cans scattered around the piste. Hopeful that this *was* the fuel dump, he set the Stearman down. Moye and Richard felt greatly relieved when they found the two sun-bleached pumps, one for water and one for fuel, sticking up from the sand. Unlocking the fuel pump, they began transferring gas to the airplane, one gallon at a time.

Airborne again, herds of gazelles, veiled Tuaregs on horseback, and a ribbon of blue in the distance signaled that Gao was near. The *Flying Carpet* would land before nightfall. Although they made their destination, Moye and Richard found the facilities on the military airport lacking; the rest house was filthy and thick with flies from off the Niger River. The conditions made the next three days miserable for Moye as he made an earnest effort to clean the sand from the airplane's engine. He couldn't wait to get away from the dreadful town.

April 23, 1931, Moye and Richard departed for Timbuctoo, 223 miles west, following the Niger at an altitude of 10,000 feet. At that height, the cooler air and absence of insects provided for a refreshing flight. Moye began his descent into the ancient city at ten miles out. At 5,000 feet, mosques, a fort, and the medina became distinguishable. Richard's excitement built as he began to see camels and white-robed natives in the market place from his vantage point of 1,000 feet. Alarm replaced anticipation when the roar of the plane's motor startled thousands of black storks from their perches atop chimneys and rooftops. The birds formed a dark, moving cloud which completely blotted out the sun. Miraculously, Moye landed without ruining the engine or damaging the plane's fabric by striking one. 7

In the absence of any vehicle at the airfield, Moye and Richard rode into town on donkeys. Richard most likely embraced the moment as he entered Timbuctoo, imagining himself a consummate merchant bringing silks and brocades to barter in the market place. Hundreds of locals lined the streets to catch a glimpse of the visitors. The procession passed through narrow lanes bordered by undistinguished yellow mud houses and ancient mosques topped with squat towers and studded with crude wooden spikes. In contrast to Richard's mythical image of Timbuctoo, he found a rather run-down, decrepit city.

Once a significant trading outpost for the great caravans that crossed northern Africa, Timbuctoo had not prospered for centuries. The thousands of merchants that exchanged European goods for gold, black slaves, ivory and other exotic goods had disappeared long ago. The gold they traded had earned Timbuctoo a reputation as the *El Dorado* of Africa long before the 18th century. The gold, however, was mined elsewhere but the myth continued. The precious metal came up the Niger from countries southwest of the Sahara. The encroaching desert now separated the river from Timbuctoo by seven miles. 8

Salt, mined 150 miles north and transported by camel caravan to the city, was the sole product that Timbuctoo traded. According to author John Norwich, Timbuctoo's economy had depended on the twice-yearly salt caravans made up of well over twelve thousand camels. Each animal carried four blocks of salt, each weighing one hundred pounds. By the 12th century, Timbuctoo earned the reputation as a center for Islamic scholarship. At its peak, the city's population of 100,000 included approximately 25,000 Muslim scholars who frequented 180 Koranic schools. This, rather than the trading of gold, may have given more credence to the European idea that Timbuctoo represented the key to Africa. 9

The legendary city of Timbuctoo had not been mechanized by the white man as other African cities. Richard and Moye discovered there were "no cafés, hotels, bars, restaurants, garages, brothels, churches, movie theaters, not one commercial advertising sign or billboard; no residence or even bungalow of European style, no pane of glass, no telephone, no newspaper; no public conveyance or vehicle of any sort; only one automobile privately owned – and publicly frowned on – brought rattling God knows how from Gao in 1931 by a worthless cousin of one of Yakouba's black sons-in-law. He drives it when he can beg, buy, or steal gas from the military field." 10

Peré Auguste Dupuis Yakouba was Richard and Moye's contact in Timbuctoo. Yakcouba, a member of the Péres Blancs, co-founded Timbuctoo's first Christian mission in 1895. After nine years, he gave up his missionary career, married Salama, a rather large local woman, and fathered eight children. Over time, he became an authority on native languages and cultures, serving as an interpreter and liaison for the French government and president of the local university. By 1931, Yakouba, stocky and powerful with twinkling blue eyes and a snowy beard, had become the patriarch of Timbuctoo. Some considered him eccentric as he shuffled about the earthen streets in a shabby khaki shirt, Arab trousers, rawhide sandals, and beret. The truth is that he had simply gone native after 35 years in the isolated town. Yet, he had gained renown for his knowledge. Distinguished visitors paid their respects to "the white monk of Timbuctoo" before engaging in any other business. 11

Yakouba and Salama, "an immense motherly Ethiop queen, in gorgeous robes, great golden earrings, bracelets, and anklets", loved to entertain on their rooftop. They shared their house pets, a baby leopard and monkey, and provided a formidable cuisine with their guests. While Moye and Dick indulged in culinary delights and imported liqueur, Yacouba shared some noteworthy information with them. 12 Some weeks prior to their arrival, Elly Beinhorn, a German woman pilot, found her way to Timbuctoo having crashed her airplane south of the city. She was returning to Berlin after participating in a scientific expedition for Austrian anthropologist Dr. Hugo Bernatzik. Flying a Klemm with floats, she assisted the researcher who was studying the indigenous peoples in Portuguese Guinea, southwest of Timbuctoo. She applied for the job as E. Beinhorn, a necessity if she wanted to be hired. The concept of a woman at the controls of an airplane in Germany seemed less acceptable than in other European countries. Although France produced 22 women pilots before WWI, Germany counted only three; Melli Beese being the first licensed German female pilot. The numbers were proportionate in 1930. 13

Dr. Bernatzik did not know E. Beinhorn was a woman until he interviewed Elly in Vienna. Impressed by her confidence, charm, and resume, he explained what her position entailed. She would fly a cameraman to take pictures of Guinea, transport necessary supplies to the camp, and improve the accuracy of maps by taking the map maker aloft. Excited to have the opportunity, Elly exchanged her airplane for a Klemm powered by a 40 hp Salmson engine, arranged for fuel with Shell, and shipped a set of floats to Bissau. The flight down the coast of Africa to Guinea went smoothly; the return trip, ten weeks later, proved the most difficult of any cross-country flight she had attempted. 14

Rather than take the coastal route back to Europe, Elly headed northeast toward Timbuctoo. Fifty miles from Timbuctoo, a broken oil line forced her down in the mosquito-infested marshes of the Niger River. Three days later, exhausted and covered with bites, Elly made her way to Timbuctoo with the help of donkeys, zebus

(Brahmin cattle), boats, and members of the Songhai tribe. She would return to Berlin weeks later in a Klemm supplied to her by the German government. Richard, familiar with the noted aviatrix, felt disappointed that he had missed an opportunity to meet her. In time, and many thousands of miles later, her path would cross that of the *Flying Carpet*. 15

A caravanserai, a shelter for visiting tradesmen, served as accommodations for Moye and Richard. The simple structure possessed no furnishings, no attendant, and no food. It did have squawking storks nesting on the roof, screeching bats, and swarms of flies. The suffocating odors of bat urine and stork droppings left nowhere else to sleep but on the sand in the courtyard. Moye and Richard could not comprehend how the building could be packed full of guests in March and September when caravans converged upon the otherwise lethargic town. Timbuctoo's central market came alive during those months and, on a smaller scale, during weekly market days. Vendors offered a variety of merchandise - melons, fruits, fowls, bootleg slaves, locally-made pottery, brassware, home-made weapons, hand-woven cotton cloth, and bottles of gin.

Moye and Richard established friendships with Timbuctoo's small white colony composed of one army colonel, six young officers, and the French postmaster, his daughter and six other French civilians. They dined frequently with the officers on the roof of their barracks. Heavy drinking and raucous singing accompanied every meal. The officers told Moye and Richard that they would die from the heat and monotony without their liquor and songs.

Timbuctoo obviously lacked the qualities of the dream city Richard imagined. Despite his idealization of the Saharan town in his book, *The Flying Carpet*, the reality of strong odors, incessant noises, and sand in everything proved difficult to overlook. No matter how much magic Richard attributed to the fading city or how many velvet skies he saw, Timbuctoo sat isolated in the middle of the desert with no remarkable characteristics.

In one episode of Richard's adventurous description of the town, he discussed the purchase of slaves. He writes that he and Moye rode camels to a Tuareg encampment outside of town to buy slaves to take care of their living quarters. As he tells the story, they bargained with the chief for two child slaves, put them to work, and then sold them back to the chief when they didn't work out. This type of acquisition would have been frowned on by the locals.

In a 1993 interview, James Cortese asked Moye about the two slave children pictured in Richard's book. "No, my God," Moye exclaimed. "There were French officers there. There was a contingent of the French military with whom we dined, fortunately . . . We much preferred not to make arrangements with a native family with their hygienic customs. So we were with them (the French) every night for dinner. I don't think they would have regarded the purchase of slaves as being quite the right thing to do." 16

In a letter to his parents, Moye describes his and Richard's last evening in Timbuctoo. "Dick spent the time exploring the starlit mysteries of the town and then celebrating the Islamic holiday, *fete de mouton*, with the natives in the central plaza. I spent the evening with the French soldiers. I brought wines, aperitifs, and champagne for my hosts. Lieutenant Barat was awarded the Legion of Honor that day so they had a huge celebration. There were two captains, Fargues and Baudet, but the real ring-leader and life of the party was a Lieutenant Chapuisat, a huge young man who knew more songs, some questionable, than any other ten men I have ever known, Dick Ranaldi included. He was full of pep and kept things going all the time. We had the good fortune to meet them through a letter of introduction from one of their officer friends in Gao, a Dr. Ghuigue. The letter was addressed to Lieutenant Delgee of the aviation department, temporarily stationed at Timbuctoo without any kind of aeronautical equipment save an empty hangar. During our stay we rode horses and played tennis with the officers. You can probably comprehend the horseback riding - but the tennis! Lieutenant Delgee and I came off champions and Delgee wasn't much better than I."

April 26, Moye and Richard returned to Gao. Finding better accommodations than previously, they rested for one day in preparation for the Sahara grilling, taking off just after dawn the following day. Moye was pleased when he discovered that the often elusive road was clearly visible. Fresh tracks created by a recent motor caravan made navigating much easier. After two hours, he noted that tremendous headwinds had slowed the *Flying Carpet* to about 40 miles an hour. Reaching the fuel stop seemed doubtful. Moye decided to turn around and go back to Gao when he recognized Tabankort, the only military emergency aviation field between Gao and Bidon Cinq. Authorized in Colomb Bechar to use military gas on the trip if necessary, they borrowed just enough to get them to Bidon Cinq.

With full tanks, Moye still believed he could reach Reganne before nightfall. Pushing the throttle forward in a race to beat the sun's descent below the horizon, the *Flying Carpet* seemed to hang stationary above the scorching desert. At dusk, Moye made the decision to land before all light disappeared. He and Richard secured the airplane by filling sacks with gravel. The bottom pneumatic seats and back parachute cushions served as beds; the motor and cockpit covers made do as blankets. The two travelers enjoyed a dinner of water and canned beef and music played on Richard's phonograph. His records included *Happy Days Are Here Again*, *Bolero*, and *St. Louis Blues*.

"It certainly makes one feel rather insignificant," Moye commented later, "to spend the night in a tiny spot in the middle of countless miles of flat desert with every star in the heavens shining brilliantly because of the clear dry air."

About three in the morning, Moye and Richard woke up shivering. Emptying their suitcases, they put on every article of clothing possible, piling the remainder on top of themselves. The rest of the night passed in comparative comfort. With no vegetation to absorb the intense heat during the day, temperatures in the Sahara can plunge to near zero at night.

At first light, the *Flying Carpet* continued on to Reganne, arriving just in time for breakfast at the Hotel Transahariene. Exhausted from the strain of the previous day and night, Richard and Moye decided to stay overnight. They checked into their rooms and slept until noon. In the afternoon, the hotel manager drove them to the airfield so Moye could change the Stearman's oil and fill it up with gas. A tour of adjacent oases and an explanation of their water system followed. Every inhabited oasis between Adrar and Reganne has *fougeras* or lines of wells radiating out in all directions for miles. Each oasis sits in the center of a slight depression so that the water will flow into it from all the *fougeras*. The water continued through very elaborate irrigation channels to the patches of cultivated land amongst the palm trees. The residents of the oases owned the water in common and no one could use it without the consent of the others. Without the *fougeras*, constructed by unknown engineers, the oases would not thrive.

A glorious tail wind, the first of their trip, sped them north the next morning. They arrived in Colomb Bechar in a remarkable four hours. Monsieur Meziah met Moye and Richard at the airport and celebrated their return with a welcome luncheon. The meal began with the usual aperitifs, followed by ten courses, champagne, coffee, and three kinds of liqueurs. Meziah appreciated Moye's huge appetite although the effects of heat, flies, and sand made eating painful for him. Moye later discovered that the intense heat from the slipstream had seared his lungs; breathing in grains of razor sharp silica sand had taken their toll as well. He just didn't

Moye and Richard, third and fourth from left, could easily pass for authentic Legionnaires. The photo is taken in Colomb Bechar. Photo courtesy of Moye F. Stephens.

want to offend his host.

Moye and Richard stayed six days on their return visit to Colomb Bechar. In the barracks, they listened to the Legionnaires' stories while sampling their favorite drink, *earthquake*. The drink contained raw white Spanish or Moroccan wine heavily laced with Pernod, a potent alcohol similar to absinthe. One evening, Richard managed to talk a rather inebriated Legionnaire into procuring field uniforms, including kepis, caps with a flat circular top and visor, for him and Moye. The uniform consisted of laced boots, duck trousers lashed at the ankles by leather gaiters, and a collared shirt. Moye looked comfortably smart in his uniform as if he had been in the Legion all his life. Richard simulated a child playing dress up in an

Moye, second from left, and Richard on the right, joined a group of Legionnaires and a native boy in the cool shade of date palms. Photo courtesy of Moye F. Stephens.

outfit two sizes too large. The 'new' recruits now freely joined the Legionnaires in their activities. They washed, swam, drank, and learned a small portion of the Legion's secret language, a mixture of French, German and international slang.

At lunch one day, Moye looked up to see his friend Monsieur Meziah standing at the table in a very excited state. He begged Moye to bring the *Flying Carpet* to Oran.

"It seems that there are two flying clubs in Oran, deadly rivals of each other," Moye explained to his parents. "Mr. Meziah is the treasurer of the Club Aeronautique d'Oran which was giving an air meet that afternoon in Oran. The other club is giving an air meet next Sunday. The club that puts on the best meet will be able to continue while the other must fail as there aren't enough supporters for both. Meziah pleaded with tears in his eyes for us to come and put on a stunt exhibition for them as he was afraid there wasn't going to be enough activity. At first I refused point blank. I learned that they had hired a professional stunt man, Pierre Lemoigne, with a special single seat monoplane. In the end, I couldn't refuse to show off the beautiful *Flying Carpet*. I flew to Oran and, according to Meziah, easily won the competition for his club."

Moye stayed in Oran for eight days. He underwent treatment for his throat and lungs and when feeling better, spent time with the local pilots. He flew their Hanriot and Caudron trainers and took them for rides in the Stearman.

Richard accompanied Moye to Oran but desperately wanted to visit Sidi Bel Abbes, the Holy City of the French Foreign Legion. His original itinerary included attending the *Centenaire de la Legion,* the Legion's one hundred year celebration, from April 29 to May 4, 1931. Whether he misunderstood the dates or lingered too long in Colomb Bechar with his Foreign Legion activities, Richard took the train from Oran to Sidi Bel Abbes, too late to witness the activities first-hand. He did acquire the centennial's program and history booklet for they are part of his collection at Princeton University. They appear to be the basis for his narrative of the celebration in his book. Because Richard's editors placed such importance on the subject of the French Foreign Legion, he may have considered it imperative to mention the centennial activities at length.

Examining the centennial's program, Richard visualized what he missed. Commanders and dignitaries, on horseback or in automobiles, paraded past an endless sea of Legionnaires, standing at arms to salute their leaders. Elite units moved down the parade route with their slow, gliding step, their arms straight and fingers outstretched singing their marching song, *Le Boudin*. Each Legionnaire strutted with majestic stature and self-assurance. At the conclusion of the opening ceremonies, the Legionnaires participated in pageants, an orchestra performing patriotic songs, speeches, and a Tournament of Gladiators that duplicated traditional competitions. Shell, Citroen, Cinzano, and Gordon's Gin were some of the sponsors of the spectacular event. 17

May 14, Moye picked up Richard in Sidi Bel Abbes en route to Fez. Moye found Richard miserable, suffering from sore and swollen feet, the result of a three day march with the Legionnaires – in slacks, tennis shoes, and a sweater! Moye shook his head at the dismal sight as he helped the lame, yet upbeat, writer into the Stearman.

When they arrived in Fez, an official letter from Russia awaited Richard. They refused to issue the *Flying Carpet* a permit to fly into their country. The news was somewhat disappointing for him but not a factor that bothered him for long. He entertained in the evening and, during the day, he and Moye wandered through Fez's medina or old city. They explored its thousands of streets, just wide enough to accommodate a donkey laden with hides for tanning or a baker's cart of fresh baked bread. The labrythinine city offered a rainbow of wares in a variety of souks or markets to delight the senses.

Fez's overall aura of ancient romance and intrigue fascinated Richard. He elaborated on this theme in his book. One chapter centers on a young girl, a more dazzling dancer than any other, who entertained Richard's guests. He weaves a tale of romantic entanglement between the dancer Gulbeyaz and Moye. 18

"At first sight, Moye and I were enslaved . . . When she danced, she scarcely even looked my way, but would cast those great black eyes of hers upon Moye, and smile . . ." Fiction or reality, the affair reflects Richard's ability to add titillating interest to his travel log. 19

"Moye added how Halliburton generally wrote a true account of their adventures," a later interview revealed, "but he often stretched it a bit in order to add more drama to the situation he was describing." William Stoneman, foreign correspondent for the Chicago Daily News, once told Richard, "You're a story teller posing as a journalist." Even Richard alluded to some 'fibs'. "When I say I did something," he once told his father, "I actually did it. But I splash a little red paint on it to make it more interesting." 20

While in Sidi bel Abbes, Richard learned of a Legionnaire outpost at Rich, deep in enemy country. Believing a visit there essential for his commentary on the French military unit, he and Moye sought permission to fly to the outpost but officials refused to grant them a permit. Berbers were constantly attacking the area which made flying there far too dangerous. They would have to fly to Mecknes and go overland to Rich. Before beginning this last Legionnaire adventure, Richard and Moye flew to Casablanca, likely for the purpose of sight-seeing. Moye's letters indicate that Richard then took the train to Marrakesh while Moye returned to Fez to pack up their belongings. Heading out to the military field, he discovered that the officers had washed and polished the Stearman in preparation for his departure. Before saying good-bye, Moye and the Frenchmen celebrated the occasion with some aperitifs.

Just after lift-off, whether by chance or by alcohol, the Stearman nearly collided with a large stork. Moye had been looking to his left when he caught a glimpse of something to his right. A stork, positioned at 2:00 and closing fast, seemed confused about which way to turn. Moye quickly responded by putting the ship in a left bank, allowing the stork to continue on his path. Had they collided, the Stearman could have been destroyed.

On May 21, Moye picked up Richard in Marrakech and flew to Mecknes. After securing the airplane, they boarded a local bus for the trip over the Atlas Mountains to Rich.

"It was the rottenest road I have ever had the particular misfortune to encounter." Moye recalled. "The bus crept along in second gear all the way. Midelt, an uninteresting little market town, existed for the sheer reason that the Legion established a post there. We didn't waste much time delving into the smelly corners of Midelt but sought the sanctuary of an also smelly hotel. After an early dinner, we turned in for some much needed rest.

"The next morning, we left for the bus station only to find that there were no buses for Rich that day. But having exhausted the novelties of our Midelt hotel, we were anxious for new worlds to conquer so hopped a truck bound for Rich, a key Legion station, and spent another day bouncing southward over a branch of the Atlas range, arriving in the afternoon."

Situated in the Ziz Valley, Rich provided the Legion with a stronghold between the north and south of Morocco. On all sides of the valley, sheer mountain walls rose completely vertical for thousands of feet - rugged masses of rock entirely devoid of any vegetation. Once part of a caravan route from the desert to the Mediterranean, the deep valley served the Legion well. A transiting river created a lush oasis, abundant with date palms and crops; narrow access from the northwest and east prevented a surprise attack. In 1930, the Legionnaires blasted a 656 foot high passage, the Tunnel du Legionnaires, through the southern end of the valley to open an additional route to the Sahara. [21]

Moye and Richard spent the night at Rich's only inn, the Hotel du Ziz. In the morning, they set out for the Legion's mile-high fort over-looking the valley. They hired burros, joining up with three mounted police and two prostitutes on their way up the steep path to the isolated fort. The women belonged to the *Bordel Mobile de Campagne*, a brothel unit overseen by the Bordel Militaire Contrôlé. The Legion provided prostitutes for the pleasure of their troops, rotating the women to outposts every pay day. [22]

The climb up the hill took the entire day. That evening, more than the usual celebratory drinking, fighting, and dancing took place on the rooftop. The previous day, Berbers had engaged the Legionnaires in a particularly vicious battle. Having held their ground and lost few troops, the festivities provided a welcome reprieve for the men. Moye did the unthinkable in the morning. He wandered out in search of shells and guns - without a weapon – unaware the enemy still lingered nearby. Spotted by a sentry who frantically motioned to him to return, Moye rushed back to the fort. If captured, he would have been killed by a Berber's curved knife, or even worse, tortured as the enemy sliced his body into pieces. 23

On the return trip to Meknes, the bus passed through cedar forests giving the passengers an occasional glimpse of Barbary apes feeding at the edge of the trees. In Azrou, a scheduled rest stop, a filthy old Arab beggar attempted to bully Moye into contributing a few coins to his cause. When Moye laughed at him, the beggar moved on to another passenger but not before flicking several lice from his grimy hair onto Moye. That evening at dinner, Moye became suspicious that he had brought a few lice along with him. As soon as he arrived back in Mecknes, he found a doctor who confirmed his suspicions. Moye started treatment immediately.

Richard, who took an extra day in Rich, arrived in Mecknes the day after Moye. Moye's logbook indicates that the *Flying Carpet* returned to Marrakesh from Mecknes on May 29, departing two days later for Spain. Studying a map of Morocco, Marrakesh is approximately 250 miles south of Mecknes. It is presumed that Moye and Richard were required to complete official paperwork in Marrakesh before and after their trip into the Atlas. There is the possibility that Richard took the train back to Marrakesh while Moye underwent treatment for lice and picked up Richard when he completed his treatments. Whatever the reason for flying south twice, Moye and Richard arrived in Seville via Rabat on May 31. They toured the city's old quarter, famous for its Moorish and Gothic architecture, and then flew west to Lisbon. Portuguese Air welcomed Moye and Richard, hangared the Stearman, and drove the two into the legendary city for a dinner of hearty seafood dishes. Three days later, they departed for Toulouse but foul weather forced them to spend the night in Biarritz on the Bay of Biscay instead of Toulouse. Moye and Richard landed in the City of Lights the next day after lunch in Poitiers.

11

PARIS TO BAGHDAD

Moye and Richard checked into Paris' Wagram Hotel where Richard intended to put his notes on the Foreign Legion into some semblance of an article. His propensity for socializing, however, left him with little material to send to his publisher. If he had any hope of putting something together, he would have to isolate himself from the gaiety of Paris. Boarding the train to Villers-sur-Mer on the Normandy Coast, he rented a farm house two miles north of town. Moye remained in Paris with the airplane.

Saharan sandstorms and extreme temperatures, sometimes exceeding 125 degrees, had taken their toll on the *Flying Carpet*'s engine. The odds of it performing efficiently or, for that matter, lasting the next 6,700 miles to Singapore, were slim. As a result, mechanics at Le Bourget, supervised by the Wright factory representative and Moye, overhauled the engine. July 20, the team completed the work. Moye flew several short test flights and found that the engine performed flawlessly. Concerned about previous irregularities after the engine warmed up, he made an hour cross-country flight to pick up Richard without any noticeable difficulties. He landed at Deauville, the nearest airport to Richard's rented farm house and, after spending the night, returned to Paris

For the next month, final preparations began for the flight through Europe to Constantinople, Turkey. Moye made a two day

186

trip to London, presumably pick up the permit to overfly Jugo-Slavia (Yugoslavia), while Richard arranged to have a spare propeller and cylinder, shipped from New York to Paris, sent on to Cairo. Two tin auto trunks went to Jerusalem and Richard's books were shipped to Baghdad and Memphis. On August 3, with baggage and supplies stowed on board, the *Flying Carpet* departed for Geneva. Two hundred and fifty miles later, Moye and Richard enjoyed a pleasant lunch overlooking Lake Geneva.

Next on Richard's agenda was the Matterhorn. He climbed the ominous mountain in 1924 and now he wanted to see it from the air. Viewing the 14,692 foot peak would require removing all unnecessary items from the Stearman and carrying a limited amount of fuel. This accomplished, the airplane could easily fly high enough to provide an incredible view of the famous mountain. Donning their fur-lined flying suits, Moye and Richard lifted off the Swiss runway and set a course for the Alps. The entire experience proved inspiring. Few words could capture the majesty of the entire range.   Pristine snow fields, glistening peaks, and craggy outcroppings seemed to fill the horizon in every direction. Richard snapped a few pictures which turned out poorly. The turbulence near the peaks made it impossible for him to steady the camera. On the return flight, the *Flying Carpet* soared past Mount Blanc before descending into the Rhone Valley. The entire trip lasted two hours.

Richard's version of the Matterhorn flight provides an additional twist to the adventure. Unsure which mountain was the iconic summit, they spotted two climbers atop a peak and dropped a note tied around a monkey wrench asking, "Where is the Matterhorn?" The next day, the airport received a phone call from two German climbers. They wanted to know who had flown the beautiful red and gold airplane that buzzed them and dropped something from the plane. It seems improbable that the airplane possessed pen, paper, string, and a spare wrench. Richard might have been impulsive enough with the right supplies to toss out a note but Moye would not have condoned throwing a perfectly good wrench away unnecessarily. The chances of the message landing within reach of the climbers seems ridiculous. [1]

Weather would prevent Richard and Moye from continuing

on to Vienna for several more days. Their first effort to cross the Simplon Pass at the eastern end of the Rhone Valley proved unsuccessful. Loaded down with baggage and fuel, the *Flying Carpet* could not climb over the ever rising clouds enveloping the Alps and was forced to return to Geneva. On their second attempt, the tops of the clouds to the east loomed even higher. The third attempt, August 5, Moye opted for the southern route toward Milan. They flew over Aiz-les-Bains and Grenoble to Turin. Moye's ability to maneuver around imposing mountains and massive cloud formations impressed Richard. His quick decision-making skills made the harrowing flight seem much less intimidating than it actually was. The night was spent in Milan where Moye and Richard boarded a bus the next morning to do a little sight-seeing.

En route to Vienna, a planned, one day stop in Venice lasted for a week. Richard wanted to swim the Grand Canal and challenge the city's law which prohibited the activity. He formulated his escapade at Harry's Bar near the entrance to the waterway. Opened on May 13, 1931 by Giuseppe Cipriani, the bar possessed a reputation for great food, a delicious drink called *Moonlight*, and a favorite rendezvous for the rich and famous to gather. Harry's seemed just the sort of place to bolster Richard's celebrity status. In addition to a trademark drink, the owner started a tradition of having his customers sign his guest book. Signatures of Toscanini, Marconi, Capote, Chaplin, and other worldly aristocrats would eventually reside next to Halliburton's. 2

Richard's race down the canal involved Moye and Jimmy Lownes, an American vagabond whom Richard met at Harry's. Richard hired a gondola and, reaching the middle of the canal, he and Jimmy stripped down to their shorts and dove in. Moye stayed on board as a referee. Half way to St. Mark's Square, the Polizia hauled the entire group off to jail, including the dismayed gondolier. Each were levied a fine of 50 cents apiece for disrespecting Venetian law. 3

A week passed before the *Flying Carpet* left Venice. Richard would have stayed longer had Moye not reminded him that the rest of the world awaited them. Undecided about where to go next, they unfolded maps of Europe and Turkey. Richard wanted to go to the island of Malta in the Mediterranean; Moye suggested Berlin. In the end, they compromised and chose Constantinople. They would follow the route of the Christian crusaders who, 900 years prior, marched off to save the Holy Land from the Turks.

August 17, Moye and Richard left Venice for Vienna, a short one and a half hour flight. The Hotel Metropole served as their home for three days while they visited historic sites and investigated the city's celebrated night life. They found one particular night club, *Femina,* most entertaining. The performances consisted of risqué skits interspersed with singing and dancing. The superior quality of the entertainment surprised Moye as did the young, good-looking girls making themselves available to the patrons after the show. "If a patron found a girl he liked," Moye recalled, "he invited her over to his table and proceeded to squander small fortunes on her, buying immense quantities of champagne, etc. If they managed to hit it off, they left the cafe together when the dancing was finished. It was all very amusing."

From Vienna, the *Flying Carpet* followed the Danube River to Budapest where they waited two days for word from Richard's agent. Hopeful that he would receive good news, the noncommittal wire left Richard discouraged. He attributed the agent's response to the Depression. Minimal magazines sales forced publishers to be more cautious about submissions than usual. Not to be deterred, Richard continued to document the historical aspects and adventures of the round-the-world trip.

The *Flying Carpet* departed Budapest for Bucharest where Richard gave a scheduled lecture. August 26, avoiding restricted areas to the north and south, the *Flying Carpet* landed in Constantinople, imperial capital of the Roman Empire. Two days of preparation for the next leg of the flight left Moye little time to explore the city. Supervising maintenance on the Stearman hangared at the British military aerodrome required his close attention. From Constantinople, the *Flying Carpet* would cross nine hundred miles before finding adequate mechanical services. Assuring that the airplane operated perfectly was crucial.

A slight breeze and clear skies greeted Moye and Richard on August 28 as they headed for Aleppo, Syria. They flew northeast through the Bosporus strait, along the southern coast of the Black Sea for 50 miles and then inland, directly south, over barren, mountainous terrain, to pick up the railroad tracks that led to Aleppo. At the midway point, they stopped for lunch and fuel at Konich (Konya). Another 350 miles, they landed in Aleppo, once the gateway to Asia for pilgrims and traders. Well-rested, they departed for Homs at daybreak. There, they hired a car to tour a 12th century Qalaat Al Marqab or Castle of the Watch Tower. Richard the Lionheart inhabited the grand castle during the third Crusade. Situated at the top of a rugged hill, the castle provided a 360 degree view of the surrounding desert. 4

Moye and Richard next flew east to the oasis of Palmyra, recently surveyed and excavated by the French. In the heart of the Syrian Desert, the oasis possessed an abundance of palms and sulfur springs that made it ideal for silk traders and their caravans to rest as they traveled between Iraq, Syria, Lebanon, the Holy Land, and Jordan. The Romans, after conquering Syria, built temples, statues, and an elaborate infrastructure at Palmyra which resulted in one of the greatest cities of the Roman Empire. Although most structures still lay buried in the sands, exposed marble colonnades and archways left enough for Moye and Dick to imagine how magnificent the city must have been in centuries past.5

August 31, they traveled southwest to Damascus, a short flight of 100 miles. There, they hired a car to drive them across the Lebanese mountains to the sacred sanctuary site of Baalbek atop a plateau in the fertile Beqaa Valley. The most outstanding of all the structures was the Temple of Baal or Jupiter, the single largest religious building erected by the Romans. Late afternoon, Moye and Richard continued on to Beirut through the coastal towns of Sidon, Tyre, Acre, and over to Nazareth, through Cana and Capernaum, and on to the Sea of Galilee. They found rooms in Tiberius at the edge of the freshwater lake. Two days later, Dick engaged a fishing boat to accompany him while he swam the seven miles to the other side of the sea. He accomplished the feat in five hours. Although proud of his achievement, the adventure left Richard with second degree burns. In Tiberius, he spent two days recuperating, two more in Damascus, and several in Jerusalem. 6

Fully recovered, Richard wandered with Moye through the historic sites of Jerusalem. One memorable night, they explored an ancient water tunnel built under the original city of David. Richard wanted to trace the route Joab took to help King David capture Jerusalem in 1048 B.C. Joab had discovered a tunnel and vertical shaft that led to the top of the mountain and the city's fortifications. Accompanied by two soldiers, he climbed to the opening, then surprised and captured the defenders. Moye agreed to the expedition. He and Richard entered the three-foot wide and six-foot high tunnel, each carrying candles to light their way. They walked in waist-high water until them came to the shaft. While Moye waited, Richard climbed to the top and attempted to exit the opening as Joab had done but centuries of debris blocked the outlet. Richard would have to be satisfied that he had, in fact, retraced Joab's route. 7

When Moye departed for Cairo on September 8, Richard remained in Jerusalem to pursue writing. Moye planned to assist mechanics at Heliopolis, the British Royal Air Force Base, in servicing the Stearman. Shortly after WWI, the British Royal Air Force made its presence known in the Middle East and other parts of the world. Their bases provided facilities for the early pilots when public airports were non-existent or inadequate. Imperial Airways was one airline that maintained facilities at Heliopolis. 8

Moye took up residence at the Victoria Hotel in central Cairo. Between visits to the airfield to check on the airplane, he replied to a letter from his parents which related his grandparents concern about him performing aerobatics.

"Had I known you were not aware that I practice aerobatics from time to time," Moye wrote, "I could have convinced you that, when executed at a proper altitude and without terrific dives that put undue stress on the machine, stunting is not only safe but quite beneficial. In aviation circles, it is no longer regarded as hare-brained dare-deviltry. It is looked upon as having a real and practical value. The Army Air Service feels that a pilot is not competent until he has been subjected to a rigorous course in aerobatics.

"Just as a horseman is not safe unless he is familiar with his mount, not only at a walk but also at a gallop, so is a pilot handicapped unless he is familiar with his machine and its reactions in all different positions. It sometimes happens that in stormy weather or in the 'bumps' found over mountains, an airplane is tossed about considerably. If the elements place the airplane in an awkward position near the ground, the pilot must react instinctively. He must not hesitate and think about what he should do because he has never flown in any than straight and level flight. Without the immediate and proper movements of the controls necessary to right the airplane, he puts himself in danger of crashing. Practicing aerobatics accustoms the pilot to these unnatural positions and the ability to coordinate the controls of the airplane and avoid an unnecessary accident. On one occasion, I was approaching a landing field in a turn when my plane was caught by a 'bump' and thrown almost on to its back at an altitude of not more than seventy-five feet. Having been voluntarily in that position before, but at a safe altitude, I was right-side-up almost before I had realized my situation. Recovery had become instinctive only through a great deal of practice."

October 5, Moye met Richard at Cairo's main train station. With just ninety-four cents in his pocket, being reunited with Richard brought more comfort to Moye than the author could have imagined.

Having no definite travel plans after Cairo, Richard and Moye discussed some of their options. Richard thought about flying south and visiting Addis Ababa, the capitol of Abyssinia, exploring the Congo, and ending up in Cape Town. The return flight included stopping in Khartoum. Adding the full length of east Africa to the itinerary easily added another nine months to the trip. The most reasonable direction, when considering time and money constraints, seemed to be crossing Asia en route to Singapore. Understandably pleased when Richard agreed, Moye put away the maps of Africa and began plotting out a route that would include Mt. Everest. Richard arranged for the *Flying Carpet*'s pontoons to be shipped to Singapore. Moye thought it best to ship the floats to Cairo first, and then to Singapore once they had a better estimation of their schedule.

Moye put on an aerobatic demonstration at Heliopolis prior to departing Cairo. In an interview with Martin Cole, he described what transpired when Richard neglected to tighten his seatbelt. Preparing to take off, Moye tapped Richard on the shoulder, signaling him to buckle his seatbelt. This was a precaution Moye habitually performed since Richard often overlooked the simple procedure. He gave Moye a nod and the *Flying Carpet* ascended into a climbing turn. Reaching altitude, he came back around to make a low pass and slow roll down the runway. Just as the airplane approached a knife-edge position, Richard's entire body, up to his knees, slid out of the cockpit. His arms flailed wildly in the slipstream in an attempt to grab on to any part of the plane within reach. Horrified, Moye instinctively stopped the roll and leveled the airplane. Richard dropped down into his seat and cinched the belt as tight as possible. Moye never had to tap Richard on the shoulder again. 9

A large crowd of Americans, including a minister, his wife and many local dignitaries, watched the *Flying Carpet* perform and then head east over the Suez Canal toward Amman. The beginning of October replaced the sizzling temperatures of summer with cool, brisk weather making the flight to Amman particularly pleasant. Moye followed the coastline of the Black Sea to Gaza and then flew direct to Amman. Situated on an isolated hilly area surrounded by desert, Moye easily located the Royal Air Force field. The new commanding officer of the post, Group Captain Fowler, greeted them. Fowler learned to fly around 1910 and flew through WWI. While indulging in whiskies and sodas, Fowler told Richard and Moye one of the most touching stories they ever heard.

Shortly before Fowler came out to Amman, his son graduated from the RAF flying school. Fowler requested that the two be stationed together at Amman - the only case of a father and son actively flying together in the RAF. Fowler left England for Amman excited over the prospect of his son joining him. Two days before his son planned to depart, an air meet took place in England. During an exhibition night flight, the inexperienced young man took off, went into a spin, and died on impact. Although some years had passed since the fatal accident, Fowler still grieved for his son.

That evening, Moye mentioned to Fowler that officials in Jerusalem refused to grant the *Flying Carpet* permission to land in Maan where they planned to take a car to Petra. Fowler lost no time in phoning headquarters in Jerusalem and obtaining the necessary permission for his new friends. In return, Fowler insisted Moye take him flying. He wanted to experience the grand Stearman with its powerful engine. An equally grand smile lit up Fowler's face when he hopped out upon landing. That seemed the least Moye could do in exchange for Fowler's help.

Later in the morning, Moye flew down the railroad tracks from Amman to Maan. The tiny Arab village and British outpost differed from the thousands of others because it possessed a landing field. Flight Lieutenant Mickey Noonan, commander of the handful of enlisted men garrisoning the post, welcomed Moye and Richard and set them up in the officers' mess for the duration of their stay. Mickey, as everyone addressed him, seemed a typically good-natured Irishman. More the sergeant type than a high ranking officer, Mickey had been stationed in Maan for as long as everyone could recall. The isolation and boredom of the small post resulted in his addiction to the bottle.

Mickey arranged for a truck and squad of soldiers to accompany Moye and Richard to Petra, a Crusaders fortress hewn from red sandstone cliffs in the 1300s. With road access ending five miles from Petra, they mounted mules for the rest of the trip. An eastern entrance to the rose-colored city was a narrow gorge, a thousand feet deep and twenty feet wide. Moye and Richard wandered all day through Petra. They passed temples, mausoleums and a magnificent amphitheater. The most remarkable was the Treasury, 150 feet high and 100 feet wide. At the end of the day Moye returned to the post for a much needed soak in the tub. Richard, having a need to mingle with ancient spirits, spent the night in the company of the site guard. He returned around noon the next day at which time they flew back to Amman. They wanted to thank Mickey for his hospitality but he seemed to have disappeared. 10

Richard and Moye next drove to the Roman ruins at Jerash,

one of the largest and most well-preserved sites of Imperial Roman architecture outside of Italy, and then continued on to Jerusalem via Jericho. They viewed all the usual sights - the Holy Sepulcher, the Wailing Wall, and the Dome of the Rock. One night, Richard returned to their hotel room covered with cobwebs and dancing on air after discovering a very "enchanting and mysterious" secret passageway while poking around debris outside the south wall of the city. He declared that his name would be indelibly engraved in the archives of archeology. Informing a resident archeologist of his miraculous unearthing, the expert pointed out to him that the "Halliburton Tunnel" appeared to be the modern sewer leading from the city to the ravine below. 11

On their third visit to Amman, Moye and Richard received some disturbing news. Major Edwards designated them as star witnesses in a case against Mickey Noonan. An hour after they left for Petra, Edwards arrived at Maan and found Mickey drinking heavily. Normally, no disciplinary action would have resulted. This occasion, however, the officer placed him under arrest and escorted him back to Amman for a court martial. Edwards filed charges against him for dereliction of duty by a display of drunkenness in the presence of two American visitors.

Moye and Richard felt responsible for the incident. Mickey, only three months away from collecting his pension, now stood to lose it. Informed that the court martial would take place in one week, they made written depositions about everything which occurred during their stay at Maan. They kept as close to the truth as possible believing that their testimony proved critical to proving Mickey's innocence. Moye, the lawyer, felt they perjured themselves in the process.

Preparing to depart for Baghdad, Moye was not comfortable with the sound of the airplane's engine. Six hundred miles lay between Amman and Baghdad and the all important motor should not present any doubts as to its reliability. Moye and the mechanics worked until lunch and discovered nothing. With Guy Fawkes' Day celebrations beginning the next day, mechanics postponed any further exploration of the engine until after the holiday. Even the most isolated British outposts celebrated Guy

Fawkes Day, similar to America's Fourth of July. In Amman, the British added an extra day to the November 5 holiday.

Had Moye and Richard left as planned, they would have missed the opportunity to participate in the festivities or meet Colonel Peake. An elderly gentleman, his fellow officers addressed him as Pasha Peake, a prestigious title conferred by an Arab king he assisted at one time. Peake recently purchased a de Havilland Moth and had begun flying instruction from officers on the field. A pilot by the name of Atcherly went up with Peake later that afternoon. Five minutes after take-off, an officer strolled into the mess and told Atcherly's brother that the Pasha's Moth had just crashed.

"Everybody rushed to the door thinking, of course, that it had been merely a nose over or something of that nature." Moye wrote. "On reaching the tarmac, we found a twisted mass of wreckage rapidly being devoured by flames. Peake and Atcherly were a pretty grim sight as they walked away from what was left of the Moth. Both of them were badly cut about the face and head. Peake had a couple of broken ribs and Atcherly's nose had almost been cut off. Patched up at the hospital, they returned in time to have whiskies and sodas with the rest of us in the mess after dinner. It seems that Atcherly had been instructing from the front seat and was taking off when his stick pulled out of the socket at about thirty feet from the ground. The ship immediately nosed into a dive. He waved the stick in the air for Peake to see but he hadn't reacted quickly enough. They dove in with the motor full on. It was one of the luckiest escapes I believe I have ever witnessed."

Moye and Richard took part in some tent-pegging during the holiday. A sport which requires spearing tent pegs with an iron lance from atop a galloping horse seemed a popular and dangerous pastime at the outpost. If the rider speared the peg recklessly, the top of the lance would spring back and crack him in the head. Atcherly's brother finished his last run, having suffered just such an injury. Moye and Richard's companions for dinner proved to be a sorry lot - Peake and Atcherly's brother swathed in head bandages, Atcherly equally bandaged, and a fourth officer, who flattened his nose diving into the swimming pool, sported a bandaged nose.

When Moye rose early to check on the airplane the RAF

mechanics assured him the motor ran perfectly. Moye took it around the field and agreed. Amidst fond farewells and promises to look them up in America, the *Flying Carpet* headed for Baghdad. Flying Officer Jarmin in a Fairey bomber escorted the Stearman out about fifty miles to make sure Moye found the track east referred to as the furrow. Satisfied, he waggled his wings and turned back, leaving the *Flying Carpet* to sail into the desert alone.

In 1922, to aid the British mail service navigating across the expanse of the Syrian Desert, the RAF plowed a furrow between Amman and Baghdad. Fordson tractors pulled weighted plows eastward from Amman and westward from Baghdad, a total of 310 miles. They marked areas composed of scattered black asphalt with white paint. Every 25 miles, emergency landing areas were scraped. Fuel was available at two of them. The furrow provided a clear line-of-sight navigational aid for pilots. Unlike many areas of the Sahara, where drifting sand can bury tracks in minutes, the mid-eastern desert contained volcanic rocks with patches of sand and hardened mud which allowed little movement of the ground cover. Six years later, Jacques and Violette de Sibour found "only a small furrowed track, 4,000 feet beneath us that at times threatened to disappear entirely." [12]

Rutbah Wells, halfway between the two cities atop a high plateau, served as the main refueling station and an overnight stop if necessary. Rutbah's square fort sufficed as a rest house with minimal services. With no heating system, guests dined in their overcoats and most likely slept in them during the winter months. A circular staircase to the roof offered a breathtaking view of a million sparkling stars and perhaps helped guests overlook the chilling temperatures. A radio and observation tower with a beacon visible to aircraft as far as 80 miles away was positioned on the roof. Imperial Airways took over the route from the RAF in 1926. [13]

Moye used the now faint furrow to navigate to Rutbah Wells and then to Baghdad. Approaching the refueling station, he and Richard saw thousands of camels, sheep, and goats surrounding the oasis. The sheer number of animals astounded them; far more gathered in Rutbah in comparison to the oases in the Sahara. It seems Rutbah served as a primary source of water for nomads and

Moye and Richard took Prince Ghazi flying. Their destination was Samarra, north of Baghdad. Moye F. Stephens' photo.

their herds for hundreds of miles.

As the last light glimmered on the golden domes of ancient mosques, the *Flying Carpet* crossed the Euphrates River and landed at the RAF's Hinaidi Airport south of Baghdad. Moye and Richard spent a memorable time in Iraq's capitol. American Consul Alexander K. Sloan, a fellow alumnus of Richard's from Princeton, gave them access everywhere - not that they actually needed it. They motored to Nejf and Kerbela, Holy cities of Iraq south of Baghdad and passed an afternoon in Babylon. When Richard learned that the Crown Prince of Iraq wanted to go flying, he and Moye happily obliged his Majesty.

King Faisal I gave his seventeen-year-old son, Prince Ghazi, permission to fly but only in the company of an escort. Two Royal Air Force planes flew in formation with the *Flying Carpet* to the ruins of Samarra. One carried the Prince's uncle; the other, a photographer. The three planes landed in a flat area near the great mosque, overlooking the Tigris. The steps of the mosque's minaret provided an excellent spot for lunch. On the return flight, Prince Ghazi requested that Moye fly over his school and do some stunting, a feat talked about at length for many years.

Several Iraqi officials entertained Richard and Moye during their stay in Baghdad. The Commander-in-Chief and the Chief Flying Officer hosted lunches for them; the British Governor held a dinner in their honor at his home. Other activities less pleasant were inoculations against typhus, cholera, and the plague. Persia would not permit them to enter the country without them. The long-term results may have protected them but they didn't anticipate becoming as sick as if they had actually contracted the diseases. With winter fast approaching and temperatures aloft expected to drop below freezing, Richard and Moye found a local shop to make them sheepskin-lined flying suits and boots.

Before departing Baghdad, Moye addressed some inconsistencies in his London maps. Comparing visible features to ones presented on his charts often proved misleading and unreliable. Moye continually gathered information from local pilots and made notations on his maps to avoid geographic hazards. The mountains between Baghdad and Tehran provided little room for navigational error. An attempt to make an emergency landing might end disastrously without proper information. Moye consulted with two Lufthansa Airline pilots flying the Bagdad-Tehran route in a single-engine Junkers. They checked his maps for accuracy and made the necessary changes. One lake, for instance, was marked over 20 miles from its actual location.

The Lufthansa pilots, anxious to help the Americans, volunteered to guide the *Flying Carpet* along the route to Tehran. Taking off at 5 a.m. on December 4, the Junkers carried a full load of passengers and mail. With approximately 100 more horsepower, the airliner flew ahead for a few miles, circling until Moye caught up. Both planes landed at Kermanshaw, halfway to Tehran, to clear Persian customs. The airliner went through without delay; red tape tied Moye and Richard up for hours. The German crew offered to wait, but Moye declined the courtesy. Navigating the second half of the flight seemed fairly simple. Moye was later disappointed that he never knew their names so he could write a note to thank them.

Above, the Flying Carpet arrives over Baghdad. Below, the ruins of Samarra and the mosque's minerate are visible. Photos courtesy of Moye F. Stephens.

12

PERSIA TO SINGAPORE

Forty-five miles northeast of Tehran, graceful Mt. Damavand stood as a beacon for the *Flying Carpet.* The towering volcano, with its dominating profile, represented peace and stability for Persians who for centuries had suffered the effects of social disorder. Changing political policies were evident when Moye touched down at Tehran's airport where he noticed an absence of British aircraft so prevalent on the RAF fields. That year, Reza Shah refused Imperial Airways permission to fly into Persian airspace, choosing to use the German owned Lufthansa Airways to service his country. Lufthansa Junkers now replaced Handley Pages as passenger and cargo transports. Compared to the German aircraft parked on the ramp, the Stearman's design and construction seemed superior. 1

Before Moye and Richard had a chance to secure the airplane, local dignitaries, pilots, and town residents surrounded them. Invitations for lunch and dinner followed. That evening, they dined at a Persian merchant's house where they met Dr. William McGovern, an explorer, scientist, scholar, teacher, and linguist. Richard greatly admired the gentleman and had hoped to cross paths with him one day. He never expected to meet him in Tehran.

McGovern, in the country for over six weeks, volunteered to act as Moye and Richard's guide. He and Richard made plans to become inmates of the Imperial Prison for aristocratic dissidents and thieves. Moye politely excused himself from this escapade. Little did he know that his accommodations at the Grand Hotel, a primitive residence with few amenities, would pale in comparison to those of the prison. Moye's bathroom was down the hall; a reservation was required to bathe; hot water had to be ordered in the morning; and, in the absence of an adequate heating system, he found it difficult to keep warm. Richard and McGovern were

Two Persian princesses go for a flight over Tehran. Note Moye and Richard's new sheepskin-lined jackets made in Baghdad. Photo courtesy of Moye F. Stephens.

released after twenty-four hours with enough stories to fill a book. 2

Richard's choice for the name of the Stearman, the *Flying Carpet*, undoubtedly had romantic origins. History notes that the Queen of Sheba presented King Solomon with a flying carpet as a token of love. She was heartbroken when the king showed no interest in such a gift. Perhaps Richard envisioned taking an exotic princess on his flying carpet to make amends for the queen's sorrow. Tehran would give him the opportunity to soar with feminine royalty.

Cautiously approaching the Shah of Persia, Richard asked permission to take his daughter flying. The Shah emphatically refused which left Richard surprised. He had heard that the Shah favored expanding freedoms for women in his county. Richard next asked the deposed Shah, Mohammed Kuli, if his nieces might join him in a flight over the city. He consented. As lovely as they might have been, the size of the princesses precluded them from going aloft together. Moye took the overly plump niece flying first and then returned to take Richard and the slimmer woman for a ride. 3

The event is described much differently in Richard's book. He writes that he was unable to accompany either princess in the airplane due to their size. He could only gaze longingly as the *Flying Carpet* became a tiny speck in the sky. Photos indicate that he did fly with the smaller of the two princesses.

An additional opportunity to share the front cockpit with a princess is related in Richard's book. ". . . Moye was being even more social than I," Richard wrote, "and attending more parties, and having more success with the local ladies generally . . . One evening he came home to our hotel reporting still another girl he had met and particularly liked . . . He suggested taking her for a ride in the *Flying Carpet*." 4

The following morning, "Moye appeared at the field with . . the prettiest, daintiest, most charming girl . . . She wore the *izzar*, the black all-enveloping mantle worn by Persian women of position, but beneath its many folds a delicate and slender figure was indicated." Not until after the flight did Moye reveal the identity of their lovely passenger. "That girl, my lad — but for the present dictator — is the Queen of Persia. 5

December storms brought an abundance of snow and heavy frost. With no room in the hangars, the *Flying Carpet* sat on the ramp, exposed to the elements. The once taut fabric now sagged, a result of the severe cold temperatures on the grade 'A' cotton covering the Stearman. Little could be done except to fly south to warmer climates. Moye and Richard discussed their options. Richard chose to go overland to the fabled cities of Isfahan, Persepolis, and Shiraz, homes to Persia's most famous poets,

Elly is seated in her Klemm Kl-26 on the ramp at Calcutta's airport. Moye is at the front of the plane. Photo courtesy of Moye F. Stephens.

mystics, and conquerors. Moye flew the Stearman to Bushire on the Persian Gulf. The city's airfield, a major stop for Imperial Airways, KLM, and Air Orient, operated several facilities that could hangar the Stearman and perform any mechanical and covering repairs needed. With clear, but bitterly cold weather, Moye followed the main road crossing the central Iranian plateau and the Zagros Mountains to Bushire, 400 kilometers south of Tehran. He made the flight in one day. Richard took two weeks to cross Persia.

Waiting for Richard, Moye supervised work on the Stearman, studied the route from Bushire to the Himalayas, and enjoyed whiskies, flying stories, and hunting north of town with local pilots and residents. One evening, he became the recipient of a pleasant surprise – Elly Beinhorn. Landing at many of the same airports in the Middle East as the German aviatrix, Moye and Richard were either ahead of her or had just missed her. They would finally meet in Bushire.

Upon receiving her pilot's license in the spring of 1929, Elly purchased a Klemm L-20 powered by a 20 hp Daimler engine. Unlike other women pilots of the era, Elly independently financed her early flying with a small inheritance. She earned additional monies performing aerobatics but preferred the scenery of cross-

An aerial view of Bandar Dilam from the Flying Carpet. Moye and Elly were returning to the town in order to fix her Klemm. Photo courtesy of Moye F. Stephens.

country flights. Although other German aviatrices, such as Thea Rasche and Marga von Etzdorf, distinguished themselves in aviation, Elly became the darling of Germany in 1936 after setting a record flight by landing a Messerschmitt ME 108 on three continents in one day. 6

December 4, 1930, Elly departed Berlin, in a Klemm Kl-26, en route to Singapore. The flight was free of major incidents until Bandar Dilam, 60 miles north of Bushire, where the motor on her airplane failed. She managed a safe landing on the hard-packed desert without damaging her Klemm and then went in search of assistance. Soon realizing the impossibility of locating a mechanic knowledgeable about airplane motors in the sleepy village, she hitched a ride with a merchant on his way to Bushire for supplies. Five hours later, through deep ruts and clouds of heavy dust, his rickety Ford truck pulled up in front of the Imperial Airways rest house.

Elly stepped down from the truck, doing her best to shake off the dirt and present some semblance of propriety before entering. Moye, penning letters at the only writing desk in the guest lounge, looked up in amazement when Elly entered. Although he knew of her impending arrival from a telegram she sent to Bushire, he didn't expect such a lovely woman. Elly thought Moye must be the manager until they introduced themselves. Several whiskies later, plans had been made to fly to Bandar Dilam in the morning and repair the Klemm which Elly referred to as *mein ehemann* (my husband).

"Stephens immediately volunteered to fly over with me in his machine to Bandar Dilam." Elly described in her autobiography. "He was sure that Halliburton – to whom the aeroplane belonged – would agree . . . He took it as a matter of course that fellow aviators should help each other in such predicaments . . . At noon the next day, the *Flying Carpet* was made ready for the flight . . . I sat helplessly in the passenger's seat in front and had to let myself be flown by a strange man." [7]

Local authorities met the Stearman at Bandar Dilam and asked for passports. Elly produced hers but Moye had left his in Bushire. Before he could begin work on the Klemm, he was obligated to retrieve the document. The next day, having satisfied the officials, Moye began troubleshooting Elly's 120 hp Argus engine. He discovered the fraulein to be self-sufficient, resolutely so. She met his every suggestion with, "I've already done that." When Moye inquired about the fuel jet, Elly, in an impatient tone, insisted she had already removed and cleaned it thoroughly. Moye reinspected the valve and found it clean but discovered a grain of sand lodged in the opening. Once the sand was removed, Elly flew alongside Moye back to Bushire. [8]

When Richard arrived, he was instantly enchanted with Elly. In his forward to her autobiography, *Flying Girl*, he makes the following remarks. "Just like everybody else, I fell in love with Elly on sight," Richard confided. "She had the youngest, gayest, most buoyant personality I'd ever met. She infected everybody with her own happiness and her own vitality. Stephens and I hadn't laughed for weeks. Now we laughed at everything – especially at Elly and her funny German accent and her broken-English curses when her engine quit." [9]

For Moye, Elly was his "Violette de Sibour", the vivacious aviatrix who had enchanted him in Paris. They both played a part in a man's world, yet they both took pride in their femininity. This is reflected in the clothes Elly took with her on the trip. She stored a selection of fashionable hats in a hatbox; a trunk held lingerie, silk stockings, shoes, evening dress, along with an assortment of skirts and blouses. 10

Richard, Moye, and Elly created the Timbuctoo Flying Club with Elly as its president. She adopted Richard and Moye as her *papas* and looked after them. She darned their worn socks, mended their shirts, and cut their hair with fingernail scissors. Discovering that she and Richard both brought phonographs, Elly proposed that they exchange records. Elly exchanged the German rendition of *Falling in Love Again* for Richard's *St. Louis Blues*.

Richard, Elly, and Moye formed the small Timbuctoo Club. Photo courtesy of Moye F. Stephens

December 20, both planes left for Djask on the Persian Gulf despite Richard's lingering fever. The cool air at altitude he thought more salutary than a long stretch in bed. The shortest and most scenic route to Djask lay along the rocky coast with occasional outcroppings of sand. An Imperial Airways and Air Orient stop, Richard and Moye expected a more developed airport than the few rock buildings and several groupings of tents they saw from the air. The guest house, however, surprised them with an exceptional meal.

The *Flying Carpet* continued on to Karachi in the morning. Moye and Richard planned to pick up the rest of their Stanford maps there but a hapless clerk had returned them to London, unaware to hold them for the *Flying Carpet*'s arrival. Richard purchased Survey of India maps to replace them. Sectioned and mounted on canvas, similar to the Stanford maps, they lacked a laminated coating and cardboard backing. Moye marked the maps in the same manner as previously, with airports, routes, mileage, and headings. RAF pilots shared practical information with Moye relevant to flying in India and beyond. He used the edges of the maps to jot down his notes.

Elly lingered an extra day in Djask to bathe in the sea. After refueling and lunch in Gwadar, she arrived at Karachi's Drigh Road Airport exhausted. The thought of doing any more flying in the next few days seemed impossible. Three weeks of steady flying - having encountered severe turbulence, gale force winds, and slicing her fingers – had taken their toll. Elly just wanted to snuggle under the covers and sleep late. Informed by Moye that they were taking off at daybreak for Delhi, Elly found it difficult to generate any enthusiasm for the 678 mile flight. A satisfying dinner and the usual whiskies in her room with Moye and Richard convinced her otherwise. She must not spend Christmas alone in Karachi, they told her. They insisted she celebrate Christmas in Delhi with their American friends. Managing only four hours of sleep, Elly joined the men at the airport in the morning.

While Moye and Elly inspected their airplanes, Richard wired the Maharajah of Jodhpur for permission to land at his aerodrome for fuel. The return wire gave them permission and an invitation for lunch. Although the Maharajah would be away, he directed his servants to take care of the flyers' every need. Upon landing, a luxurious Mercedes took the three travelers to the Maharajah's imposing residence set amidst 26 acres of lush gardens. His estate contained a well-stocked library, a subterranean pool and spa, and "rooms of untold treasure. All the jewelry in the state of Jodhpur was safely guarded here. Rubies, emeralds, pearls, and diamonds – any stone was insignificant that was not as big as at least a plover's egg." 11

The 300 mile flight to Delhi proved refreshing compared to the recent stretches of desolate terrain. The two airplanes flew over gentle rolling plains with an occasional range of mossy green hills sprinkled with solitary peaks. The colorful landscape made the flight seem much shorter than those over hundreds of miles of brown sand and scattered black rock.

Touching down at Delhi's Willingdon Airport, the *Flying Carpet* and its crew were met by a crowd of friends and Delhi residents on what became a wonderful Christmas Eve day. Richard dined with friends; Moye and Elly enjoyed the evening meal in each other's company. The majority of their conversations, when separated from Richard, focused on flying but they also talked politics and responsibilities upon returning home. As he listened and observed the lovely Elly, Moye began falling in love with her. It would be easy to surmise that they became lovers along the way but Moye never lost sight of his views on marriage and sex. He respected Elly and held her in the highest regard. Elly trusted Moye implicitly. She took his advice with confidence and, most importantly, allowed him to look after her airplane, something she rarely allowed anyone but herself to do.

A quote from one of Moye's letters supports his continued celibacy. "The European attitude toward promiscuity on the part of men is very interesting," he reflected. "They think it the most natural thing in the world. I have talked to several men about it. They were genuinely amazed to hear that American men are instructed from childhood to remain chaste. The European parent apparently expects his offspring to start going the rounds as soon as he is physically able."

Richard, Moye, and Elly celebrated Christmas Eve in Delhi at a traditional British ball. According to Elly, the three wanted to dress as elegantly as possible for the occasion but Moye found himself in a predicament. He arrived at her hotel room with a handful of tangled collars, ruined by a leaking bottle of shampoo. "Moye, the great man who had flown all around the world, sat on my arm-chair in utter despair and gave me a wrathful glance because I could not help laughing so heartily," Elly wrote in *Flying Girl*. "He explained his anger by the fact that he had been looking forward to dancing with me ever since Bandar Dilam and now this was impossible. He only cheered up when I reminded him that we were no longer in Timbuctoo, but in Delhi, and that in all probability he could simply get the porter to go to a Chinese shop and buy him some fresh collars." 12

Christmas 1931, sharing holiday toasts with friends and thinking about loved ones, evoked mixed emotions for Moye and Richard and caused them to reflect on the past year. The few minor incidents that the airplane presented had been resolved satisfactorily. They had survived severe weather conditions; adjusted reasonably well to sometimes squalid living accommodations; and endured insects, storks, bats, fetid smells, and eaten sand. With the exception of lice, seared lungs, second degree burns, and an occasional cold, their health had been excellent. The *Flying Carpet* had taken them to wondrous ruins, flown them over stately mountains and unparalleled panoramas, and provided them with the opportunity to meet remarkable people. Richard and Moye were living the life they wanted. Expectations for the next part of the world flight were optimistic.

Before leaving Delhi, Richard arranged for another aircraft to photograph the *Flying Carpet* over the Taj Mahal. He wanted to create an exceptional photo for his book about the round-the-world flight. On New Year's Eve day, at an altitude of 1,000 feet, the *Flying Carpet* soared inverted over the white marble domes and minarets of the magnificent mausoleum. Years later, Moye recalled the brilliant contrast of colors - the scarlet red Stearman, the pristine ivory Taj Mahal, and the surrounding green countryside – a once in a life time moment. Richard related an incident that purportedly occurred during the flight. While flying upside down, a section of the main fuel tank worked loose and dumped forty gallons of gasoline into his lap. A few drops flowing from the vent system seems much more plausible than an exaggerated forty gallons. 13

Richard received a telegram in Delhi from Calcutta's Bengal Flying Club inviting him, Moye, and Elly to participate in a Flying Day for the Maharajah of Nepal. The club intended to impress the Maharajah, on holiday in Calcutta with his entourage, with their superb flying. Richard saw the opportunity as a stroke of good luck.

Moye flew inverted over the pristineTaj Mahal on the banks of the Yamuna River in Agra. Built by Mugal emperor Shah Jahan in memory of his third wife, it is the most recognizable structure in the world. Moye F. Stephens photo.

211

Obtaining travel permits to fly over Mt. Everest, situated on an invisible line between Nepal and Tibet, had proven difficult. Nepalese and Tibetan officials typically refused entry to foreigners even though Tibet's leader, the Dalai Lama, permitted access to climbers to scale Mt. Everest in 1921. The heads of state wished to keep European influence outside their borders. As a result, they rejected Richard's formal application. Richard hoped that the Maharajah might be inclined to grant them permission after Moye performed in the powerful *Flying Carpet*. He also believed his own stature, similar to that of a cultural ambassador, combined with Elly's charm and exceptional piloting skills, might further sway the Maharajah.

Following the photo opportunity over the Taj Mahal, Richard and Moye followed the Ganges River to Calcutta where they met Elly. She had departed Delhi earlier in order to celebrate the New Year at Calcutta's German Club. In preparation for the air show at Dum Dum Airport, Moye and Elly hired several young Indians to polish their airplanes until sunlight danced on their fuselages. They then practiced stunting on the outskirts of town and felt ready to dazzle the Maharajah, his staff, and the mostly European spectators.

Richard, riding with Moye, described the affair in his book. "Calcutta probably never saw such a stunting exhibition as Stephens put on. With the very first wide-open dive at the royal tent, the Maharajah was on his feet, white beard flowing in the wind, hat in hand, looking up in amazement at the wild-flying Carpet. He was wondering, no doubt, how the airplane ever held together – and so was I. Moye had stunted with me before but never like this. After exhausting our bag of tricks, as one last stroke we shot past the tent upside down and, hanging on our safety-belts, waved at the grand old King. Elly was startling him with gyrations hardly less intricate than Moye's. In fact, her slip-stall, three hundred feet off the ground, was a stunt we did not dare to do so close to earth." 14

So delighted by the air show, the Maharajah presented an airplane to the flying club to show his appreciation and granted Elly, Moye and Richard permission to fly over Nepal to Mt. Everest.

Elly sits next to the Maharajah of Nepal as they watch Moye stunt overhead in the Flying Carpet. Moye F. Stephens photo.

While members of the European set enjoyed their privileged status in India during a depression felt worldwide, the rest of the country fared poorly. Striving for independence from British rule, civil disobedience primarily led by Mahatma Gandhi, became prevalent in the country's major cities, more so in Calcutta. The new Viceroy and Governor General, Freeman-Thomas incarcerated Gandhi and made every effort to suppress the public's outcry. As a precaution against being attacked or shot, the Viceroy surrounded himself with body guards whenever he left his residence. The three fliers arrived in Calcutta eight months after Gandhi's arrest to find the uprising still in progress. Shop owners marched the streets with anti-British banners; large crowds gathered to listen to heated speeches. Armed soldiers kept angry natives in check. The three fliers proceeded cautiously when venturing out from their hotel. They didn't want to be mistaken as British and have their trip come to an unfortunate end. As soon as they received the proper paperwork to enter Nepal, they would depart for the Himalayas. 15

Moye and Elly removed all unnecessary gear from their airplanes and loaded enough fuel for five hours flying time. The lighter load would enable the planes to achieve a higher altitude. With the Stearman's ceiling of 18,000 feet, Moye thought he could fly within twenty miles of the mountain. Discovering that Darjeeling, gateway to the Himalayas, had no landing site, he and Elly inquired about landing areas near the town. Elly found that a Mr. M. Dupuis, a Frenchman from Darjeeling, knew of a possible landing area near Baghdogra. He marked the spot on Elly and Moye's map, volunteering to drive ahead in his Baby Austin and arrange for their arrival. Elly took off ahead of the *Flying Carpet* and followed the train tracks north. Three hours later, she reached the area designated by Dupuis. The level stretch of ground, at an elevation of 1,000 feet, was situated on the southern slope of the mountains near Baghdora.

Moye and Richard arrived in the late afternoon. Securing the Stearman and Klemm, Dupuis hired the local police to guard the

Moye had the Stearman waxed and polished until it sparkled in the sunlight before performing for the Maharajah of Nepal. Photo courtesy of Moye F. Stephens.

two airplanes. People could look at the planes but if anyone touched them, they would provoke evil spirits that dwelled within or so the pilots told the police. Dupuis then drove Elly, Moye and Richard to the little town of Siliguri which provided lodging for the flyers. In the morning, they continued north to Darjeeling. With an elevation of 6,710 feet, it provided an almost spiritual view of the world's grandest mountains. "In the background, appallingly immense, loomed Kinchinjunga," wrote Richard, "thrusting its ice peaks five and a half miles into the clear cold blue - a mountain normally clothed in purest white, but now turned gold and purple by the sunrise glow. The early morning light fell full upon the shining flukes and spires, the castles of snow, the cascades of ice. From ten thousand feet we could see this glorious peak." 16

From Darjeeling, Moye visually calculated possible routes to Everest, compared them with altitudes on his maps, and then rechecked them. The flight over the Himalayas presented far more danger than any mountains previously encountered by him. His airline experience taught him how unfamiliar weather conditions could slam an airplane into the ground without warning. Moye wanted to be sufficiently prepared for whatever the mountains and weather offered him. Briefing Richard and Elly about flying conditions and the possibility of turning back at any time, Moye felt satisfied that he had thought everything through as meticulously as any pilot could.

January 9, Richard's 32nd birthday, the *Flying Carpet* turned west across Nepal's border after passing over Darjeeling. Fifty miles later, the airplane turned north. The bitter cold at 15,000 feet made breathing labored. Moye kept a vigilant eye on the airplane for signs of icing. As the terrain rose skyward, villages and vegetation quickly disappeared. The Stearman struggled in the thin air; the power-starved engine provided little assistance as mountain waves drew the plane close to the jagged peaks. At twenty-five miles from Everest, freezing blasts off the glaciers penetrated the flyers fur-lined suits and numbed their gloved hands. Moye realized that flying much closer was out of the question. At fifteen miles, the airplane cleared the mountains by only 500 feet. No margin of safety remained. And then, just as Moye began a turn to take them away from the rising summits, Richard stood up in a desperate attempt to take a picture. His action changed the plane's center of gravity, increased drag, and nearly caused the airplane to smash into the rocky crests below. Quick recovery skills by Moye prevented what seemed certain death. After five miles, clearing the terrain by a sizable distance, did Moye allow Richard to try for another photo of Mt. Everest. Continued turbulence and a vibrating engine gave no chance for a clear picture. Richard would have to settle for a blurred image of Everest, still the first aerial photograph of the peak and an achievement which made him proud. The majestic and awe-inspiring sight of Mt Everest, looming thousands of feet above them, would forever be etched in Moye's memories.

"Halliburton knew nothing about flight," Moye stated when asked about Richard's fool-hardy stunt that nearly cost them their lives. "I reached up and batted him on the head. He said, 'What did you do that for? Now we'll have to go back up and get more pictures.' I said, 'You and who else?'" 17

Clearing the foothills, Moye leveled off to 1,000 feet and stayed at that altitude until reaching Calcutta. Once on the tarmac, Richard informed the waiting press of his unsuccessful attempt to fly over Mt. Everest. His failure to meet such a lofty and

Thousands of miles after departing Grand Central, the Stearman performed well and attracted a great deal of attention wherever it landed. Calcutta photo courtesy of Moye F. Stephens.

unobtainable goal was posted in several newspapers and proved to be an unwelcome and disappointing report for Richard. In all probability, a subsequent announcement by Richard was an effort to overshadow the previous accounts of the Everest flight. He informed reporters that he planned to make a second attempt to fly over Everest the following year in a specifically-equipped, 500 hp airplane, however improbable that might be. 18

A Westland PV3, renamed the Houston Westland, succeeded flying over the tallest mountain in the world in 1933. Douglas Douglas-Hamilton, better known as Lord Clydesdale, piloted the open-cockpit biplane powered by a supercharged Bristol IS3 Pegasus engine. 19

Elly spent a day in Sikkim before attempting her flight to Mt. Everest. Passing through a cloud layer, she reached an altitude of 10,000 feet which gave her and Dupuis an excellent view of Mt. Everest. She then returned to Calcutta to meet Richard and Moye.

Anxious to take off for Singapore and prepare for the final phase of their world flight, Moye repacked the Stearman and checked his map to Rangoon. On January 16, 1932, satisfied with his route, Moye flew directly east over the Bay of Bengal and then followed Burma's coastline to Akyab for fuel. Villages and roads soon gave way to thick jungle and thousands of low, flat islands or mangrove swamp. River channels separated them from each other and from the mainland. Crocodiles and sharks occupied the treacherous waters.

At Bawmi, using Pontamau Island and his calculated mileage as a marker, Moye turned inland toward Rangoon, a flourishing, modern city filled with yellow-robed Buddhist monks. The next morning, the *Flying Carpet* crossed Martaban Bay and then headed southeast direct to Bangkok. The Moulmein Pagoda verified Moye's heading before he navigated through the range of heavily forested mountains that lay between the coast and Bangkok. With elevations between 3,000 and 7,000 feet, it was critical that he track the right course in the event of a sudden downpour and possible loss of visibility. Once he cleared the range, the *Flying Carpet* would easily sail over the central plains of Siam (Thailand) and into the country's capital.

As noted in his letters home, Richard felt very uncomfortable these last legs of the trip. Having listened to pilots who had flown through these areas, he knew that there was no chance of survival if the airplane went down. Wild beasts and venomous serpents inhabited the jungles; man-eating sharks circled in the ocean; crocodiles hid beneath the surface of murky rivers; hostile natives boiled humans alive; and dense vegetation would hide an airplane forever. Richard's overactive imagination put him in an acute state of anxiety. Only when they neared their destinations of Rangoon and Bangkok did he find relief. [20]

After a restful overnight stay in Bangkok, Moye flew down the Siam peninsula toward Singapore, stopping for fuel in Prachuabkirikhan and Alor Setar where they also spent the night. Weather held for the entire thousand mile flight over idyllic scenery. Countless rivers wound their way south like snakes through tropical forests; occasional groups of clustered huts and primitive boats hugged the river banks. Late afternoon, January 19, 1932, Moye touched down on the tarmac at the British Royal Army Base in Singapore.

Elly took the same route to Singapore as the *Flying Carpet* but her flight did not fare as well as Moye's. Five minutes out of Calcutta, a loss of oil pressure forced her to return. Swift repairs enabled her to arrive in Rangoon by dusk. Although she had been given geographic references, Elly, unable to locate the airport in the diminishing daylight, landed next to a rice field for directions. A lone worker managed to give her the airport's location by pointing and using other animated gestures. During her take-off roll, natives appeared from out of nowhere, forcing her to swerve and make an unconventional lift-off. She later discovered that the Klemm's tailskid and undercarriage had been damaged. With repairs completed in Rangoon, she continued her trip to Singapore to join Moye and Richard. [21]

Singapore marked the final leg of the *Flying Carpet*'s world flight. The open ocean now replaced barren deserts and required exchanging the Stearman's landing gear with pontoons. Richard had purchased a set of floats in California and shipped them ahead to Cairo, then to Singapore. Designed for the Fairchild 71-A, a single engine, high-wing monoplane, they arrived in twenty foot long crates. An equal number of *coolies* transported them from the truck into the hangar. When Moye opened the crates, he discovered the struts that attached the pontoons to the airplane were missing. Richard had contracted with Stearman representatives to fabricate a set of struts but apparently they neglected to fulfill their promise. This left Moye, with the assistance of British mechanics in their spare time, to design and construct a set. Because the Fairchild weighed 3,800 pounds and the Stearman, 1,650 lbs, Moye wired the Stearman factory to determine the center of gravity (c.g.) for the *Flying Carpet* excluding the landing gear. He estimated the center of gravity for the pontoons by balancing them on saw horses. With the aid of a plumb bob, he aligned the center of gravity for both pontoons and the Stearman. Steel tubing used in the construction of steam boilers served as material for the struts.

Configuring the pontoons extended Richard's planned two week stay in Singapore to two months. Impatient, he almost canceled the rest of the flight. When he announced his decision to terminate the air adventure, Moye was extremely disappointed. To cancel the trip after months of constructing pontoons, installing them, and charting the flight over water made no sense. "Look at it this way," Moye responded. "I know there are no archeological ruins in Borneo and the Philippines, and the countries are without classical lore, still – we're now equipped to fly on, so let's do so in anticipation something worthwhile will turn up."

Moye eventually persuaded Richard to continue. Richard's original plans encompassed a larger itinerary for the Pacific. After a visit to the headhunters in Borneo, they would fly to Manila where the engine would be overhauled once again, return to Borneo and island hop to Australia. The next three destinations, Tahiti, Hawaii, and San Francisco required shipping the airplane aboard a steamer. Moye plotted out the route on a March 1932 U.S. Hydrographic Chart of the Pacific Ocean. He confined ocean crossings to no more than one hundred miles, in some instances, going a thousand miles out of their way to accomplish this. Richard's route contained several crossings of five to six hundred miles. His ideas, according to Moye, were not based on bravery, just sheer ignorance. The

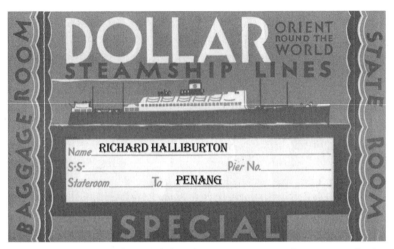

Richard grew restless while the struts were being made in Singapore and took a Dollar Line to Penang. Author's original Dollar Steamship boarding ticket.

costs and duration of such a flight, however, outweighed its possibility.

While mechanics fabricated the struts, Moye took seaplane lessons at the local flying club. His training consisted of landing and taking off from a variety of water conditions and confined areas, surveying landing sites, maneuvering on water, docking, and securing the plane. He and Richard would later practice propping the Stearman while standing on one pontoon, securing it to buoys, and releasing the anchor. Other duties to perform in Singapore were crating and shipping the airplane wheels and parachutes to Hong Kong, purchasing food supplies, bathing suits, sunburn cream, rope, anchors, and anchorage lights. Richard and Moye gave talks about the trip to the Rotary Club. Despite his reluctance to speak in front of crowds at the beginning of the trip, Moye conceded at least this one time.

When local pilots suggested to Moye that he use maritime and local maps for navigating through Borneo and the Philippines, he purchased the appropriate ones. They outlined the coastlines and waterways more accurately than Stanford's maps of the East Indies. The maritime maps consisted of British Admiralty Charts and

U.S. Department of Commerce Charts of the Philippines. Moye also used Shell Autoline Maps of Sumatra, British and Foreign Government Surveys, and the Airway Map of the Philippine Islands which indicated moorings and landings.

Pilots who frequented the islands gave Moye additional navigational information. Captain Kamen with the Philippine Aerial Taxi requested a draftsman from the Asiatic Petroleum Company draw a map for the Halliburton flight from Kudat to Manila. Although not to scale, the chart detailed fuel ports, elevations to fly, places to avoid, and the location of their hangar in Pasay, six kilometers south of Manila. The map gave specific instructions. "Our hangar on the beach, you can run on the beach, no stones at all, but be careful with fish traps." One other hand-drawn map highlighted the waterways and seaplane mooring point for Kuching and Sarawak in Borneo.

Without the diversion and support of the British Royal Air Force, the Shell Oil Company, and Elly, Moye and Richard's stay in Singapore would have proved much more tedious. Shell, often their only link with civilization, had assisted in making the world flight successful. They had provided gas, oil, and professional courtesy at nearly every stop, even in the most desolate locations. The company continued its support for the *Flying Carpet* crew in Singapore, providing mechanical assistance, dinners, entertainment and anything else the two might need. Although Elly was anxious to continue on to Australia, her *papas* persuaded her to stay an additional month. Moye couldn't have been happier. He believed that their feelings for each other were mutual. He wanted to spend the rest of his life with her. She possessed an excess of social energy; she was smart and pretty; she also loved flying and hunting. What he didn't realize was that she was neither warm-hearted nor a romantic. Although her public persona alluded to these qualities, they were only superficial.

Moye proposed to Elly, but she turned him down. She found him handsome and, when he smiled, endearingly boyish, but Elly wasn't ready to settle down nor was she willing to leave her home country for the United States. Certainly disappointed, Moye understood. Returning to their respective homes, they would cherish the fond memories of their time together, one of trust and freedom. But, like a teenager's 'endless summer' where a first love is discovered, the salient affair would always be remembered with nostalgia. They would reaffirm their friendship when Elly visited California in 1934. The pictures she took of Moye at that time reflect the genuine warmth he felt for her. The two flyers would have other interactions through the years but none comparable to those adventurous months traveling through Asia. 22

When Elly left Berlin, she intended to end her journey in Bali. A meeting with Australian pilot Charles Kingsford Smith in Calcutta convinced her to continue on to Australia. After several weeks in Singapore, she could not delay her flight any longer. Elly circled over the airport for one last good-bye before heading south toward Indonesia. Richard and Moye barely managed smiles as they waved her off. The sentimental favorite of the Timbuctoo Club would be missed.

Within days, Elly sent a note postmarked Batavia.

"My Dear Papas,

Batavia was easy - only six hours - but it seemed such a long time with no *Flying Carpet* to keep me company. The world became very big and very empty again after I left Singapore. *What Good Am I* - without my two Papas? And what will you do without Elly? Who will keep Moye from talking about aviation, and who will make Dick wear his sun-helmet? I'm sure you both will go to the dogs. But I'll play *St. Louis Blues* for you on my phonograph each day and you must play *Falling in Love Again* for me, and love me very much.

I kiss you both on your sunburned noses - and will always stay your good child -
                    Elly" 23

Touching down in Darwin on March 21, Elly became the second woman to fly from Europe to the land down under. British aviatrix Amy Johnson made the flight in 1930. Elly decided to return to Berlin by continuing east and completing a round-the-world flight. Shipping her Klemm to Panama, Elly flew down the west coast of South America, over the Andes in Peru, and across the lowlands to Brazil. In Rio de Janero, a steamer took the Klemm across the Atlantic. Elly arrived home in June 1932, the same month that the *Flying Carpet* landed in Glendale. Her homeland lauded her as a heroine. Receiving the Hindenburg Cup, her country's highest civilian aviation award which included a 10,000 mark cash prize, Elly was able to continue flying. 24

On March 23, 1932, the *Flying Carpet* lifted off the South China Sea, a fine mist of sea spray coating the crew's goggles. The new experience of a water take-off and expectations of the unknown imbued Richard and Moye with an excitement not felt since arriving in Singapore. Realizing the latitude a seaplane provided them, the probability existed that Richard conjured up images of isolated beaches, swaying palms, and maybe a mermaid or two. Moye most certainly anticipated safe landings on rolling seas and narrow inland tributaries.

13

BORNEO TO MANILA

The most direct route to Borneo lay over 400 miles of open water. Not completely confident of the pontoon and strut assembly, Moye chose to stay close to the islands between Singapore and Sumatra. A torrential rainstorm which severely limited visibility was another reason to remain near land. Moye kept the *Flying Carpet* at 1,000 feet above the rolling seas until he located the island of Banca. He had only flown 50 miles, but anxious to attempt a landing in choppier water to test his skills and the pontoons, he landed without incident on the leeward side of Banca. Moments later, he took off and continued up the Musi River to Palembang where he and Richard spent their first night away from Singapore. In the morning, Moye topped off the fuel tanks and calculated the Stearman's speed with the pontoons installed – only ten mph slower.

Richard and Moye's next destination, Pontianak, was 300 miles north on the west coast of Borneo. As a precaution, Moye typically avoided long distances over water. Numerous small islands scattered along the first 200 miles of his route, however, could provide shelter in the advent of a storm or other emergency. Enjoying fair weather and the steady hum of the engine, Richard soon spotted an isolated cove on the easterly side of an island. He tried to convince Moye to land for a morning of swimming and sunbathing but Moye rejected the idea. There were too many risks if the Stearman failed to start or the weather changed dramatically.

The small village of Pontianak sat in the delta of the Kapau River. On approach to landing, Moye nervously watched as what seemed like a hundred dugouts rushed out from shore. He feared one of the exuberant paddlers might ram a pontoon or, worse, be decapitated by the whirling propellers. Fortunately, the locals stayed their distance and then something very strange happened. When the engine shut down, every paddle lay silent. The natives appeared awe-struck. Not until Moye and Richard climbed onto the pontoons and began motioning for a ride to shore did they see any movement. A single dugout cautiously approached the *Flying Carpet* and ferried Moye and Richard to the dock. More movement followed as the locals realized that the airplane and its crew presented no danger to them.

What should have been a simple water departure the next morning nearly ended in disaster. The Kapau River, the longest in Borneo, emptied directly into the South China Sea. At low tide, the river's current reached tremendous speeds as the water rushed seaward. Although Moye understood air currents, he may not have been familiar with the dangerous effect of tidal currents. Richard described how the situation played out in his book.

"By the time I'd pulled the anchor up and cranked the engine, we were already rushing downstream. Moye, in order to hold us against the flow, had to accelerate the engine. With the propeller whirling two feet away from me, I stood on the pontoon and tried to coil up the new and stubborn anchor rope, and unshackle the anchor. But an especially fierce blast from the propeller caused me to lose my balance; and as I clutched wildly at a strut to keep from going overboard, a blade of the prop caught a flying loop of the rope - and I still had most of it wrapped around my arm. In a flash, the rope and the anchor and I were all jerked toward the prop. Moye, hearing the banging and the clatter and my cry, instantly cut the engine and looked around to see what was happening." [1]

Moye's version of the incident tells another story. The force of the current pulling the Stearman downstream caused the anchor to dig deeper into the river and impossible to retrieve. Starting the engine and taxiing over the anchor was the only way the anchor could be loosened. Moye instructed Richard to throw the slack of the rope over the wing as he brought up the anchor – and to be careful not to swing the rope near the propeller.

"Halliburton was a Wild Bill as a crew member," he related to Ron Gilliam. "He had no idea of anything mechanical . . . Playing to an audience of hundreds of natives lining the river, Halliburton coolly began flipping the rope off the wing and coiling it around his elbow and shoulder. Somehow a bight of rope got into the propeller arc. In a flash the prop whipped the rope – and some skin – off his arm, winding it around the propeller shaft and jerking the 40 pound anchor into the blades with a resounding clang, missing the writer's head by an inch.

"We were drifting downstream," Moye continued. "I put the anchor on a spare rope, hooked it into the bottom and hailed a motorboat to tow us to dock. Here we were, in a small port in Borneo with a propeller bent ten degrees out of line!"

Moye located a local mechanic who knew how to straighten boat propellers bent by submerged logs. "He went to work on that thing with a block of wood, a clamp, and a thickness gauge and in five hours straightened it where there was no vibration at all and it flew right from then on." 2

Moye indicated the following in the airplane logbook. "Straightened prop. Dick threw a log into it."

The *Flying Carpet*'s second attempt to lift off the river proved successful. Once airborne, Moye flew north to Kuching, home of the last white Raja and Ranee of Sarawak, Indonesia. His concern over the near catastrophe and the current condition of the airplane diminished as the engine performed to the standard of the last several thousand miles. A few miles inland, on the Sarawak River, Moye spotted Kuching. Circling overhead to determine water conditions, he saw a horse race in progress. The scarlet and black Stearman caused a sensation as it soared past the royal box. The local radio station, covering the race, broadcast the American's arrival to all of Sarawak!

After a smooth landing, Moye and Richard secured the

seaplane to a buoy and lounged leisurely on the pontoons until someone arrived to take them ashore. They didn't mind waiting. A slight breeze cooled the sunlight filtering through the humid air as they gazed at the simplistic beauty of the royal Astana. Built in 1870 by British Rajah Charles as a wedding present for his Ranee, the palace's elaborate landscaping contributed to its overall elegance. The path that led from the river to the palace, shaded by bamboos, frangipani trees, palms, and clumps of red and white lilies, was a hint of the Rajah's love of gardening. Before the manicured lawn gave way to an endless rainforest, beds of gardenias, tuberoses, and cape jessamine filled the air with their perfume. 3

The royal yacht pulled alongside the *Flying Carpet* within the hour. Transported to the dock or landing stage, Richard and Moye received a summons from Ranee Sylvia to attend the Grand Prix Ball that evening at the Astana. Though exhausted, they graciously accepted the invitation and had the honor of leading the procession into the palace accompanied by Sylvia's two younger daughters – Princesses Pearl (Elizabeth) and Baba (Valerie). The oldest, Princess Gold (Lenora), was in England.

Richard, Princess Pearl, Ranee Sylvia, Princess Baba, and Moye relax on the grounds of the Astana landscaped by the Raja. Photo courtesy of Moye F. Stephens.

The people of Sarawak, including the Dyak headhunters, admired Ranee Sylvia. Married to Vyner Brook, the third Rajah of Sarawak, she was treated like a queen. In fact, she referred to herself as the 'Queen of the Headhunters' - an intriguing title but an irrelevant one. Her husband's grandfather James Brook, in the mid-1880s, greatly discouraged headhunting to the point of eradication. Britain considered Sylvia outrageous, extravagant, and foul-mouthed. Richard and Moye found her quite adventurous, gracious, and very beautiful. Invited to go flying, she lost no time accepting the offer despite objections from her Secretary of State. If something happened to her, who would rule the country with the Raja away on business? 4

Newspapers blasted her frivolity. "Kidnappers in Airplane Steal White Queen of Borneo – Rajah Hurries Home – Army Called Out. Government officials warned the head-hunters not to behead any English woman wandering in the jungle." As it turned out,

The Ranee's two daughters and Moye. Moye F. Stephens' photo.

Sylvia's husband had cabled to tell her to enjoy the opportunity. The Ranee Sylvia became the first woman in Borneo to fly in an airplane. 5

Richard happily added flying a Ranee, along with a prince and princesses, to his list of accomplishments. His next adventures would surpass those of his French Foreign Legion exploits. He and Moye planned on sampling Dyak life in its purest form. They would visit the long house of Koh, the Punulu Delam or

The Ranee Sylvia and Richard relax while Moye prepares for a flight over Sarawak. Photo courtesy of Moye F. Stephens.

warrior chief of all the Dyaks, located two hundred miles up the Rejang River. Sylvia marked the Dyak village and Kapit, the station of the British Resident for the area, on Moye's map. Moye and Richard were directed to stop at Kapit to deliver supplies and notify the Resident that he was to act as a liaison and interpreter during their visit to head hunter country.

Kapit's accommodations appeared far more primitive than expected and the house orangutan, an intimidating pest. Richard and Moye wondered what possessed the young man to consider the position. The isolation experienced in the middle of the jungle would be enough to discourage most humans. Crocodiles resided on the beach below his bamboo dwelling; boas and an assortment of deadly snakes slithered silently nearby; and insects of legendary proportions occasionally dropped in through the thatched roof.

After an uncomfortable night at the outpost, the Resident agreed to accompany them, but not by plane. He and his servants would take his motored dugout. In the morning, dodging floating logs on take-off, the Stearman flew upriver to the chief's long

229

Above, the Flying Carpet arrives at the Dyak village. The Resident, wearing a hat, can be seen on the dock. Moye is on the pontoon; Richard is in the front cockpit. The Dyak longhouse can be seen in the bottom photo. Moye F. Stephens' photo.

house. The flight took 30 minutes; the Resident arrived five and a half hours later.

The *Flying Carpet* roared over the Dyak's long house situated in a large clearing on the river. Observing the results of his thunderous announcement, Moye wished he had foregone the low pass. More than three hundred Dyaks fled the long-house in complete panic. Some ran into the jungle; others hid under the structure. Moye imagined that the Dyaks undoubtedly equated the

Moye tests his strength with a few Dyak boys. Photo courtesy of Moye F. Stephens.

plane to a demonic creature, swooping down to devour them. Not wanting to disturb the natives any further, he shut the engine down as soon as possible after landing.

Observing from the safety of the Stearman, Richard and Moye saw not a single Dyak which left them wondering how they would reach the shore. With no way to determine the depth of the water or the extent of hidden obstacles, Moye and Richard dared not taxi any closer. Their only option seemed to be waiting for the Resident to arrive, that is, until they spotted a dugout gliding noiselessly toward them. A handsome young Dyak, sitting cross-legged in the middle of the dugout, waved and smiled as he neared the airplane. He was yelling something that neither Moye nor Richard understood. They later learned that he was Jugah, the son of the chief and had been in Kuching when the *Flying Carpet* arrived a few days earlier.

The entire area came alive as the three climbed out of the dugout and up the ladder to the longhouse. Dyaks began peeking, ever so shyly, from around corners, behind trees, and from the tops of ladders. As more began inching their way toward Moye and Richard, a sense of courage began to circulate among the tribe. Adults and children soon swarmed the two flyers. Their physical appearance differed from any native peoples Richard had previously encountered.

"The men were dressed uniformly in red loincloths and narrow aprons, heavy earrings, anklets and wristlets of twisted grass. The women were dressed as simply – bare from the waist up, with their hips wrapped in a single cotton cloth . . . Everybody was adorned with the same tattoo, always dark blue in color. . . But what gave them all such a surprised expression? It was their eyebrows and eyelashes – there weren't any. Every eyelash and eyebrow had been pulled out . . . Each mouth was black from betel-nut." 7

Less than five feet tall, Chief Koh commanded respect and attention. Almost regal with a muscular frame, he had a chiseled

face and eyes that reflected kindness. His curiosity about the airplane led to many questions. He wanted to know if it was a bird and, if so, could it drop eggs on his enemy? Richard, of course, fabricated a mythical story through the interpreter. His son, not believing a word, quickly informed his father otherwise. Moye and Richard asked the chief if he would like to fly over his territories; it would bring him much prestige and glory. Not totally convinced, the chief went out to the plane to inspect it and, finding it harmless, agreed to go for a ride in three days. The chief's messengers then spread the word of the historic event, inviting all his chiefs to attend the impending flight and festivities.

Chief Koh, chief of all Dyaks.
Moye F. Stephens photo.

Their first evening in the longhouse, a sort of primitive apartment complex, Moye and Richard participated in several ceremonies. They carefully observed the chief performing the Dyak rituals in order to repeat them correctly and not to offend their host. In ceremonious fashion, five young, unmarried maidens knelt before them and held gourds full of rice wine to their lips. A live rooster, held by its legs, was passed over the food to instill good luck from the gods. The procession of diners visited every family's quarters, repeating the ceremony in exactly the same manner. Making his way to their assigned sleeping quarters at the end of the evening's events, Moye had another surprise.

"That night, our pygmy hosts insisted that we sleep in a special straw hut, supported ten feet above the swampy ground on pilings. Neither Dick nor I could stand up in our hut. As I prepared for bed my 190-pound body was too much for the fragile floor and I broke through, landing with a splash in the swamp of a pig sty below." 8

Jugah took Moye and Richard fishing in his dugout. He demonstrated how his tribe customarily poisoned an area of the river with tuba root to catch fish. As the poison began to suffocate the fish, they jumped out of the water into the nets of waiting fishermen. Jugah showed Moye and Richard how to use blowpipes to kill pigs and birds. The two used up all of their darts without hitting either animal.

Boats began arriving in waves the third day of their visit. Over five hundred guests, adorned in their finest, stood ready to watch Chief Koh soar into the sky. Richard wondered if he would back out at the last moment. With his guests anxiously waiting, no other option remained for the chief other than to take his chances in the airplane. The chief stood on the pontoon, drunk as a man could get, and climbed into the cockpit with all eyes upon him. Moye strapped his helmet and goggles on and cinched his belt tight over his naked belly. He didn't want the chief falling into the river. The responsibility for killing him would certainly result in horrific consequences. After cranking the engine, Richard hopped in beside the chief and Moye maneuvered the plane away from the dock. Hundreds of dugouts surrounded the *Flying Carpet* as Moye positioned the plane for take-off. With Richard motioning for them to keep back, the *Flying Carpet* gained speed and lifted off the jungle river. Chief Koh went from trembling to great excitement as the biplane leveled off at two hundred feet over the trees.

Moye put on a good show for the guests below. He zoomed down, just thirty feet above the canoes, and then pulled the Stearman straight up like a rocket. He flew low over the long-house and roared up the river, just skimming the waves as he raced past the neighbors' long-houses. For ten minutes, Moye gave the Dyaks an unforgettable performance. Chief Koh began his flight as the most important of all Dyak chiefs. He returned, elevated to a god-like status.

"We invited the pygmy chief to take a ride with us and, as we took off and circled their camp," Moye recalled later, "I thought that our passenger would fall out of the open cockpit as he stood up and frantically waved at his cheering tribesmen below. After landing and returning to the village, the chief was encircled by his faithful villagers, and he began to talk about his ten-minute flight. The talk continued long into the night. Villagers sat in stony silence, fascinated by his account of his airplane ride." 9

Richard holds Chief Koh's gift of shrunken heads. Moye refused to take them on board the Stearman. Moye F. Stephens' photo.

Rice wine flowed copiously that evening. An orchestra of bagpipes, drums, and gongs echoed throughout the territory and an endless array of foods circulated around the longhouse. Ranee Sylvia's message of good-will was translated by the Resident. She loved him and trusted him to continue instilling his people with dignity, and honor. She also sent a precious gift for the great warrior - a hunting rifle. Not to be outdone, the chief praised the Rajah and Ranee and swore eternal allegiance to them. He had kind words for Richard and Moye and offered them one dozen human heads, weighing twelve pounds a piece and measuring six to eight inches in diameter. To lighten the Stearman's load, Richard gave the chief his phonograph and records.

Contrary to Richard's treatment in his book, the shrunken heads remained in the Dyak settlement. For the entire round-the-world flight, the plane, with a full load of fuel, exceeded its maximum pay load of 445 pounds. The addition of the pontoons decreased the pay load further. As Moye argued, "besides being heavy, they took up all the baggage space, and smelled to heaven of stale Dyak and old smoke." Richard wrote that they accepted the dozen heads and wove an elaborate tale, from Kuching to Manila, about the misfortune the cursed heads created. 10

The morning after the chief's historic flight, Moye flew north to Sibu, a small Malay-Chinese town for fuel. They could not take off the glassy water, however. When the pontoons were installed in Singapore, they were set at the wrong angle and did not allow the airplane to rotate properly into lift-off attitude and break the surface of the water. As a result, Moye hired a local motorboat to tow them out to sea at Brunei. The buoyancy of the sea water and the unlimited area of the open ocean guaranteed the plane's successful departure. Other than striking a floating log, the airplane was airborne without further delay. Moye examined the pontoons for damage in Sandakan, their last stop in Malaysia. Happily, one pontoon received only a small dent and didn't require repairs.

From Sandakan, Moye skirted the north coast of Borneo and then flew up the Sulu Archipelago to the volcanic island of Jolo, a 200 mile flight. The plane remained anchored in the harbor while Moye and Richard visited the Sultan of Sulu, the only Sultan ruling under the American flag. Finding the island serene, with its white sands and warm waters, the two intended to stay a few days but an early seasonal typhoon thwarted their plans. As Jolo prepared for the worst, Moye and Richard immediately headed to Zamboanga which lay 150 miles to the north. A natural breakwater created by the Santa Cruz Islands to the south protected the *Flying Carpet* from the storm's fury. As a precaution, Moye and Richard rode out the storm in the airplane. They later learned that their quick departure from Jolo proved fortunate. The storm thrust ships moored in Jolo's harbor onto the shore. Houses, huts, and the Sultan's palace lay in shambles. When the gale subsided, three fourths of the town had disappeared. The archipelago counted over 600 deaths. 11

The *Flying Carpet* flew directly east from Zamboanga over Moro Gulf to Cotabata and then north to Cebu to visit Magellan's grave. En route to Manila, Moye and Richard landed in two different lakes. Richard heard stories about Lake Buluan, teeming with crocodiles, snails, and ducks, and thought it worth visiting. Richard's account states they spent several days on the lake, shooting ducks by day and harpooning crocodiles by night. The time frame, from leaving Jolo to arriving in Manila, allowed for only one night's stay. In addition, the pungent smells, swarming mosquitoes, and large crocodiles would have proved physically challenging after a few hours.

Fifty miles from Manila, the *Flying Carpet* landed on Lake Taal near Luzon. In the middle of the extraordinarily beautiful lake, a volcanic crater held another lake about five miles wide. An eruption in 1911 created a new crater inside of this one. Now filled with water, the crater measured a half mile in diameter. Moye put the Stearman down near the shore of the largest of the three lakes. A native from a lakeside village rowed the two out to the volcano for a better view. Warned that the brownish water was unsuitable for swimming, Richard jumped in any way and began swimming out to the lava formation. Within minutes, caustic chemicals began burning his skin. Richard took refuge in the larger lake to soak his inflamed skin with clean water. Several applications of coconut oil helped to soothe his burns.

Manila, the capitol of the Philippines, welcomed Moye and Richard when they arrived May 2, 1932. Governor-General Theodore Roosevelt II and his wife hosted a dinner in their honor. Within a week, harbor personnel had crated and placed the *Flying Carpet* aboard American Mail Line's *President McKinley*. Moye watched over the process to ensure they loaded the airplane properly. The Stearman, faded and worn, still deserved the highest level of care after a reliable 30,000 miles of dedicated service. Having some free time before the steamship departed, Moye

Above, the Flying Carpet arrives in Manila. Below, Richard prepares to secure the Stearman to a buoy in Manila's harbor. Photo courtesy of Moye F. Stephens.

indulged in some island hopping. He flew the mail in a Waco J-5 twice, from Manila to Baguio, the summer capital of the Philippines. The regular pilot, the only commercially licensed flyer on the islands, hadn't taken a day off in nearly two years. Moye was pleased to give the veteran some much needed rest. 12

May 10, the *McKinley* steamed out of Manila's harbor for Hong Kong where the Stearman's wheels and parachutes were placed on board. After stops in Shanghai, Kobe, Yokohama, and Honolulu, the *McKinley* entered the San Francisco Bay on May 31, 1932. The sea water sparkled as the morning fog lifted, presenting a magnificent view of the city's striking skyline. Moye and Richard took little notice, eager to disembark and unload the airplane. In contrast to Richard's previous trips, where large crowds of fans gathered to celebrate his return, a small group greeted Richard and Moye as they walked down the ship's ramp. The next morning, the two attended a reception in their honor

By late afternoon on the day of their arrival, mechanics began to assemble the *Flying Carpet* in Alameda. They removed the pontoons, installed the landing gear, and bolted the wings in place. Moye gave it a thorough inspection and a test hop before he and Richard returned to Grand Central and completed their round-the-world flight on June 2, 1932. Newspaper announcements of their arrival were scarce and relegated to the last pages of section one. Amelia Earhart's solo trans-Atlantic flight on May 21 and preparations for the summer Olympics in Los Angeles received preferential treatment on the front pages. 13

After 33,660 miles and 178 landings on every surface, from major airports to polo fields, cow pastures, the vast Sahara Desert and, as a seaplane, from sheltered harbors, Borneo rivers, and the open ocean, the *Flying Carpet* and its crew arrived home safely. The trip took 18 months and Moye logged 374 hours flying over 34 countries. He considered applying for an official record as the slowest round-the-world flight, but not having flown the Atlantic and Pacific, he decided his application would be rejected. In comparison to the *Flying Carpet*'s trip, the 1924 Douglas Cruiser world flight took just over a year and covered approximately 22,000 miles.

"Moye and I wheeled the old Carpet into the hangar," wrote Richard, . . . and there for the first time, we realized how much it showed the marks of battle, with the elements in a hundred lands . . . Through desert and jungle, Africa and Arabia, Himalaya and the islands of the sea . . . these brave and sturdy wings, had brought us safely home." 14

Richard spent a total of $50,000 for the trip. He owed Shell $14,000 but they canceled the debt due to the extremely favorable publicity they received from it. Nearly broke, Richard sold the airplane to help offset expenses for the trip. Naval officers in Honolulu bought the Stearman. Soon after, the plane crashed on takeoff from John Rogers Airport, killing one passenger and seriously injuring the pilot, co-partner Jerry Leach, and one other passenger. An undated newspaper clipping listed the passenger's names as Charboneaux and Stamatics. Mechanics had installed the ailerons upside down when attaching them. With hopes of rebuilding the airplane, the same broker that sold Richard the Stearman arranged to have it shipped back to Burbank. Realizing the plane could not be rebuilt, the broker parted it out. One wing went to Honduras as a replacement on a Stearman hauling gold out of the interior. The tail assembly was shipped to Fairbanks, Alaska for a bush plane. Polar explorer Donald B. Macmillan installed the wheels on his Lockheed *Vega*. An Arizona Stinson claimed the J-5 engine. A private pilot in the state of Washington bought the landing struts. 15

Richard would star in a travel film, *India Speaks*, in 1933. Rosina Schulse played his love interest. *Seven League Boots,* another book project based on his travels, was completed two years later. In March of 1939, Richard set out from Hong Kong on what became his last adventure. He planned to sail across the Pacific in a tenuously constructed Chinese junk named the *Sea Dragon*, recording his voyage in a book by the same name. Fair weather followed the *Sea Dragon* for the first two and a half weeks. Richard felt certain he would arrive in time for the opening of the Golden Gate International Exposition in San Francisco but that was not to be. Disaster struck in the form of a typhoon somewhere in the northern Pacific. With winds in excess of seventy miles per hour and waves towering over thirty feet, the top-heavy junk's fate was sealed. On March 23, the *President Coolidge,* a Dollar Liner, received a final radio message from the *Sea Dragon*'s captain describing the weather conditions. Richard was declared legally dead October 5, 1939 by the Memphis Chancery Court. 16

The survival of the *Flying Carpet*, preserved intact in an aviation museum, would have been an enduring celebration of a well-executed flight. The gold and scarlet Stearman might have stood tall, painstakingly refurbished by dedicated volunteers, as an airplane that beat the odds. Very few thought the airplane could persevere over uncharted country and extreme weather changes. If it didn't crash, it most certainly would need constant servicing and, at times, thorough maintenance. Could such a young pilot and a romantic adventurer possess the forethought and responsibility to succeed? Much can be said for Moye's careful flight planning and meticulous attention to detail when it came to the operation of the *Flying Carpet*. Unlike Richard, Moye knew the fate of those who took piloting lightly. Extreme weather tested his flying skills. He gained confidence with each lesson the skies offered up. Learning to respect the integrity of his aircraft and Mother Nature, the pilot of the *Flying Carpet* crafted a remarkable journey and remains the sole testament to a job well done.

Boarding the McKinley, Moye appears exceptionally happy to have successfully completed the eighteen-month flight and to be on his way home. After docking in San Francisco, the plane would be reassembled and flown to Grand Central Airport. Photo courtesy of Princeton University Library.

14

FROM FLYING CARPETS
TO FLYING WINGS

Emotions ran high when Moye reunited with friends and family at Grand Central. Regardless of their confidence in their son's skills, Moye's letters had given Mr. and Mrs. Stephens a sense of comfort during the trip. The absence of any word, particularly between Calcutta and Singapore, undoubtedly gave them concern. They must have imagined inescapable scenarios of a downed airplane, serious illness, or attack by fierce natives. Now, the pleasure of having Moye home left them overwhelmed. Moye felt the same, elated to stand on familiar ground surrounded by family, including Suzanne and Trow who recently returned from a world trip of his own. Moye missed connecting with him in Paris; in Singapore, they spent several days together.

Moye's friends, whose greetings were lighthearted and reaffirming, gave him a brief report on aviation happenings as they helped him push the *Flying Carpet* into a hangar. They had not worried about him. If anyone could succeed flying a single-engine Stearman around the world, Moye could. He possessed a great deal of common sense and an understanding of mechanics that would help him survive the toughest of situations.

Rounds of parties with family and friends, Richard's commitments, and his own kept Moye busy for several weeks. He spoke about the flight to social and aviation groups including the Southern California Chapter of the National Aeronautic Association on June 12. A month later, he was a guest speaker at an event recognizing Amelia Earhart for her recent Atlantic crossing. [1]

When *Flying Carpet* activities slowed, Moye discussed the immediate future with his father. Not surprisingly, Moye Sr. encouraged his son to finish law school and join the family firm. Moye found working for the law firm as a law clerk far more agreeable than returning to the confines of a classroom. Western Airlines offered him a job but flying for the airlines no longer appealed to him. The new rules and regulations seemed oppressive after his eighteen-month tour. Moye wanted to continue his involvement in aviation, but with few opportunities available, he agreed to work in his father's law firm while looking for a position worthy of his talents. [2]

One issue raised by his father was the matter of Moye 'settling down'. Now 26 years old, Moye agreed that he had a social obligation to continue the family legacy and marry someone within his social ranking. Louise Janss, a 22-year-old debutante and close friend of Moye's sister Suzanne, belonged to the extremely wealthy Janss family, developers of Holmby Hills, Westwood Village, and other architectural projects in the Los Angeles area. Her father, Dr. Herman Janss, invested in real estate and maintained a consulting position with the California Real Estate Association. Other than her social obligations, Louise's interests were limited to sculpting, an activity inspired by her father. She displayed her work at the 1931 Artist's Fiesta in Los Angeles. [3]

In early November 1932, Richard Halliburton dined with the couple at the Stephens' Kings Road estate. Reading about the engagement in the newspaper, just 24 days after they landed at Grand Central, he wanted to meet the soon-to-be Mrs. Moye Stephens. He also took the occasion to announce the completion of his book, *The Flying Carpet* which he dedicated to Moye. The honor humbled him. Published by Bobbs-Merrill Company, the text romanticized the round-the-world-flight and was a huge success. Sales reports range from 50,000 to 250,000. Richard toured the country to promote the book. In the spring of 1933, Moye and Louise attended a book signing and lecture of Richard's in San Diego.

Moye and Louise's wedding took place at Los Angeles' premier Ambassador Hotel on Saturday, December 3, 1932. The week before the ceremony, Moye and Louise, declared the most popular and beautiful bride-elect of the season, attended a number of celebrations in the homes of their friends. One possessed a notable pedigree. Ross Clark, grandson of Montana Senator William A. Clark hosted a dinner party for the couple in his home. Having fulfilled their pre-wedding social obligations, Moye and Louise took their vows in the Ambassador's Fiesta Ballroom which overflowed with flowers and guests. The best man, Trow, stood by his brother; the matron of honor, Suzanne, held Louise's bouquet. As the *Los Angeles Times*' social column noted, "the wedding was a brilliant event." Moye and Louise Stephens. left for their honeymoon to an undisclosed location one week later. 4

Although they enjoyed each other's company, Louise and Moye's engagement and subsequent marriage served to unite families and fortunes, not hearts. Stunningly beautiful, Louise possessed few of the qualities that Moye loved in Elly. Louise was neither adventurous nor spontaneous. When Moye discussed having children with Louise, she was quick to reject the idea. Her reluctance to consider Moye having a career in aviation and her increased lack of intimacy resulted in the couple's separation in May 1934. They divorced July 3 in Reno. 5

In early 1933, Moye took a job with Glass Containers, Inc., a company owned by his family. He filled the position of production supervisor and later, that of vice president. He referred to the experience as an unhappy three-year period of non-aviation employment. When an opportunity arose to join Pacific Aircraft Sales in 1936, Moye jumped at the chance. He became partners with Ivar Axelson and Norm Larson who learned to fly with Moye while at Stanford. Pacific received a contract from Fairchild, based in New York, to distribute their aircraft. They offered the public an airplane with a fully-enclosed cockpit and hydraulic shock landing gear, the first of its kind built in America. Moye promoted sales, gave demonstration flights, and occasionally flew mapping flights for Lee Eliel of Fairchild Aerial Surveys based at United Airport.

Moye had joined flamboyant Sheriff Eugene Biscailuz's Aero Squadron in 1933 and continued to fly for the organization in one of Pacific's Fairchilds. Launched as the "Sheriff's Aero Detail" in 1929, the squadron policed Los Angeles County's 55 airports and 500 airplanes. Captain Claude Morgan was appointed commander of the squadron. His responsibility was to supervise the handful of civilian volunteer pilots who flew their own aircraft. The squadron searched for lost individuals in the mountains and deserts, aided in capturing fugitives, and were trained to assist in major disasters.

The famous Mission Inn in Riverside, California hosted the Aero Squadron soon after the organization formed. The group is posing in front of the Flyer's Wall adjacent to the International Shrine of Aviators. The wall displays autographed wings from notable aviation-minded individuals from around the world. Sheriff Biscailuz is standing center; Moye is behind him to his left. University of Southern California photo. 6

FROM FLYING WINGS TO FLYING CARPETS

In June 1933, the Los Angeles Board of Supervisors, realizing the critical services the Sheriff's detail provided, officially authorized Biscailuz to form the Aero Squadron, the first of its kind in the United States. Moye became one of 25 original members to be sworn in as special deputy sheriffs. The 1933 Long Beach earthquake provided the squadron with an opportunity to demonstrate their capabilities. With all means of ground communication down, air units, as they were called, flew over the devastated area to assess damages and locate victims. In 1935, members ferried Mexican dignitaries from Agua Caliente in a Junkers trimotor to the California Pacific International Exposition. Actor Robert Taylor donated the squadron's first airplane, a Fairchild 24, in 1947. Movie director Clarence Brown donated a Stinson L-5 soon after. 7

Over coffee in front of Wally Timm's hangar at Grand Central, Moye, Norm Larson, Charles Kidder, and Ben McGlashan conceived the idea of a flying club for private airplane owners. Rather than let their planes accumulate dust, they wanted to organize flying tours to various parts of California. Their inspiration might have been the recent derby to Ensenada. January 1936, fifteen planes left Union Terminal and raced down the Baja for an evening at the Playa Ensenada Hotel. Marty Bowen won the competition, taxiing past a squad of Mexican soldiers, courtesy of the Mayor, to claim her prize. The pilots and their guests enjoyed a night of dinner, dancing, and gambling before departing in the morning. Moye flew his cousin Jeff Stephens and wife Sally in one of Pacific's Fairchilds. 8

Over 20 pilots gathered at Grand Central Air Terminal for a more formal meeting following the Ensenada trip. Tentatively called Sports Wings, the group incorporated in February 1936 as the Aviation Country Club of California. The club's first official tour occurred in May. Nearly 100 planes flew to Sonoma, California. "All types of flying contests were held on these tours including navigation, target bombing, best ETA and even golf from the air, an event at the Furnace Creek Inn at Death Valley. This consisted of the contestants flying over the golf course and dropping their golf balls by parachute as close as possible to a designated green. They

245

would then land and play out the hole." Included among its early members were Senator Barry Goldwater, Paul Mantz, Claude Ryan, Edgar Bergen, Wallace Berry, and three future Northrop flying wing pilots - John Myers, Max Stanley, and Moye. 9

Two months after the Aviation Country Club became a reality, Los Angeles declared the third week in May as Will Rogers Week. To honor the American icon killed on August 15, 1935 near Barrow, Alaska, a group of respected Los Angeles aviators were chosen to pay tribute to the beloved humorist. Moye, Paul Mantz, Amelia Earhart, Clyde Pangborn and Roscoe Turner dropped rose petals from their planes as they flew in formation over Rogers' vault at Forest Lawn Memorial Park. Earlier in the day, in the company of more than a hundred silent film actors, they attended a tribute to Rogers at the Riverside Drive Breakfast Club. 10

Lockheed Aircraft approached Moye in early 1937, offering him a position as sales representative and demonstration pilot for the new Electra, the company's first all-metal, twin-engine design. Excited by the idea of flying a ground-breaking aircraft, he readily accepted the offer. He obtained a six-month leave from Pacific Aircraft and, on March 22, 1937, ferried an Electra to the east coast for a Lockheed customer. In June, he and Milo Burcham, former stunt pilot and barnstormer who hired on with Moye, were responsible for the delivery of three Model 10E Electras to New Zealand and Australia. Powered by two 550 hp Pratt & Whitney Wasp engines, the airplane could easily depart a high-altitude runway with a gross load. Moye checked out pilots from Ansett, Union, and Guinea Airways as well as demonstrated the plane's capabilities to pilots, charter operators, and additional airlines in both countries. 11

While visiting Darwin on the northwest shore of Australia, Moye learned that Earhart had departed two weeks earlier. He had taken a personal interest in Earhart's flight and subsequent disappearance. The two sat down together before her last flight to discuss the portions of her route coinciding with that of the *Flying Carpet*. Refueling in Karachi, she flew direct to Calcutta where she picked up Moye's route. She made fuel stops in Akyab, Rangoon, Bangkok, and Singapore. The meteorologist in Darwin shared some

Lockheed hired Moye as a demonstration pilot and sales representative for the Lockheed Electra. The photo shows him standing in front of an Electra at the Lockheed factory. Photo courtesy of the Museum of Flight.

of his theories about Earhart and her disappearance. He felt that all of her flying could be considered 'stunts' created by her husband George Putnam. She did little flying in between the newsworthy events. Because Earhart flew through the treetops at Auckland, unable to climb above them with full tanks, she didn't fill her tanks completely at Lae. Another contributing factor was an unfavorable weather forecast which would make it almost impossible to locate Howland visually. 12

Moye spent the last few weeks in Australia enjoying his honeymoon. April 26, 1937, he wed 29-year-old Countess Inez Buttora, Gadina de Turiani. The ceremony took place at the Stephens' home on Kings Road. Born in Trieste, Italy, Inez's family possessed vast holdings in Russia and Europe. She sailed to the United States in 1928 to visit relatives in New York and California, her parent's solution to ending a romance with an older man. A cousin, Bank of America director Howard Buttora, hosted her in San Marino, California. Inez spoke three languages – Italian, Spanish, and French, but not English. She did manage, however, to have a few bit parts in films. On the train to Los Angeles, she chanced to meet one of the Warner brothers who afforded her the opportunity. A year later, Inez returned to Italy at her parent's insistence and entered medical school. When the career she once found attractive no longer interested her, she withdrew from the program. Inez loved the outdoors, sports, and fashion. She raced cars until a near fatal crash convinced her take up a less dangerous sport. It didn't take long for her to find one.

Inez met Ross Hadley during his 1929 European tour. Arriving in France on the *Il de France*, Ross and co-pilot

Ross and Inez and the Stearman C-3B he flew to Singapore as noted in the picture. Moye F. Stephens' photo.

Chet Loomis flew their Stearman C-3B through France, Italy, Austria, Germany, Holland, Belgium and England.   At Dijon, France, Ross cracked up in a windstorm, putting him and Inez in the hospital. Inez, smitten with the sports pilot, traveled to California following Ross's world tour in May 1931. They married in 1932. 13

Ross' wealth was attributed to his father's business, Chas. R. Hadley Co., a Los Angeles bookbindery, and Ross' partnership in Pacific Airmotive Corporation.   Organized by W. E. Thomas, A. L. Patterson, and Ross, the company began operations in February 1928. They moved from their Angeles Mesa Drive location to Metropolitan Airport at the end of that year. Moye and Ross were good friends and both members of the Aviation Country Club. Pacific had been responsible for the overhaul of the *Flying Carpet's* engine. 14

Inez, with Ross as her instructor, received her pilot's license on May 22, 1932. She often stated that she was the first Italian woman to receive a pilot license.   Research gives credit to Italian Rosina Ferrario for that achievement. Ferrario received her license in 1913. Inez did make use of her royal relatives, however, to pilot an Italian military aircraft. Related in some manner to the Duke of Aosta or Prince Aimone, Inez stated that he allowed her to fly his personal fighter and also awarded her an Honorary Lieutenant's position in the Regia Aeronautica.   Further, Inez claimed to have flown the Keith-Rider R-2 owned by George McGrew, first husband of actress Jean Harlow.

Moye met the beautiful Inez at Mines Field. She loved to fly and was just as charming and daring as Elly and Violette. Moye F. Stephens' photo.

Renamed the *Bumblebee*, McGrew entered the racer in the Los Angeles Nationals that year. 15

Inez spent nearly every day at Mines Field, quickly accumulating over sixty hours of aerobatics. To gain cross-country experience, she frequently flew down to Ensenada. A popular destination for the social set, the seaside town offered a variety of activities. Besides excellent fishing and sailing, Ensenada possessed a luxurious resort, the Hotel Playa Ensenada and Casino. Inez and Ross enjoyed the indulgent comforts offered by the club. Most popular with the pilots was Walter Hussong's Cantina. Founded by his father, Juan Hussong, in 1892, the cantina earned a reputation as the friendliest place in town. The Hussong's employees graciously welcomed anyone who stepped through the front door as did Madame Cecile at her "house of ill-repute" where the flyers often went to dance. 16

Before landing, pilots buzzed Hussong's to signal the need for a ride. By the time the airplane descended over the pasture of grazing cows at the end of the strip, a car was on its way. One trip, Inez signaled Hussong's by performing aerobatics over town. The stunting not only alerted the establishment that someone needed a ride but captured the attention of the police.

"Ross arrived (in Ensenada) about an hour later," Inez remembered with a twinkle in her eye. "He followed the coast; I took a straight compass course. Ross had just landed when a policeman approached Ross and said, 'You're under arrest.' Ross says, 'What for?' 'For stunting over Ensenada.' Well, I decided I couldn't let that go by so I said, 'Ah Capitan! It was not him; it was me!' Then he came over and kissed my hand . . . and everything was forgotten!" 17

Ross and Inez's marriage ended in divorce on April 19, 1937. Because Ross didn't want any children; his relationship with Inez lacked intimacy. Five years earlier, Moye and Inez had met at Mines Field. Vivacious, intelligent, and lovely, Inez instantly captivated him. She further impressed Moye with her ability to handle an airplane and her eagerness to improve her skills. When her love for Moye exceeded her religious beliefs concerning divorce, she left Ross. One week later, Inez and Moye were married. On the couple's return from Australia, Moye's mother and sister entertained 300 guests at a cocktail party honoring the new Mrs. Moye Stephens. 18

Following his employment with Lockheed, Moye began formulating plans to develop a company whose primary purpose would be the design and construction of state-of-the-art aircraft. His managerial skills and aviation experience would prove a strong foundation for such a project. During dinner one evening at his sister Suzanne's home, he discussed his aspirations with her husband, Wesley LeFever. Employed by Banks Huntley, a securities firm, LeFever possessed a keen sense of finance and organization. He also knew a number of financially solvent investors.

In March 1981, Moye described his involvement in the development of what would become Northrop Corporation.

"The way it happened . . . Tom Ellsworth, a salesman for Banks, was talking to my brother-in-law Wesley LeFever. He said. 'It's a shame for that fellow Northrop to be working for other people. He should head his own company.' Wesley told Tom, 'Why don't you talk to Moye Stephens. He has much the same idea.' Well, Tom came to me and we got together with Eddie Bellande, who was then a commercial pilot for TWA. It was Eddie, by the way, who taught me to fly.

"Eddie was very enthusiastic. We approached Jack Northrop and he was agreeable, but only if someone else handled the administration of the company. Jack was primarily interested in designing aircraft. Eddie presented the idea to TWA President LaMotte Cohu who proved to be as enthusiastic as the rest of us. He brought in his brother who also became a member of the board of directors. We first tried to interest private capital by approaching people in both the movie and oil industries." 19

Recently resigned as Douglas' Chief Engineer for its El Segundo Division, Jack Northrop received a call from Bellande and Moye encouraging him to locate a financial partner who could assist him in founding his own aircraft company. Bellande suggested Northrop contact his boss and LaMott Cohu in New York to discuss funding. Cohu was quite receptive and sought backing through his contacts on Wall Street. Unable to create any interest, Northrop and Cohu returned to Los Angeles to meet with Bellande and Ted Coleman, Vice President of Corporate Finance for Banks Huntley. Occasionally dining with Coleman in Albuquerque where Banks maintained an office, Bellande suggested to him that his firm might consider backing Northrop. A premier aircraft designer, Northrop was on the verge of pioneering something exciting. Coleman agreed to a meeting.

Moye also discussed the opportunity with Coleman. After learning that the New York firm of E. H. Rollins and Sons rejected Cohu and Northrop's proposal, Moye began contacting several of his wealthy friends to assist Northrop. Two week later, Northrop, Cohu, Bellande, Coleman, Banks-Huntley President Earl Huntley, and Bert Lester, a former Vice President for Banks Huntley & developer of many young and promising west coast companies, sat down for what would become a historic meeting at Huntley's Spring Street office. Although Moye did not attend the meeting, Coleman and Bellande kept him apprised of any decisions made.

Jack spoke first, as always in a subdued, straight-forward manner.

"I believe this is an ideal time to start a new aviation company. Not only because war may break out anytime in Europe, but because the industry is facing an unlimited future due to rapid technological advances." [20]

After assuring the potential investors that many experienced engineers and technicians from Douglas would be on board, Northrop presented his goals for a new company. Foremost, he wanted to develop an all-wing airplane with a tail that would fly faster and further on less fuel because of its high lift and low drag. Introduced to this idea in 1923 by Tony Stadlman, former co-worker at Lockheed and now Douglas Company plant manager, Northrop "believed that the ideal aircraft of the future was in the true 'flying wing' design. From that day, Northrop's goal was to design and perfect a flying wing." Northrop had formed the Avion Company in 1928 to begin construction on this unique concept. Collecting valuable data from numerous flights, Northrop closed shop when the Depression hit. [21]

The gregarious and dynamic Cohu followed Northrop's

genuine presentation by praising Northrop's abilities and the direction his dreams were taking him. Cohu reiterated his strong feelings about the new company; he was ready to leave TWA and move his family to Los Angeles to assist in its start-up. He proposed financing the new company by selling the initial stock to the public, a rather unconventional method at the time. Both he and Northrop believed acquiring funding through private investors resulted in too many unnecessary obligations. Cohu stressed the importance of keeping "the company small — a company built on Jack's research ability — he is a genius. A company specializing in advanced design can easily be supported by U.S. government contracts. It is essential for our national defense. War is coming soon. It is inevitable that the United States will become involved." 22

Earl Huntley relied on Cohu's aviation background as well as Coleman's degree in engineering and economics from Caltech. He based his opinions on their familiarity, experience, and knowledge of aircraft. Before committing, however, Huntley wanted to determine if Douglas and Bob Gross, head of Lockheed, would put up any road-blocks to the new company's success. Both gentlemen welcomed the competition and wished Northrop well. Bert Lester concurred. His new firm, Batson, Barnes, and Lester joined Banks Huntley in forming an underwriting group in Los Angeles with two eastern partners. Walter Cohu's firm in New York City and Rolly O'Brian & Mitchell's in Buffalo also became partners with Banks Huntley. They sold 250,000 shares of Northrop Class A common stock to the public at $6.00 a share, raising the 1.5 million dollars needed to start the company. Moye and Bellande provided a list of prospective investors. With the purchase of the remaining 50,000 shares by Floyd Odlum's Atlas Corporation, Northrop had sufficient funds to launch the new company.

Cohu was appointed Northrop's chairman of the board and general manager. His experience as a financial manager and labor-relations man proved a great asset to the new company. Gage H. Irving, a long time associate of Northrop, left Douglas for a position as vice-president and assistant general manager. The corporate secretary position went to Ted Coleman. When Bellande decided to stay with TWA, Coleman took Bellande's promised job as vice president of sales. Moye, originally assistant corporate secretary, assumed Coleman's position. Both he and Coleman earned places on the Board of Directors that year. Moye's starting salary was $250 a month for the dual assignment of corporate secretary and chief test pilot. 23

Needing a site for the new company, Moye scouted the Los Angeles basin and located a 72-acre, former asparagus field in Inglewood, southeast of the Los Angeles Municipal Airport. September 1939, construction began on Northrop's manufacturing facility and the fulfillment of Jack Northrop's dream of building a true flying wing. Soon after, a successful wind tunnel model, created by many of Northrop's earlier calculations, led to the design of Northrop's Model 1 Mockup (N-1M). 24

The N-1M, nicknamed the *Jeep* after the small military vehicle of the same name, was a wood mockup with welded steel tubing. Northrop intended to use the N-1M to explore the controllability and stability of the all-wing aircraft concept. Vastly overweight, sorely underpowered, and plagued with constant engine problems, the ship fulfilled its design purpose and produced the general configuration for the subsequent Northrop flying wings.

Northrop consulted with Dr. Theodore Von Karman, Director of the Daniel Guggenheim School of Aeronautics at California Institute of Technology, and his assistant, Dr. William R. Sears, on the wing design. As the project developed, Northrop employed Von Karman as Aerodynamic Consultant and Dr. Sears as Chief Aerodynamicist. Moye related some rather unconventional testing that took place to provide additional input for the wing design. He invited Northrop and his wife to visit the Stephens ranch in La Verne to enjoy a day outdoors – hiking, riding, and perhaps a little hunting. When rain and gusty winds forced them indoors, Moye and Northrop climbed the stairs armed with paper airplanes to experiment with a variety of flying wing configurations. They discovered that a wing with downward tips performed the most efficiently. 25

Northrop selected Vance Breese as pilot for the initial ground runs of the N-1M. Born in 1904, Breese left school in the sixth grade to help support his family. He worked at a number of jobs including one at the Young Men's Business Club in Seattle where he studied how successful men carried themselves. According to Breese's son by the same name, his father seemed to be resentful that he came from a 'dirt-poor' family. He imitated the behavior of accomplished individuals, even wearing a business suit when he flew. It was important for him to dissociate himself from the indigent appearance of local pilots on the airfield. Breese began his aviation career as a wing-walker. Discovering a place in the cockpit paid more, he learned to fly. Breese flew a Ryan M-1 in the 1926 Ford Reliability Tour, an event created to increase the popularity of flying. He finished in eighth place. Competing in the 1928 National Air tour, flying a Mahoney-Ryan B-1, he was ninth. 26

In 1927, Breese and Arthur Pop Wilde, a former member of the Lafayette Escadrille, founded the Breese Aircraft Company. The Breese-Wilde 5 monoplane ranked as their most successful design. Assisted by John Northrop in designing the plane, the final product consisted of parts salvaged from miscellaneous sources, including a Lockheed fuselage. The company sold five, two of which were entered in the 1927 Dole Race. One, the Pabco Pacific Flyer, crashed on take-off; the other, the *Aloha* flown by Martin Jensen, landed second in Hawaii. Detroit Aircraft absorbed Breese Aircraft in the late 1920s. 27

Breese's early flying earned him the descriptive moniker, "hard-charging Vance Breese". "He could fly anything", his peers said, "even a barn door". As a result, he performed the first flights on aircraft for Northrop, Bennett, Lockheed, and North American aircraft companies from the 1930s until the late 1960s. His son stated that airplane designers chose his father for intrinsically dangerous flights to determine if the plane possessed sufficient stability for further tests. The companies, specifically Northrop, then used another test pilot with the appropriate experience and one less expensive. Although Breese integrated several test parameters into a single flight, he charged, in foot increments, by the width of the plane's wingspan. An exorbitant fee resulted. Bob Hoover believed that Breese laid the foundation for future test pilots with his innate feel for an airplane and the dynamics of flight. Breese's experience with Northrop set the ground work for a

Amelia Earhart and Vance Breese admire the Vultee, believed to be the Model V-1 prototype which was later designated as the V-1A built for American Airlines. Photo courtesy of Vance Breese.

successful career as a well-respected engineering test pilot. 28

Waldo Waterman, pioneering aviator described an incident which involved his Arrowbile and Vance Breese. Considered by some as a flying wing and by others, as a car with wings, Waterman successfully tested the Arrowbile in February 1937. Studebaker placed an order for five at that year's National Air Races in Cleveland. Mechanical problems and a sharp downturn in America's economy the following year ended the production of the innovative vehicle. When Breese strolled over to Waterman's Santa Monica facilities in June 1940, under the pretext that North American was interested in providing financial support for the Arrowbile, Waterman provided him with the plane's manufacturing details and flight characteristics. Breese, as it turned out, only wanted to determine the flying characteristics of the tailless plane.

"I went into considerable detail," Waterman related in his autobiography, "explaining to Vance all of the many problems we'd originally had . . . I was quite surprised to read in the papers about a week later that Northrop had designed a new aircraft dubbed a

Moye and Jack Northrop prepare for a test run of the N1M on December 4, 1941. Roy Wolford Collection, Harvey Mudd College.

Flying Wing which Vance Breese was putting through flight tests on Rosamond Dry Lake! . . . Vance had been 'picking my brains' to learn how to do it. By moving the landing gear around, like I'd told him, they succeeded." 29

The initial flight of the N-1M, July 3, 1940 at Baker Dry Lake, took place quite by accident. Powered by two four-cylinder, air-cooled Lycoming engines, the N-1M hit a rough spot on the dry lake during one of Breese's scheduled high-speed taxi runs. The plane immediately bounced into the air and became airborne, entering controllable flight for a few hundred yards. No one considered that the prototype required little power to become airborne because of its decrease in drag. By November 1941, Moye and Breese had completed over 50 flights in the N1M. 30

December 6, 1941, one day before the Japanese released havoc on Pearl Harbor, Northrop invited the press and newsreel cameramen to Muroc Dry Lake to observe the N-1M in flight. Moye adeptly demonstrated the flying wing's capabilities to the line of excited newsmen. Much to the satisfaction of Jack Northrop, the world now shared his vision for future aircraft.

"The Northrop N-1M Flying Wing," Moye later related, "was a flying mock-up built for the purpose of exploring the

The location for this photo of the N-1M is Muroc Dry Lake. The wing sweepback and dihedral could be adjusted at the joint covered by the metal strips outboard of the engines. Roy Wolford Collection, Harvey Mudd College.

controllability and stability of an all-wing, tailless aircraft. To facilitate the program, the ship incorporated features which permitted adjustment, on the ground, of its dihedral, sweep back, and wing tip deflection. As performance was considered of secondary importance, during its design, insufficient attention was paid to weight. As a consequence, if I remember correctly, the ship weighed close to 4,000 lbs upon completion. The two, 65 hp Lycomings initially installed were unable to lift it out of the ground effect. The two replacement 120 hp Franklins did somewhat better, though scarcely provided fighter performance.

"At the start of the test program, Northrop Aircraft had no staff of pilots. I was the corporate secretary but due to my piloting background, took an intense interest in the N-1M program and accompanied Jack Northrop to Muroc Dry Lake to witness the start. Vance Breese, a free lance test pilot, made the first flight and I made the second. We then more or less alternated on the flights until Vance became involved in the testing of the North American B-25. At that point, I took over and was responsible for the major portion of the N-1M test program.

"On one flight, just after breaking ground, I heard what seemed to be an explosion followed by an extremely violent shaking of the entire ship. Fortunately, an adequate stretch of dry lake enabled me to instantly chop the power and land straight ahead. Upon examination, the rear spar of the right wing was broken when six inches of a right hand propeller blade snapped off.

"In the initial flights with the Lycomings, the ship would climb to about five feet and the increased induced drag associated with attempts to force it higher would bring it down to a landing. Continuous flight called for maintenance of a precise angle of attack. Any increase in the angle of attack and the ship would land. Any decrease in the angle of attack and the ship would land.

"The situation was complicated by a dead area in elevator effectiveness. In order to nose down, it was necessary to move the wheel forward a disturbing amount with no response when the elevons would suddenly take over. In order to keep from banging into the ground it was then necessary to traverse the dead elevator area in the opposite direction to find the start of effectiveness.

"This was moderately unsettling while flying along five feet off the ground. I temporarily overcame the difficulty by use of the longitudinal trim flap, a control surface spanning the trailing edge of the center section. With this adjusted to create a nose heavy condition, flight was maintained with a constant back pressure on the wheel. To nose down, it was simply necessary to ease off the back pressure.

"When the condition was explained to aerodynamicist Dr. Theodore von Karman, he unhesitatingly came up with a quick fix. "Vell, I tink ve choost poot a cusp on de elevons."

"He realized that the extremely thick wing was creating an airflow separation which was not coming together until aft of the wing. The cusps extended the trailing edge of the elevons into the closure of the airflow. It was thought that this also tended to move closure farther ahead.

"Before the installation of the more powerful engines, flights were made in a straight line over the length of the dry lake. Following the landing and a taxied turn-around, a return flight was made with another taxied turn-around, another flight, and so on.

"Following the installation of the 120 hp Franklins, considerable time was consumed in adapting the new engines to the requirements. The manufacturer's specifications stipulated

2,500 take-off rpm, not to exceed three minutes, followed by a reduction to 2,300 maximum rpm for continuous operation. It was found necessary to turn the engines 2,800 rpm to accomplish a take-off in less than a mile run and to establish a climb of around 200 feet per minute. It was necessary to turn 2,500 rpm to maintain altitude in level flight.

"The manufacturer's specifications stipulated maximum cylinder head temperatures of 272° C not to exceed three minutes, followed by a reduction to a maximum of 232°C for continuous operation. In the beginning, I was unable to ascertain what the head temperatures went to as the gauge pegged at over 300°C. After considerable work on the engine installations, we were able to reduce the temperature to around 270°C in level flight, continuous operation.

"In order to get on with the primary objective of the test program it was necessary to condone exceeding, by a large margin, the maximum allowable rpms and head temperatures in both the take-off-climb and continuous operation regimes.

"During the program, I flew the N-1M with numerous combinations of wing tip deflection, dihedral, and sweepback. Initially, it was thought that downward deflecting wing tips would contribute to directional stability. It was soon found that they had little if any effect in this connection but did lessen lift noticeably.

"Also, the configuration incorporating the maximum tip deflection, the least dihedral angle, and the maximum sweepback did little to add to my peace of mind. With the ship at rests on the tricycle gear, the wing tips were only a foot off the ground. In this position, manually raising the nose lowered the wing tips until they touched the ground while the tail wheel, installed in a small, aft fin to prevent banging the pusher propellers on the ground, was still six inches in the air. On one flight, I just skinned the paint off one wing tip during a landing.

"In some configurations, yawing the ship and releasing the controls induced Dutch roll which continued to intensify until I wondered if, without any intervention, it would ever stop increasing – and what the result would be if it did not. I found the burden of an unsatisfied curiosity in this connection not overly irksome.

Jack Northrop and Moye discuss the performance of the N-1M for newsreel footage after Moye demonstrated the flying wing to the press. Roy Wolford Collection, Harvey Mudd College.

"The ship was longitudinally unstable with the minimum degree of sweepback, the configuration in which the trailing edge of the wing formed a straight line from wing tip to wing tip. It was the configuration which resulted in the rearmost positioning of the center of gravity. The instability was evidenced at low speeds and under acceleration.

"In landing, the ship exhibited positive stability during the approach, increasing nose heaviness with decreasing speed. But following the flare-out, increasing elevator stick force reversal resulted in an eventual full forward control position in order to maintain the holding-off altitude. In steep turns, nose heaviness was exhibited initially, but, as the g-force increased, a point was reached at which the ship would want to root into the turn necessitating forward control pressure to prevent it from doing so. Sweeping the wings back to the rearmost position moved the center of gravity forward and achieved longitudinal stability.

"The test program resulted in the configuration adopted for

Engineering, flight and ground crew members at Muroc Dry Lake. L to R: Walt Cerny (N-1M project supervisor),Moye, Dr. Bill Sears (Northrop Chief of Aeronautics), Tom Ruble, Harold Pedersen, Ed Lesnick, Earl Paton, and Ralph Winiger. Roy Wolford Collection, Harvey Mudd College.

incorporation in the design of the N-9M – straight wing tips, minimum dihedral, and the greatest degree of sweepback. In this form, longitudinal, directional, and lateral stability were considerably acceptable. Induced Dutch roll damped out in three to four oscillations.

"It is noteworthy that much of the difficulty encountered in the program was due to the N-1M being overweight and under powered, factors intrinsic to the investigation for which the ship was intended. In spite of its poor performance and continuous engine problems, the ship was a success. It accomplished the purpose of its design.

"As we neared the end of the program, Jack wanted to move the ship to the Northrop Airport in Hawthorne. I told him, in view of our continuous and drastic abuse of the engines coupled with the marginal performance of the ship, that I considered the move too risky. It was questionable that the ship, even with everything operating up to par, could take off from the Hawthorne field and clear the wires at the end. I expressed the opinion that the loss of as little as one cylinder toward the end of a take-off attempt would result in the start of an N-1M Avenue in the heart of Hawthorne. I stated that I would be happy to continue flights at Muroc where the possibility of serious consequences resulting from an all-too-likely engine failure would be reduced considerably in operations from the large expanse of the dry lake.

"Jack did not appreciate my viewpoint. He suggested that I get another pilot to carry on the experimental test flying. I contacted John Myers, a Lockheed test pilot, and recommended him to Northrop.

"As the N-1M was incapable of attaining sufficient altitude to make the flight to Hawthorne, piloted by John Meyers, it was towed behind a C-47 but was landed at LAX which provided somewhat more favorable take-off accommodations. Johnny Myers made several flights from LAX and then the N-1M was returned to Muroc. Its last flight was in early 1943.

"Northrop released the N-1M to the Army Air Corps in 1945 with hopes that it would eventually be put on display. The National Air Museum maintained the prototype in storage until 1979. At that time, a complete restoration began which took four years to complete." 31

The Smithsonian Air and Space Udvar-Hazey Annex now houses the N-1M in its original configuration.

Like Moye, John Meyers attended Stanford, studied law, played polo, and had a passion for aviation. He even built his own airplane during his college years. Graduating three years after Moye, Meyers earned a law degree at Harvard and joined his father at the O'Melveny and Meyers law firm. When WWII started, Meyers took a low level job in Lockheed's law department to avoid being drafted as a field artillery officer. He began ferrying Hudson bombers when the company discovered he possessed a wealth of

Moye sits in the center of this September 22, 1943 Northrop photo of the flying wing, surrounded by Northrop engineers. Jack Northrop is to Moye's left. Katy Ranaldi image.

flying knowledge and experience. Transferring to flight test, Meyers flew P-38s until he became Northrop's chief engineering pilot in 1941. [32]

Completing the test program for the N-1M, the Army Air Corps awarded Northrop a contract to develop a long-range, flying wing bomber designated the XB-35. To gather flight research data, Northrop constructed four, 60-foot one-third scale models, aerodynamically equivalents of the XB-35 design. Designated N-9Ms, they differed only in propellers and power plants. Moye inadvertently made the first unofficial flight in the N-9M when he substituted for Meyers for preliminary taxi runs. Once airborne, the flying wing easily traveled several yards until Moye pushed the nose down and landed. In an interview with the Society of Experimental Test Pilots Moye stated, "The N-9M was much more lively than the N-1M. The test unintentionally progressed beyond the taxi stage with surprising abruptness." [33]

Roy Wolford, an employee of Northrop for over 60 years, convinced Jack Northrop that photographing different elements of a test flight would substantially benefit the engineers on the ground. Northrop agreed and Wolford began the process of recording data to support the flight test programs. He took thousands of photos over the years which, when combined with the pilots' notes recorded on small notepads taped to their legs, expedited the process of certifying a new aircraft.

Wolford remembered Moye as a very thoughtful individual and excellent test pilot. He displayed a professional confidence, noticeably lacking the flamboyance that other test pilots possessed. After reviewing flight parameters, Moye interjected previous scenarios into the new expectations and knew what he had to do. Most flight tests took place on Rosamond Dry Lake near Muroc Army Air Corp Base, later Edwards Air Force Base. During its periodic flooding, the flight test crew moved its operations to an alternate site, Roach Dry Lake on the California-Nevada border. A small hangar sheltered the N1M, N9M, and XP-56 from the harsh sun and occasional sandstorm. The crew stayed in Las Vegas, Roy recalled, driving a distance of 40 miles to the site until someone determined that flying the company airplane would be much faster.

Moye normally piloted the crew from Las Vegas to the Roach test site. 34

In March 1940, the Norwegian Buying Commission contracted Northrop to design and build twenty-four N-3PB seaplane patrol bombers. Bernt Balchen, Norwegian adventurer who made considerable use of Northrop's Gamma during his explorations of the Arctic regions, was responsible for the referral. Designed in 1939, the N-3PB seaplane prototype first flew on November 1, 1940, piloted by Vance Breese off Lake Elsinore in southern California. Moye flew the remainder. At 17,000 feet, the seaplane reached a speed of 256 mph, exceeding Northrop's expectations and became the world's fastest seaplane to date. Hitler, already advancing on Norway, made prompt delivery of the seaplanes imperative. "By the end of March 1941, all 24 aircraft had been accepted by the Norwegian government, the fastest delivery on record and a remarkable achievement by the embryonic aircraft company." Even more remarkable was the fact that the development and production of the N-3PB took place concurrently with that of the flying wing program. 35

Performing test flights for the N1M and N-3PB, serving as a member of Northrop's Board of Directors, and assuming the role of a father made 1940 a very busy year for Moye. Inez gave birth to Moye Francesco Stephens on February 19, 1940. Affectionately known as *Moyito* (little Moye) by his grandmother, Moye's son loved flying as much as his father. As a teenager, he rode his bike to Cable Airport as often as school permitted and traded washing airplanes for flying lessons. His instructor, Linn Pearson, gave him the opportunity to fly in a variety of airplanes. Although he never received a pilot license, he maintained his enthusiasm for flying, learning as much as he could about aviation from his father. During Moye's employment with Northrop, he moved his family to a rented house just north of Hawthorne. This gave his son occasional opportunities to accompany his father to the airport and watch airplanes fly or ride in one of the corporate airplanes piloted by his father.

In June 1941, Moye became involved in another test program when Northrop received an order from the United States

Moye enjoyed flying the Vultee Vengeance. The all-metal airplane was powered by a 1,700 hp Wright Cyclone R-2600-13 air-cooled radial engine. Museum of Flight photo.

Army for 200 A-31s, single-engine bombers. V-72s, the British designation for the A-31 or Vultee Vengeance, were already being produced at a fast pace. Designed by Vultee Aircraft Inc., Northrop paid Vultee a royalty to use their design and engineering specifications after receiving the significant order from the British. The first Northrop-produced Vengeance took off from Northrop's Hawthorne facility on November 10, 1941.

"By 1944, 400 Vengeance dive bombers had been built and test flown from the mile-long runway at Hawthorne without a single serious accident." Coleman stated. "This spoke well for Moye Stephens, chief of production test flying, who was meticulous, careful, and thorough, traits that he instilled in all the test pilots working under him. To insure that factory production was properly completed, Moye insisted that a flight mechanic from the factory fly with the pilot on all delivery flights. One of Moye's favorite sayings reflected this cautious attitude, 'I want to be known as one of the

The P-61 was Northrop's first large scale production order. It had a maximum speed of 370 mph and carried a crew of three in the nacelle located between the engines. L to R - Ted Coleman, Moye, Jack Northrop, and Gage Irving. Museum of Flight photo.

oldest, not one of the hottest test pilots, when I terminate my flying career.'" 36

In a later interview for AOPA, Moye mentioned an incident involving the Vultee when asked about the various mishaps that a test pilot might experience.

"One flap collapsed on a Vultee A-31 Vengeance just as I came in on final approach to the Northrop airport in Hawthorne. It took nose down control, full opposite rudder and aileron plus full power to make the field right side up. The ship touched down at about 150 mph on the 5,000 foot runway." With only seconds to react to the malfunction, Moye did so instinctively and avoided a catastrophic outcome. 37

Moye avoided risk-taking and he instructed the test pilots he trained to err on the side of caution. Nine pilots reported to Moye during war time production. All nine, five production test pilots and four engineering test pilots, brought a wealth of experience to Northrop. Their air time, including Moye's, totaled 48,000 hours; their years of experience added up to 183 years.

Bill Wharton, a production pilot, flew for regional airlines, demonstrated Fairchilds for Pacific Aircraft Sales, and shared a few harrowing experiences with George Armistead in a Sikorsky S-39 flying boat. Armistead, motion picture and race pilot, tested the Harvard AT6, B-25, and Mustang before coming to Northrop in 1944. Max Stanley, with the fewest flying hours of the nine, joined the company in 1943 as an engineering test pilot. Previous to that, he ferried Lockheed Hudson bombers from Burbank to New York and Montreal, Lodestars and Douglas DC3s from Miami to British West Africa, and served as a captain for Pan American Air Ferries, Inc. and United Airlines.

The United States government authorized Romanian Alex Papana to test fly for Northrop in 1944. A world aerobatic champion, he set many records performing outside loops at low altitude. Prior to hiring on with Northrop in 1941, Charles A. La Jotte flew as an instructor in the WWI Signal and Air Corps, carried 50 pounds of mail on the first air mail flight in 1920 from New York to Washington, D.C., and tested North American aircraft. Dick Ranaldi joined Moye at Northrop in 1941. He became assistant production manager and test pilot for the A-31 Vengeance and P-61 Black Widow. Ranaldi, according to his log book, made one flight in the N-1M Flying Wing on August 15, 1942.

Two Northrop pilots under Moye's guidance were involved in fatal crashes, a result of aircraft design, not pilot error. Former

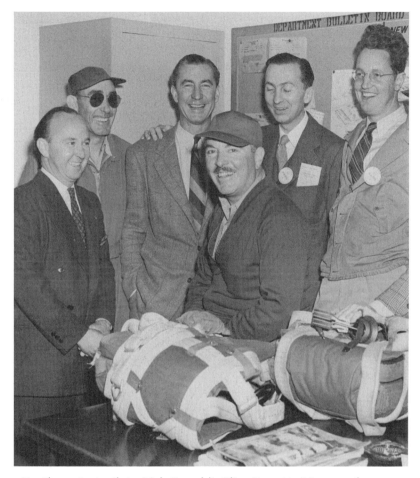

Northrop test pilots Dick Ranaldi, Slim Perrett, Moye, unknown, and newspaper reporters, Roy Zerman (Los Angeles Times) and Bill Payette (United Press). Katy Ranaldi photo.

war instructor and transport captain Harry Crosby flew gold out of Central America, designed and raced the smallest all-metal airplane, and worked as an aviation technical advisor and cameraman in Hollywood. In September 1945, a crash in the prototype XP-79B, a flying wing fighter-interceptor, ended Crosby's life. L. S. *Slim* Perrett, airline pilot and test pilot for Douglas and North American, died when he chose to stay with a Northrop *Pioneer* rather than parachute to safety shortly after the war ended. Had he jumped, the uncontrollable airplane would have crashed into a refinery. 38

Al Morgan, Moye's pal from Clover, came to work for Northrop in May 1940. He had resigned from the airlines in 1935, giving up that type of flying completely. His positions with Northrop were in management. Al eventually became Director of Customer Relations and then a Vice President of Marketing, retiring in 1970. He brought with him his experience from Clover Field, the airlines, and Douglas where he worked as a test pilot. In addition to his aviation resume, Morgan won a gold medal at the 1932 Olympics in the eight meter sailing event as a crew member on the *Angelita*. 39

Concurrent with the A-31 test flights, Moye participated in the P-61 *Black Widow* test program. In May 1942, Vance Breese flew the first flight in the night fighter prototype, the XP-61. Many more successful flights followed which incorporated necessary modifications and design changes. During August and September 1943, the Army Air Corps took delivery of thirteen service model YP-61s and one static test airframe. Moye alternated with Breese on the test flights of the XP-61 and YP-61. Moye also demonstrated the capabilities of the Black Widow for the press and military. Making a low pass, prop tips three feet off the ground, Moye shut down the engine on the spectator side, pulled straight up, stalled, leveled off, and performed one more spectacular pass. By VJ Day, August 14, 1945, Northrop had produced a total of 706 P-61 Black Widows.

Although not an aircraft designer, Moye formed a personal opinion about the process of developing a prototype.

"The designing of a new airplane is a painful process." Moye wrote in his autobiographical notes. "Each group in the engineering department is responsible for a particular portion of the completed product. The designing of each such portion calls for highly specialized knowledge as well as countless complex mathematical computations. In addition, each group is obliged to engage in continuous and often bitter battles with other groups to adapt its part to the whole while, at the same time, maintaining the integrity of the ultimate airplane.

"The aerodynamics group is primarily concerned with the

George Armistead and Dick Ranaldi listen while Boris Karloff illustrates an action for a movie scene. Katy Ranaldi photo.

outer configuration of the ship and woe unto any group that threatens those sacred external contours. The controls group, for various reasons, wants to run their cables from the cockpit to the control surfaces in as short a distance as possible. If, in their obstinacy, they poke a hole in a jealously cherished structural member and cause undisclosed damage of a critical nature during flight, the end result may be a disgraceful belly landing in a convenient cornfield.

"After years of blood, sweat, and tears, the experimental prototype is rolled out on the flight line. The engineering groups, having put their antagonisms aside for the occasion, gather about admiring the results of their hard work, slapping one another's backs and giving utterance to grudging compliments and considerable self-approbation. And there the airplane sits - to

271

them, in itself, a thing of beauty and a joy forever.

"And, in spite of their adulation, it continues to sit . . . lifeless. Totally useless . . . until the arrival of an individual they equate with a mechanic deprived of his grey matter or an upstart who knows little or nothing of the agonies endured in its creation, takes it aloft. An intruder climbs into the cockpit to snatch away their brain child; to take it up and experience for himself the achievements they had dreamed for it.

"The engineers are left relegated to the background. They are earthbound, never to taste the joy of mastering their creation, never to thrill to the sensitiveness of its responses nor guide it to its destiny." [40]

It is clear that Moye understood the integral steps necessary to create a prototype. The process depended upon explicit communication, precise calculations, and skilled fabrication. The test pilot held the responsibility of transitioning the prototype into a proficient flying machine. He undertook the challenge of converting unique flying characteristics into reliable and stable control factors. When Moye went aloft, he did so with forethought and respect for the entire process.

15

FINAL RECOGNITION

Near the end of World War II, politics took a heavy toll on Northrop Corporation. The company's government contract to build the XB-49, a flying wing jet bomber, was cancelled when Jack Northrop refused to meet the demands of Secretary of State Symington. Symington strongly urged Northrop to merge with Floyd Odlum's company, Consolidated Vultee. Odlum, a close friend of Symington, wanted to buy out Northrop in order to profit from guaranteed government funding. Jack knew that his shareholders would be cheated and the integrity of his company compromised if he consented to the merger. He would rather lose money than watch that happen. As a result, some Northrop employees lost confidence in the corporation's future and looked for opportunities elsewhere. Included among them were Gage Irving, LaMotte Cohu, Ted Coleman and Moye. Before Cohu departed, Cohu assigned Ted with the task of postwar planning for the company. Ted was responsible "with the problem of what we were to do with 12,000 war workers soon to become laid off employees . . . how could we keep Northrop alive?" 1

Ted, accompanied by assistant chief engineer Walt Cerny, met with several U.S. airline executives to promote future business.

Only Jack Frye, president of TWA, left them optimistic. Frye suggested that Northrop build a new trimotor transport for use in developing countries. Cohu and Ted spent the next two months in Brazil assessing Northrop's prospects. Neither local airlines nor the Brazilian government showed any interest in purchasing new planes when war surplus equipment was inexpensive and plentiful. Despite the absence of Brazilian interest and Coleman's opposition, Cohu encouraged Northrop to pursue development of a trimotor. The resulting *Pioneer* proved costly. No sales were made to any airlines.

During his stay in Brazil, Ted saw an opportunity to begin his own business. "The trip to Brazil played an important part in my decision to leave Northrop and organize my own airplane export company," Ted reflected in his book documenting the Northrop story. "Brazil seemed like a good place to start, and I had already received a wonderful introduction to this rapidly developing country." 2

Ted sold his shares in Northrop, moved his wife and two children to Rio, and brokered Fairchild 24s and Luscombs to Brazilian citizens. Ted also planned to import C-47s or DC-3s purchased from Glendale's used airplane dealer Charlie Babb. After a year, Ted realized additional profit could be made transporting factory merchandise into the rural areas of the country. He would need a financial partner, preferably one with flying experience to ferry aircraft from the states to Brazil, to implement his plan. His first choice was Moye. 3

Moye was not optimistic about Northrop's post-war prospects and liked the idea of being his own boss. According to his son, Moye had grown frustrated with Jack Northrop's inability to accept a test pilot's report that reflected an element that needed correcting. Jack became so unpleasant that Moye felt reticent to turn in a poor account of a flight. Inez presented no objections. For her, living in Brazil sounded very exciting. Moye accepted Ted's proposal, packed up his family, and moved to Rio, temporarily sharing hotel rooms with the Colemans in Ipanema.

While the Brazilian government processed the necessary paperwork for a franchise permit, Ted and Moye discovered the easiest and most profitable goods to deliver were finished clothing manufactured in Sao Paulo. They moved their families to Brazil's economic center, located homes, and made plans to obtain an airplane. They chose a Canadian-built Noorduyn Norseman. Designed by Robert B.C. Noorduyn, the Norseman was a single-engine monoplane that could accommodate pontoons, skis, or traditional landing gear and carry a pay load of approximately 1,500 pounds. Its STOL characteristics made it the ultimate bush plane. Moye purchased a Norseman in California and ferried the plane, accompanied by his mother, through Mexico, Central America, east over Columbia and Venezuela, and then southeast to Rio. Every time he landed for fuel and customs, the procedural red tape delayed his departure for days.

One year passed before Moye and Ted received their official permits and began delivering ready-made goods into remote regions. On the return trip, they brought harvested hardwoods to Rio and Sao Paulo. Moye and Ted's ultimate goal was transporting cattle. At the time, cattle were driven great distances to rail heads on the coast to be fattened and then slaughtered. With proper freight planes, the aerial merchandising of beef and other commodities promised a potential of better than one million dollars annually. 4

The opportunities seemed abundant for the two partners. As the business began to succeed, however, Moye's son developed chronic asthma. He was unable to adapt to the humidity and high temperatures of the tropical country. As a result, Moye sold his share of the business to Ted and returned to La Verne. Ted remained for one more year. Exasperated with the Brazilian's way of doing business and not seeing the profit he expected, Ted moved his family to San Francisco where he worked as an assistant treasurer for Standard Oil Company of California. In 1950, Ted formed his own company, the Coleman Engineering Corporation in Torrance. Two of the corporation's products were vote counting machines and bank surveillance cameras. Following his retirement in 1972, Ted became South Pasadena's City Manager and Chairman of the city's downtown revitalization committee. He passed away in 1980 at the age of 76. 5

Upon his return from Brazil in 1947, Moye established a machine shop in Pomona. The Moye W. Stephens Company filled orders for large manufacturing companies including Northrop. As orders increased, Moye placed ads in the *Los Angeles Times* for machinists. He also took the opportunity to design and fabricate a finely polished steel trigger guard for the Remington Model 270 rifle. *Rifleman Magazine* advertised his finished product. Gun collectors & Pac Myer Gun Works purchased the creative trigger. In 1954, with sales declining, Moye liquidated the business and bought Patrick Taber's Specifacts in Pasadena and began manufacturing precision measuring equipment including electronic comparators. The business provided him and Inez with a comfortable income. To increase his line of products, he traveled east to convince manufacturers on the Atlantic coast that they could profit substantially by having a west coast representative. Several companies signed on. Webber and Van Keuren Gauge were two. 6

Hughes Tool Company in Culver City purchased equipment from Moye to calculate exact tolerances for lasers. An engineering

Inez and Moye look over a sectional chart in front of their Bonanza Model H. Photo courtesy of Moye F. Stephens.

school hired Moye to assist with the development of a technically precise ruby laser. Fruehauf Trucking Company ordered measuring equipment. Van Keuren Gauge, who supplied gauges to companies such as Western Gear and Garrett Supply, became Moye's largest account. To expedite service to his clients and customers, Moye purchased a 1947 Model 35B Bonanza. Norm Larson, his former partner and distributor for Beechcraft at the time, helped Moye find just the right airplane, updated with laminated blades and a 225 hp Continental to replace the original 165 hp engine. Moye and Inez referred to the plane as "The Little Pot" in reference to the pot of money it took to pay for fuel and upkeep. The Model 35B was traded for a Model H six years later. In addition to calling on customers throughout California and Arizona, Moye flew east once a year to visit equipment manufacturers for updates. When Van Keuren died in 1965, an associate of the new owner replaced Moye despite the fact that he was the company's top salesman. Moye struggled to find meaningful work after that and made the decision to retire.

With the exception of a brief job working in a dress shop in Beverly Hills, Inez retired along with Moye. She had opened a dress shop, *Petite Paris,* in Claremont when Moye operated his machine shop. Inez provided high-end, sophisticated attire for the residents of the college town. She even designed her own line. The shop did well its first year but profits dwindled after that, forcing her to close her doors in mid-1950.

During their retirement, Moye and Inez led a quiet life in comparison to their social commitments in the 1930s and 1940s. The *Los Angeles Times'* social column often noted their attendance at an assortment of events around town — from the Sunday Nighter's Flagship Frolic at the Zebra Room to a southern themed party at the Beverly Hills Hotel. At an event honoring mutual friends at the Ambassador Hotel, Moye and Inez sat back-to-back with the former Mrs. Moye Stephens. Now, Inez occasionally volunteered for the Assistance League of Pomona and Moye worked on his autobiography. He remained in contact with the early Maddux/TAT pilots including Ben Hoy, Gordon *Parky* Parkinson, Al Morgan, and Dick Ranaldi. He may not have seen them as frequently as he wished but he never forgot to call them on New Year's Day. 7

Moye's closet friend, Dick Ranaldi, remained an active pilot until his death. In June 1931, he took a position with Century Pacific Lines. The airline used Stinson trimotors to carry passengers between San Diego, Los Angeles, and San Francisco. When Century went out of business, Dick flew passenger hops, towed signs, did movie work, and filled in as an airline captain in Ford trimotors. In April 1932, he flew for Metro-Golden-Mayer Studios and United Air Service. Lineas Aereas Occidentales hired Dick to fly the Los Angeles to Mazatlan route in October 1934. Three months later, he quit and an assortment of flying jobs followed. In 1935, he added stunt flying in *Tailspin Tommy in the Great Air Mystery*, a twelve chapter serial based on Hal Forest's comic strip, to his movie credits. He had previously flown in *Hell's Angels, Air Circus, Dawn Patrol*, and *Night Flight*.

Dick's aviation career took an interesting turn in September 1935. Philip P. Whitmarsh hired him to pilot a Lockheed *Vega* 5C from Manila to Nairobi (Kenya) in order to explore a shorter route to Africa than that of Royal Dutch Airlines. Whitmarsh, along with

Dick flew commercially to east Africa to determine suitable landing areas for Whitmarsh. Photo courtesy of Katy Ranaldi.

his wife and a radio operator, planned to accompany the aerial expedition. The trip was postponed, however, when a test flight revealed problems with the *Vega*'s motor.   Dick returned to California to secure a larger motor with a controllable prop and larger wheels suitable for muddy conditions. No information exists of the expedition after that. A fact that remains curious is the occupation that Dick listed on the San Francisco to Manila steamship log – that of mining engineer. 8

In June 1936, Dick completed Grand Central's two-month course in blind flying in order to qualify for a captain's position with Grand Canyon Airlines. He flew a Ford trimotor between Canyon Airport and Boulder until the end of 1937 when he went to work for Hearst Publications. Living in a cottage on the San Simeon pier, he had a short distance to travel to the airport up the hill. He flew the Hearst family and associates between San Simeon and Burbank in a Vultee G5. One year later, Dick was flying for C.H. *Pete* Jackson Jr. who amassed a sizable fortune through real estate investments, ranching, and horse breeding. Dick had flown a Lockheed *Vega* for Jackson in the late 1920s. Now, he piloted a Lockheed Lodestar between Santa Barbara and the Jackson's ranch north of Elko, Nevada.

Dick returned to work for the Jackson family after his employment with Northrop ended. A Howard 500 had replaced the Lodestar. Dick thoroughly enjoyed flying the pressurized, 350 mph executive airplane.   John Ferguson served as Dick's copilot and mechanic on both the Lodestar and Howard. In the summer of 1967, they flew the Howard to San Antonio, Texas for a maintenance check. The flight went well but Dick began displaying symptoms of a heart condition. On September 23, he passed away from a heart attack in the family's Santa Barbara home. He was 52 years old. When Moye learned of Dick's death, he wept. He would miss his little friend. 9

Although Moye enjoyed living quietly on the La Verne ranch, Inez wanted to move to Ensenada. She clung to her memories of the 1930s, thinking that she could still hobnob with Ensenada's 'first class citizens' but the upper class she and Moye would encounter belonged to another generation. When Mexican

President Cardenas outlawed gambling casinos in 1935, the elegant hotels closed for lack of business. Migration from the interior of Mexico and flourishing fish canneries contributed to the rapid growth of Ensenada's population, from 5,000 in 1930 to 100,000 in 1986. The small seaside town they remembered had disappeared. The only familiar site that remained was Hussong's, operated by Ricardo, the founder's grandson. 10

Inez hoped they could find an inexpensive beach house that included maid service. Instead, she and Moye settled for a small house inland, amid rows and rows of identical homes. They moved their belongings from the La Verne ranch to Ensenada in 1986. The experience of life in Mexico was far from what Inez and Moye imagined. They waited months to have all their utilities operating smoothly. Weekly trips were made to the United States to access their bank account and purchase necessities not available in Ensenada. The Campaneros de Baja Norte, a group of Americans living in Ensenada and nearby towns, constituted most of their social life. Moye and Inez looked forward to attending the club's weekly luncheons, dancing, and card games.

In 1992, Moye became extremely ill. Transported by helicopter to a San Diego hospital, doctors discovered a brain aneurism. Moye refused surgery and returned to Ensenada. By 1995, an earlier hip injury suffered by Inez and her mental state seriously concerned the family as did Moye's aneurism, an inevitable time bomb. Their son packed up his parents' belongings in June of that year and brought them home to La Verne. He also convinced his father to have surgery to repair the aneurism. During the operation, the physician discovered that cancer had spread throughout Moye's body. Nothing more could be done. Moye W. Stephens passed away December 12, 1995, just two months short of his 90th birthday. Inez followed six months later, on June 30, 1996. Their son scattered his parent's ashes in the sky over the Pacific, a perfect place for two individuals who loved flying.

For his accomplishments, Moye received many prestigious rewards. Not one to seek notoriety, he remained humble as his colleagues acknowledged his significant contributions to aviation.

FINAL RECOGNITION

The first came in 1942. The Los Angeles Chamber of Commerce presented him with the Award of Distinguished Service in the field of foreign trade in connection with his Australia-New Zealand mission for Lockheed. Six years later, in 1948, John Northrop recognized Moye's invaluable contributions with a lifetime membership in the Flying Wing Club "as one of a small group of distinguished pilots who have participated in the historical development and pioneered in the public acceptance of this revolutionary and highly efficient type of aircraft." [11]

Several years retired, Moye became a member of the OX5 Aviation Pioneers, an international organization founded in 1955. Among other educational and scientific purposes, the organization perpetuates the memory of pioneer airmen and their great sacrifices, their accomplishments and contributions to the development of civil aviation and to do honor to all who pioneered in aviation, especially to the thousands of pilots who learned to fly and operationally flew aircraft powered by the OX5 engine; and persons who owned, were associated with, or who participated in the design, construction and maintenance of OX5 powered aircraft prior to December 31, 1940. Moye received his membership in 1982. He would be inducted into the OX5 Aviation Pioneers Hall of Fame at the San Diego Aerospace Museum seven years later. [12]

In 1983, the Society of Experimental Test Pilots selected Moye to become an Honorary Fellow of the Society. An extremely prestigious award from his peers, the recognition represented his outstanding contributions to test flight as an experimental test pilot and an individual who had achieved distinction in the aerospace field. Don Downie, author, pilot, and photographer, submitted Moye's name in 1972. When the Society chose not to select him, Downie resubmitted Moye's name every year after that. Prominent test pilots Fitz Fulton and Tony Levier joined Downie's efforts in 1982. They both spoke highly of Moye's experience and contributions. And finally, on May 25, 1983, Moye received his selection letter from T. D. Benefield, president of the Society. Moye wrote the following response.

"The decision of your Board of Directors to add my name to the illustrious list of your Honorary Fellows is probably as great a

In 1983, the Society of Experimental Test Pilots awarded Moye's outstanding contributions to test flight by selecting him to become an Honorary Fellow of the Society. The award is presented by SETP President T. D. Benefield. Photo courtesy of the Society of Experimental Test Pilots.

distinction as I will receive in my lifetime. It is deeply appreciated. Needless to say, I will be delighted to attend the Awards Banquet to accept the Honor." 13

On October 1, 1983, the Beverly Hilton set the backdrop for the Society's annual symposium and banquet. The Society began in September 1955 near Edwards Air Force Base. From a meager group of six civilian test pilots, an internationally recognized organization emerged. The tradition of the banquet began in

FINAL RECOGNITION

October 1957. The warm welcome given Moye and Inez overwhelmed them.

"Inez and I were truly impressed with the Awards Banquet." he wrote to Clyde Good, Executive Director of the Society. "As I told Joe Jordan, it made up many times over for the necessity of having to wear a black tie. We particularly want to thank you for having taken us under your wing upon our arrival. It helped immensely in easing us through the 'new boy in school' feeling." 14

Moye joined a select few of eminent members, past and present, in the field of aviation. Among them were his flying instructor Eddie Bellande, Vance Breese, Jacqueline Cochran, General James H. Doolittle, Howard Hughes, Charles A. Lindbergh, Igor Sikorsky, and Roscoe Turner. Former TWA pilots made the list too – Larry Fritz, Ben Howard, and Waldo Waterman.

Tony Levier summed up Moye's aviation career in his letter which nominated Moye as an Honorary Fellow.

"The 1930s were indeed one of the harshest periods in aviation history. Only those believing in aviation and the 'sheer guts' to hang in there went on to make their mark in aviation.

"Moye Stephens was just such a man and became recognized as being one of the leading pilots in the southwest United States. This resulted in his services being sought by the aircraft manufacturers. On leave from his own company, Pacific Aircraft Sales, Moye was hired by Lockheed and sent to Australia and New Zealand to demonstrate and instruct pilots on the new Model 10 Electra transport.

"As the 1930s drew to a close, war clouds in Europe became the main topic and in August of 1939 WWII started. The United States, woefully lacking in military preparedness started scrambling to catch-up. It was at this juncture point in American aviation history that Moye Stephens probably made his greatest contribution. He was a prime innovator and organizer of the Northrop Corporation as we know it today.

"I have known Moye for about fifty years. I regard him as one of the finest gentlemen I have had the pleasure of knowing. He did his test flying with great skill and dispatch, with little or no fanfare. .." 15

Of all Moye's accomplishments, the *Flying Carpet* flight remained the most important for him. He shared his stories with pride and a great sense of accomplishment. The trip's ultimate triumph had depended upon his skills as a pilot, navigator, and overseer. As a test pilot, his superior skills created productive test programs designed by others. He could not claim full responsibility for their outcome, be it success or failure. The successful completion of the round-the-world flight had been Moye's responsibility and his alone.

Moye wondered when he began his autobiography, where all those lazy days of summer and the freedom of blue skies had gone. What happened to the time when a pilot could perform a string of wing overs and loops without permission?

Although he abhorred government regulations, he promoted safety in the air. As management ignored the human factor of flying, Moye joined with others to protect pilots' rights.

Not a man who found satisfaction dreaming of success, Moye trusted his instincts and created his own opportunities. Straightforward and sincere, he respected his fellow pilots and loved his friends, and family.

Moye started flying as a young boy, electrified by a fifteen minute flight; he ended his career as a seasoned veteran. Having been part of aviation's transformation, from WWI wood and linen airplanes to flying wings, humbled him.

Foremost, Moye loved to fly.

APPENDIX

T.A.T. - MADDUX AIR LINES

BOOK OF RULES

General Rules

2.01 Employees whose duties are prescribed by these rules must provide themselves with a copy.

2.02 Employees whose duties are in any way affected by the scheduled time of airplanes must have a copy of the current schedules with them while on duty.

2.03 Employees must be conversant with and obey the rules and special instructions. If in doubt as to their meaning they must apply to proper authority for an explanation.

2.04 Employees may be examined from time to time on the rules and special instructions.

2.05 Persons employed in connection with the operation of airplanes are subject to the rules and general instructions.

2.06 Employees must render every assistance in their power, in carrying out rules and general instructions and must report to the proper official any violation thereof.

2.07 Accidents, failure of gasoline or oil supply, defects in the airplane, or any unusual conditions which may affect the movements of airplanes on regular or special scheduled must be promptly reported to the Operations Manager by teletype, commercial telegraph or telephone.

2.08 Accident reports shall be made to the Operations Manager of the Division over which the flight is being made.

2.09 The use of intoxicants by employees while on duty is prohibited. Their use, or the frequenting of places where they are sold, is sufficient cause for dismissal.

2.10 The use of tobacco by employees while on duty in or about passenger or loading stations or on airplanes is prohibited.

2.11 Smoking or the carrying of lighted cigars, cigarettes, etc., in hangars is prohibited. When not on duty, employees shall confine their smoking to locations officially designated.

2.12 Employees on duty must wear the prescribed insignia and uniform and be neat in their appearance.

2.13 Employees and others authorized to transact business at stations or on or about airplanes must be courteous, orderly, and avoid annoyance to patrons.

2.14 Employees while on duty connected with airplanes on any division or sub-division are under the authority and must conform to the orders of the officers of that Division.

2.15 All employees shall thoroughly acquaint themselves with the Aviation Laws of the Department of Commerce and of the various States in which they may be working.

APPENDIX

2.15A Employees must exercise care to avoid injury to themselves or others by observing the condition of equipment and the tools which they use in performing their duties and when found defective will, if practical, put them in safe condition, reporting defects to the proper authority.

2.16 Employees must inform themselves as to the condition of all permanent and emergency fields within the prescribed course over which the airplanes will fly, within their division. They must also observe and obey all airport rules.

2.17 Routine contact with the Press will be maintained by representatives of the traffic department in each city served by TAT-MADDUX AIR LINES. Company statements will be released to the Press only through these authorized representatives. Other employees are not permitted to give out information concerning the company without specific authority from the publicity department.

2.17A Representatives of the Press should be extended every possible courtesy consistent with this rule, however.

2.17B In the event of an accident to a TAT-MADDUX plane courtesy to the Press is secondary only to care of injured passengers or personnel. The cause of the accident, if positively known, should be made available to the Press with as full information as can be obtained. Under no circumstances, however, will TAT-MADDUX representatives be permitted to advance theories or guesses on the probable cause of an accident.

2.17C Although photographs of damaged planes are not desired in the public prints, bona fide Press photographers should be permitted to take pictures if they insist.

General Definitions

CAPTAIN; The employee in charge of and responsible for an airplane in flight. (This responsibility corresponds to that of a Master of a ship at sea.)

MATE: The employee who is responsible for the collection of tickets and comfort of passengers on airplane during flight.

REGULAR AIRPLANE: An airplane authorized by a time table schedule.

SECTION: One of two or more airplanes running on the same schedule, properly marked.

EXTRA AIRPLANE: An airplane not authorized by a time table schedule, but properly authorized for special service.

TIME TABLE: The authority for the operation of regular airplanes over specified routes subject to the rules.

SCHEDULE: That part of a time table which prescribes the direction, route number, and movement of a regular airplane.

STATION OR AIRPORT: A place designated on the time table by name, at which an airplane may stop for passengers, mail, and Express.

FLYING CARPETS, FLYING WINGS

OPERATION RULES
Standard Time

4.01 United States Eastern Standard Time, United States Central Standard Time, United States Mountain Standard Time, and United States Pacific Standard Time, as specified on time tables, is the Standard Time.

4.02 The government radio time signal should be checked each day at 12:00 noon, Eastern Standard Time, by the Radio Ground Station operators for the purpose of checking standard clocks over the route.

4.03 Captains, Mates, and other employees connected with airplane operation must use reliable watches.

4.04 Captains and Mates must, before starting a trip, compare their watches with a clock designated by time table as a standard clock and adjust them to show correct time.

Time Tables

4.05 Each time table, from the moment it takes effect, supersedes the preceding time table, and its schedules take effect on any division or section at the leaving time at their initial station or airport on such division or section.

4.06 Schedules on each division or section date from their initial stations or airports on such division or section.

4.07 Where two times are shown on a time table for an airplane at any station or airport, the one is arriving time and the other leaving time.

4.08 Where an airplane is scheduled to stop at a regular station or airport, and the airplane is filled to carrying capacity, with no passengers to be discharged; no fuel or oil required, can, by proper order to the Captain pass such station or airport. The stop can be annulled by order from the Operations Manager to the Captain and the Passenger Agent.

4.09 The following letters when placed before the figures of the schedule indicate:

    s – regular stop
    f – stop on order to receive or discharge passengers
    e – stop on order to pick up or discharge passengers eastbound
    w – stop on order to pick up or discharge passengers westbound

Time tables may provide additional letters to indicate specific instructions.

Signals

4.10 Employees whose duties may require them to give signals to airplanes must provide themselves with the proper appliances; keep them in good order and ready for immediate use.

APPENDIX

4.11 Flags of the prescribed color and dimensions must be used by day, and lights of the prescribed color and kind by night. Flag signals for day service shall be a piece of white or yellow canvas 4 ft. wide and 20 ft. long. Such flags should always be provided in duplicate. Red fusees (flares) shall be used a signals at night.

Airplane Signals

4.12 Between one half hour after sunset and one half hour before sunrise airplanes must display the lights on wings and tail as prescribed by the Department of Commerce.

4.13 The landing lights on an airplane may be displayed between sundown and sunrise:

    (a) When landing on a field designated in the time table as a regular or flag stop.

    (b) When landing on any field in emergency.

    (c) To indicate by a prescribed number of flashes certain information to the field.

Field Signals

4.14 Permanent or fixed signals at airports are those signals or lights that have been prescribed and fixed to indicate:

    1 – obstacles

    2 – boundary lines

    3 – runways

    4 – wind direction indicators

4.15 Hand or flag signals are those signals or lights that are used, when required to convey information to Captains during the flight of an airplane. White or bright yellow day flag signals to apply, color to be determined by background, in figures or positions prescribed by Division Operations Manager.

4.16 In night flying, signals are given by the use of red fusees displayed in a fixed location.

4.17 ONE OR TWO RED FUSEE, as prescribed by Division Operation Manager indicates to the Captain that he must land in the field where such signal is displayed.

4.19 If at any time the field flood lights are displayed and are not desired by the Captain in making a landing, the Captain shall flash one landing light repeatedly until flood light is extinguished.

4.20 If field flood lights are not displayed, but are desired by the Captain in making a landing, the Captain shall flash one landing light repeatedly until flood light is turned on.

Airplane Movements

4.21 An airplane must not leave a station or airport before scheduled time unless authorized.

4.22 An airplane must not start until the proper signal or order is given to the Captain.

4.23 All airplanes must carry their proper marking to indicate their route, the same to be displayed at all points where airplanes stop to receive or discharge passengers.

4.24 Where airplanes of opposing traffic directions meet, at the same airport at approximately the same time, the first airplane arriving shall take precedence over the other airplane, unless special orders have been issued by the Operations Manager.

4.25 All airplanes must stop at points scheduled on the time table unless orders have been given by the Operations Manager to pass a regular scheduled stop.

4.26 Before an airplane leaves a station or airport, all orders and weather reports must be placed in the hands of the Captain and receipt therefore taken for same.

4.27 Two or more sections of a route may be run on the same schedule. Each section has equal time table authority.   Each section should be provided with proper markings to show route and section thereof.

4.28 Extra airplanes must not be run without orders governing their movement.

4.29 The departure time of an airplane from a terminal shall be reported to each station along the route over which airplane is scheduled to fly and stop.

4.30 The arrival and departure time of an airplane at any station shall be reported to the office of the Operations Manager.

4.31 The arrival time of an airplane at any station shall be reported to the station from which the airplane left.

4.32 The radio ground stations operator shall obtain from the Captain of any airplane, or the Field Manager, the arrival and departure time at any station in his assigned area, and keep record thereof.

Airplane Orders

4.33 Orders for the movement of extra or special airplanes will be issued by authority and over the signature of the Operations Manager. They must be brief and only contain information essential to such movements.

4.34 Airplane orders must be addressed to those who are to execute them, naming the place at which each is to receive a copy.

4.35 Orders addressed to Field Managers regarding movement of airplanes must be respected by Captains or other employees

4.36 Orders for annulment of regular scheduled stops shall be made when there are no passengers to discharge; no passengers to load and when it is not necessary to add fuel or oil to the airplane.

4.37 Orders for the annulment of regular scheduled stops shall be sent to the Captains and to the Field Managers at the stations where annulment is effective.

4.38 Orders for the annulment of regular scheduled stops will be issued by the authority of and over the signature of the Operations Manager.

4.39 Orders regarding the movement of airplanes must be acknowledged by the office receiving them.

4.40 The acknowledgment of an order should give the number of the order, number of the plane and the route number.

4.41 When an order is put out to an airplane for special stop or annulment, a copy of the order should be given to the radio ground station controlling the section over which the airplane is flying, so that a further check can be made with the Captain that the order has been received and understood.

FLYING RULES

5.01 A tabulated report shall be made during the flight of an airplane, showing all inoperative or defective parts that have come to notice.

5.02 If, in the opinion of the Captain, a noticed defect during the flight may create an unfavorable fling condition, he should take immediate action to bring the airplane to the ground.

5.03 If, in the opinion of the Captain, a noticed defect during the flight will not impair the flight, he may continue the flight to the next destined stop and have the noticed defect repaired before taking off for the next distant station or airport.

5.04 In the event of the failure of one motor on an airplane, the Captain should be governed by the following:

    (a) Safety of passengers

    (b) If possible, proceed to the nearest authorized field.

5.05 A Captain shall not hesitate to land or turn back when dangerous flying conditions are encountered.

5.06 It is better that an airplane be brought to the ground, even though damage to it may result, than fly blindly through storm conditions that may result in a tragedy by crashing out of control.

5.07 Airplanes must not be loaded in excess of the gross load allowed by the Department of Commerce for each airplane so licensed. The Captain shall be responsible for any infringement of the licensed allowable gross loading.

5.08 After the loading of passengers, and signal has been given for release of the airplane, the Captain will taxi the airplane to the runway to be used for take-off. Before take-off the Captain will head plane downwind and each motor will be given a full throttle test, also each switch will be tried. Failure of the motors or instruments to function properly makes it compulsory that the airplane shall be returned to the hangar. This test also includes the brakes and the failure of either brake to function properly requires that the airplane shall return to the hangar.

5.09 In every case the full length of a runway, or where there is no runway, the full length of the field shall always be used in a take-off.

5.10 Only normal take-offs shall be made. On smooth runways, the tail may be brought up and the airplane held on the runway until the air speed is ten to fifteen miles above the flying speed. The airplane shall then be gently pulled off the ground and continued in a normal climb with the air speed always at least 10 to fifteen miles above the flying speed. On fields without runways, where the surface is not hard and smooth, the airplane need not be held on the ground after flying speed has been attained.

5.11 The climb from take-off shall be gradual with a constant air speed or not less than 15 mph above flying speed. Zooms and sharp or uneven climbs are strictly prohibited.

5.12 Except in case of actual emergency, or where surrounding terrain demands, climbs shall not be made at full throttle. Under normal conditions of take-off de-acceleration of the motors shall begin when the airplane has reached an altitude of 300 feet.

5.13 Climbs to altitude shall be made very gradually. The full distance from the point of take-off to the point where the maximum altitude is required should be used to gain that altitude.

5.14 Under normal conditions, a minimum altitude of 500 feet shall be attained before commencing a turn.

5.15 Airplanes shall not be banked in excess of 40 degrees and care shall be taken that all turns be perfect. "Bubble in Center"

5.16 Motors shall be carefully synchronized for cruising speed and by maximum economy. The technical instructions issued by the Mechanical department limiting cruising rpm and describing the use of the mixture control shall be rigidly observed.

5.17 Upon approaching a landing point the airplane shall be brought down from altitude in a gradual power glide, at 1400 rpm. Weather conditions permitting altitude shall not be lost at a rate in excess of 500 feet per minute.

5.18 When approaching a landing point and before the motors are throttled, the Captain shall test each engine switch.

APPENDIX

5.19 Before commencing a glide the Captain shall see that the mixture controls are closed, the motors shall be throttled gradually, and under no conditions other than in an emergency, shall the throttles be completely closed when approaching to a landing until the airplane is over the last obstruction and within dead stick gliding distance of the field.

5.20 Steep banked spirals shall not be made except in cast of emergency when such maneuver is absolutely necessary in order that the Captain may maintain ground contact while descending through a hole in the clouds.

5.21 Skids or slips shall not be made except in case of emergency landing or in landing cross-wind when a slip or skid may be necessary to compensate for the drift. When skids or slips are necessary in affecting cross-wind landings they shall be made smoothly. Captains shall not use the rudder sharply in the execution of a skid or slip, nor shall they fish tail to kill their speed.

5.22 Brakes shall not be used immediately on landing to shorten the normal roll of the airplane. The airplane should be allowed to de-accelerate without the use of brakes until the speed has decreased to 20 mph. This procedure may be deviated from when necessary to prevent ground looping on a cross-wind landing or in actual emergency.

5.23 No flying shall be carried on during the day at an altitude of less than 500 feet, or at night at an altitude of less than 1,000 feet, except in landing or taking off.

5.24 No flying shall be carried on below clouds by day when the visibility is less than three miles from the airplane.

5.25 No flying shall be carried on below clouds by day when the visibility is less than one mile from airplane. When flying below clouds either objects or lights must be visible at all times.

5.26 No flying shall be carried on above clouds at an altitude which cannot be maintained with one motor stopped. No flying above clouds shall be carried on unless the port of destination or an intermediate field is known to be clear or only partly overcast and there is reliable information that it will not become completely overcast before the arrival of the airplane.

5.27 No blind flying shall be carried on unless the port of destination or an intermediate landing field is known to be clear or only partly overcast, and there is reliable information that it will not become completely overcast before the arrival of the airplane. Blind flying shall not be carried on except in climbing through fog or a stratus cloud layer. Blind flying shall not be attempted in storms of any kind. The climbing through fog or a stratus cloud layer the Captain shall allow for a course error of 30 degrees to either side of his course. There must be no obstacles higher than the altitude of the airplane at the start of blind flying in the area included in this angle and within a distance of twice the cruising range of the plane during the period of blind flying.

5.28 The only exception to these rules shall be in an emergency when it is not possible for the Captain to reach any suitable landing field without their violation

GENERAL ORDERS

6.01 In addition to the rules and regulations, there will issued general orders and notices concerning specific matters. It shall be the duty of employees to acquaint themselves with all general orders and notices posted on the Bulletin Boards. Captains and Mates shall sign for all general orders governing airplane movements and operations.

MISCELLANEOUS RULES

7.01 The rules and regulations issued by the Department of Commerce shall be strictly observed.

7.02 Only properly authorized and licensed employees will be permitted in the cockpit of airplanes while in flight unless special permission is given by Manager of Operations to licensed persons.

7.03 Captains and Mates are prohibited from flying airplanes which have not been approved by the Department of Commerce. They are also prohibited from flying for hire any airplane not owned or controlled by this Company.

7.04 Airplanes shall not be moved under their own power, unless a Captain, Mate or properly licensed person is in the cockpit.

7.05 Airplane engines must not be supplied with fuel and/or oil while the engine is running.

7.06 When a landing is made on a company field or any other field, and such landing is not a scheduled stop, the Captain will report immediately to the Field Manager and check out. On a company field where a release is required, such release shall be secured through the Field Manager.

7.07 In the event that it is necessary to ground an airplane, either on account of bad weather or mechanical defect, at other than a company airport, Captain of the ship will be governed by the same rules applying to station passenger agents for forwarding of passengers on interrupted flights and when passengers elect to stay with the ship, will secure automobile transportation and conduct passengers to a hotel or other suitable place, and in cases where passengers prefer to proceed by rail, will see that Mate secures rail and Pullman transportation for them and forwards them as expeditiously as possible, reporting manner of handling to nearest traffic representative.

7.08 Captains and Mates shall report at designated place, one half hour before the scheduled time for the departure of airplanes.

APPENDIX

7.09 VISION: Employees whose vision requires the use of glasses, must, while on duty, have the proper glasses. For distant vision two pair of spectacles are required. Where glasses are required for both distant vision and reading, two pairs of distant and one pair of reading glasses or two pair of bifocal spectacles should be provided.

7.10 Designated uniformed employees shall wear the prescribed uniform and color with the proper insignia. The uniform must be neat in appearance, and when the coat is worn it must be buttoned.

7.11 Door of airplanes: Upon arrival at a station the door of an airplane shall not be opened until the airplane comes to a complete stop, and the wheels are properly blocked, or brakes set.

7.12 No passenger shall be permitted to leave the airplane while the engines are running unless proper protection has been provided in the form of a canopy or other suitable precaution has been taken.

7.13 Employees must not permit the throwing of anything from a moving airplane.

7.14 Disarrangement of service: When airplane service is disarranged, the Passenger Agent should announce to the passengers that there will be a delay in the leaving time or that the airplane schedule has been canceled.

7.15 Baggage trucks, loading platforms, or airplane wheel blocks, when not in use, must be placed to avoid inconvenience to patrons and unsightly appearance.

7.16 When reporting cases of personal injury, as is possible should be given. The time, place, and manner in which accident occurred, together with any other information must be given promptly by telegraph or telephone to Operations Manger, Traffic Manager, and Secretary of Company.

7.17 Employees are required to report promptly, all accidents to passengers, which may come to their notice; the report to include the initial point and destination of the passenger and kind of transportation.

7.18 All cases of personal injury should be reported to the Operations Manager and, if surgical service was rendered, the name of the attending surgeon must be given. The standard form provided by the Company shall be used in making accident reports.

7.19 At stations or airports the employee who is loading the passengers should announce the route of the airplane and the name of the next station stop.

7.20 Blind, or other persons who are not capable of traveling alone will not be carried on an airplane, unless accompanied by a caretaker.

7.21 Any person under the influence of intoxicants or otherwise incapacitated will not be carried on an airplane.

7.22 If, during the flight of an airplane, any person should become intoxicated, they shall be ejected at the next station or airport. When ejection is necessary, the Captain shall make complete report to the Operations Manager.

7.23 Contagious and Infectious Diseases: Persons suffering from Smallpox, Asiatic Cholera, Yellow Fever, Bubonic Plague, Diphtheria, Scarlet Fever, Typhus Fever or other contagious diseases will not be accepted for transportation.

7.24 No officer or employee shall be absent from duty without permission from the proper authority.

7.25 Every precaution must be exercised for the sake of SAFETY. Employees when in the vicinity of an airplane on the ground, the engines of which are running, shall always keep the revolving propellers in mind.

GENERAL REGULATIONS FOR EMPLOYERS
Operations Manager

8.01 The Operations Manager of a Division shall report to and receive his instructions from the President-General Manager or other designated official.

8.02 He shall be responsible for the operation and movement of all airplanes over his division

8.03 It shall be his duty to see that the airplanes are properly maintained.

8.04 He shall be responsible for all expenses incurred in connection with the operation of his division, and for the discipline of the forces engaged therein.

Chief Engineer

8.05 The Chief Engineer shall report to and receive his instructions from the Operations Manager. He is responsible for the proper and economical management of mechanical operations, hangars, heating and power plants, and for the discipline, and proper discharge of duties of persons employed therein; for the economical use of materials, fuel, oil and for keeping the proper record of those supplied; for airplanes and other vehicles being in proper condition for efficient service, and for the proper maintenance of tools and machinery in his charge.

8.06 He must adhere to the authorized standards in construction and repairs.

8.07 He must not permit work to be done in the shops outside of regular assigned hours of duty, unless absolutely necessary, not permit lights in the shop or hangars after working hours, except those required by the watchman on duty and must not allow visitors in the shops nor hangars without permits, nor allow them to converse or interfere with the workmen.

8.08 He must consult and advise with the Captains and Mates respecting the economical performance of the airplane engines and their mechanical requirements and efficiency.

Service Foreman

8.09 The Service Foreman shall report to and receive instructions from the Chief Engineer. He has charge of the hangar and the workmen employed therein. It is his duty to see that the hangar is kept clean and in good order; that the workmen perform their duties properly' that the supplies are economically used' that the airplanes are prepared for service promptly and are in good working order and properly equipped. He is responsible for the detailed mechanical inspection of all airplanes at the end of each trip. An Assistant Service Foreman, in the duties assigned him has the same authority as the Service Foreman.

Foreman – Engine Overhaul

8.10 The Foreman of Engine Overhaul shall report to and receive instructions from the Chief Engineer or Service Foreman. He has charge of all airplane engine overhauls. It is his duty to see that the workmen perform their duties properly, and that the supplies are economically used; that the engines are properly inspected after overhaul.

8.11   He must record all piece part changes, and also record the necessity for the change. He is responsible for the continuity of the engine numbers.

Chief Pilot

8.12 The Chief Pilot shall report to and receive instructions for the Operations Manager.

8.13 He is responsible for the approval and "Checking-" of Mates being promoted to reserve pilots.

8.14 He is responsible for the testing of new or modified airplanes and instruments.

8.15 He will inspect and make recommendations regarding emergency fields and will perform other special duties as may be assigned.

8.16 He will be assigned as Captain when not performing other duties and when performing duties of a Captain shall be subject to the same rules and regulations.

Captain

8.17 The Captain reports to and receives instructions from the Operations Manager or designated officer.

8.18 He must inspect the airplane and see that the sanitary conditions are correct before departure at all times.

8.19 He must be familiar with the rules of the Department of Commerce governing aviation.

8.20 He must obey the rules and regulations of the Department of Commerce.

8.21 He must be familiar with and obey special rules and regulations governing an "Airport" permanently or temporarily used by this Company.

8.22 He must be familiar with and obey rules and regulations or general orders issued from time to time regarding the general operations of airplane service.

8.22A He must keep an accurate record of his solo flying time in a log book, and the entries must be certified. He must present his log book on the first day of each month to the Operations Manager for certification.

8.23 He is responsible for the airplane under his command and for the observance of the Department of Commerce and Company rules governing airplanes in flight.

8.24 He must see that the rules prohibiting smoking on the airplane are enforced; see that proper report is made regarding the condition of the airplane on each trip, and must report any misconduct or neglect of duty.

8.25 He must report for duty at the appointed time and place, and secure the following information:

      (a) The weather condition at the destined terminal.

      (b) The weather condition along the route.

      (c) Information regarding anticipated weather changes.

      (d) Wind velocity for various altitudes.

8.26 He must have a reliable watch and a copy of the time table or airplane schedules' compare time before starting and, if necessary adjust his watch to show correct time; examine the bulletin board when reporting for duty, and compare time with the Mate or co-pilot before departure of the airplane.

8.26A He will be responsible that the Mate is familiar with, and carries out his duties, while on the plane.

8.27 He must exercise caution and good judgment in take-off, landing, and taxiing, so as to avoid disturbance to passengers and injury to passengers or damage to airplane.

8.28 He must keep in contact with the assigned radio ground station, at regular stated intervals, reporting his position weather in which he is flying; make inquiry regarding weather; receive or give other information required.

8.29 He must not permit any person to occupy the cockpit or handle the airplane unless that person is duly authorized and licensed.

8.30 He must not leave the airplane unprotected while on the ground and the engines running.

8.31 He must not use intoxicating liquor, cocaine, or other habit forming drugs, while off or on duty. Their use will be sufficient cause for immediate dismissal from the service.

8.32 He just sign for all weather reports and orders governing special airplane movements.

Mates or Co-pilots

8.33 The Mate reports to and receives his instructions from the Chief Engineer or designated official.

8.34 He must be familiar at all times with the rules or the Department of Commerce governing aviation. He must obey the rules and regulations of the Department of Commerce governing air traffic.

8.35 He must be familiar with and obey special rules and regulations governing any "airport" used by this Company.

8.36 He must be familiar with and obey rules and regulations or general orders issued from time to time regarding the general operations of airplane service.

8.37 The Mates shall report for duty at the appointed time and place, examine the Bulletin Board, have a reliable watch, and compare time with the Captain of the plane.

8.37A He shall obey the orders of the Captain while on the airplane or during flights.

8.38 He must not leave the airplane unprotected while the plane is on the ground and the engines running.

8.39 He shall act as Courier while the airplane is in flight, attend courteously to the comforts and wants of the passengers, check and collect tickets from passengers in flight, prohibit smoking or the use of any intoxicating liquors on the plane, explain to passengers how to adjust the seats, point out and explain to passengers the places of interest along the route, assist passengers in getting on and off the airplane, oversee and assist in the loading and unloading of baggage.

8.39A Before airplane leaves hangar to load passengers at a terminal station prior to the start of a flight, the Mate will see that the airplane is properly stocked with all necessary passengers' supplies. In the event that airplane is not properly stocked, Mate will secure necessary supplies from Supply Department.

8.39B In addition to regular airplane supplies, the mate will at all times carry with him a supply of air-sickness remedies. While in flight the mate will keep a careful watch on all passengers, and at first sign of anyone becoming ill, shall attempt to render passenger every possible assistance.

8.39C At intermediate field stops Mate will notify Field Manager of any airplane supplies that he might require to replenish his stock.

8.40 It shall be the duty of the mate to be the last one aboard the airplane and to securely lock the door on the inside The Mate must be at the door of the airplane upon landing, so as to unlock the same and permit the discharge of passengers as soon as the airplane has come to a stop and the wheels have been properly blocked.

8.40A The Mate shall warn all passengers to remain seated while airplane is taking off, and not move around in the cabin until altitude has been reached and airplane leveled off on its course.

8.40B Mate will pass through the passenger cabin at intervals of twenty minutes while the airplane is in flight to ascertain if passengers are comfortable and if there is anything he can do to add to their enjoyment of the flight.

8.40C The Mate will announce arrival at each station to the passengers a few minutes before the airplane is going to make a landing.

8.41 The Mate is responsible for the general condition of the interior of the airplane and the sanitary condition of the same.

8.41A It shall be the duty of the Mate to allow no passenger to board his airplane who is not entitled to ride, and who is not in possession of valid transportation.

8.41B Mates serving luncheons aloft will be governed by special instructions issued to cover this service.

8.41C The Mate will thoroughly acquaint himself with the necessary reports and forms that he is to complete and promptly forward the same as per current instructions.

8.41D In the event that the airplane receives orders to pass over a scheduled stop without landing and continue the journey to the next city on its schedule, the Mate shall advise the passengers of this change in the plans.

8.42 He must make note of all mechanical defects while airplane is in flight and make record thereof; record all instrument readings; thoroughly familiarize the maintenance foreman at the terminal with work to be done other than routine.

8.43 He must inspect the airplane and assure himself that special and routine maintenance has been performed before the inspection sheet is offered for acceptance of the airplane.

8.44 He must be familiar with the gross loading of the airplane, and report to the Captain any seemingly infraction of the Department of Commerce rules regarding the loading.

8.45 He must, in conjunction with the Captain, keep in touch with the assigned radio ground station at the regularly stated intervals.

8.46 He must cooperate with the Field Managers regarding the servicing of the airplane.

8.47 He must read all weather information and airplane movement orders given to the Captain.

Field Manager

8.48 The Field Manager shall report to and receive his instructions from the Manager of Operations or other designated official.

8.49 He is in charge of the Company building, grounds and other property of his station or airport; and must preserve order about the airport; keep buildings and grounds in proper condition, and give proper attention to fire protection.

8.50 He must not permit unauthorized persons to have access to buildings or grounds.

8.51 He must see that the airplane, upon arrival at a station or airport, is properly serviced; that all mechanical defects which are brought to his attention are repaired or corrected if possible.

8.52 He must see that the airplane is in proper sanitary condition before departure.

8.52A Before departure of any airplane on a scheduled flight, he must see that it is completely stocked with all necessary ship supplies.

8.52B Before departure of ship from any intermediate field, field manager must ascertain if any ship supplies have been exhausted and if so he should replenish same before allowing his ship to depart.

8.53 When assigned the duties of Service Foreman, he is responsible for the proper and economical management of hangars, heating and power plants, and for the proper discharge of duties of persons employed therein; for the economical use of supplies; for the airplanes and other vehicles being in proper condition for efficient service.

8.53A At airports where field manager has joint operating and traffic responsibilities in matters pertaining solely to traffic he shall report to and receive his instructions from the traffic manager.

8.54 He must cooperate in the loading and unloading of passengers, and the loading and unloading of baggage.

8.55 He must cooperate with the Captains regarding the departure of planes, see that the weather information is prepared and furnished, and when necessary secure order for release of airplane for departure.

8.56 He must keep records of all fuel, oil and supplies received and distributed, furnish an invoice to the Captain for fuel and oil furnished to airplane.

8.57 He must cooperate and obey instructions that may be issued by the Traffic Department in which he may be concerned.

8.58 He must cooperate with the Passenger Agent and assist when necessary, in the checking of passengers and extend every courtesy possible to them.

8.59 He must be familiar with and obey the rules and regulations governing any airport used by this Company He must see that other employees obey the rules of the airport

8.60 He must be familiar with the rules and regulations of the Department of Commerce regarding take-off and landing.

8.61 He must see that other employees obey the rules and regulations of the Department of Commerce.

8.63 It shall be his duty to make report, in writing, to the Manager of Operations any disobedience of the Department of Commerce rules and regulations, Local Airport rules and regulations, or rules and regulations made by the Company.

Meteorologist

8.64 The Meteorologist shall report to and receive instructions from the Manger of Operations or Field Manager, when do designated.

8.65 He must collect data from prescribed locations and prepare a weather map daily. He may secure some of his data through the radio ground station operator or Government Weather Bureau.

8.66 He must report all adverse weather conditions to the Operations Manager or properly designated official who will decide whether or not airplane will fly.

8.67 He must make balloon runs to determine the ceiling wind velocity and wind direction at various altitudes.

8.68 He must prepare a statement before each flight, for the use of each Captain, showing the weather as follows:

    (a) The weather conditions at the destination terminal.

    (b) The weather along the route.

    (c) Any change and anticipated weather changes along the route.

    (d) What is the visibility, ceiling height, wind direction and velocity, at certain altitudes.

8.69 He must secure the signature of all captains for weather information furnished thereto.

8.70 He must see that the standard clock is properly adjusted and show the correct time.

8.71 Where the meteorologist also performs the duties of field clerk, he will report to and receive his instructions from the Field Manager.

Radio Engineer

8.72 The Radio Engineer shall report to and receive instructions from the Operations Manager.

8.73 He will be responsible for the installation and maintenance of radio receiving and transmitting sets in airplanes.

8.74 He must cooperate with the mechanical department regarding the installation of radio receiving and transmitting sets.

8.75 He must obey instructions issued regarding standardization of radio equipment.

Radio Station Operator

8.76 The Radio Station Operator will report to and receive his instructions from the Operations Manager or other designated officer.

8.77 He must contact each airplane in his area at stated intervals, make record of the airplane's location, secure from the Captain the condition of the weather in which the airplane is flying; receive or transmit any other information that may be necessary.

8.78 He must contact with the Captain of each airplane in his area and ascertain whether or not certain orders have been received and understood.

8.79 He must check Government Radio Time signals each day at 12:00 noon Eastern Standard Time, for the purpose of checking standard clocks over the Line.

8.80 He must receive and copy each day, such weather information as is furnished and transmitted by radio from the Government Weather Bureau.

8.81 He must obey orders received from the Radio Engineer regarding radio equipment.

8.82 He will be responsible for the condition of the Radio Ground station and the equipment therein.

8.83 He must be properly licensed, and shall only conduct such business as is permitted within the scope of the radio station license issued by the Department of Commerce.

Field Clerk

8.84 The Field Clerk shall report to and receive instructions from the Field Manager or other designated official.

8.85 He must keep the records of field operations; supplies received and consumed; be responsible for the transmission and receiving of telegraph or other messages; secure the signature of Captains for orders governing airplane movements.

8.86 When the duties of meteorologist are assigned to him, he will also be governed by the rules governing meteorologists.

8.87 He must cooperate with the Passenger Agent in handling of passengers and baggage and extend every courtesy to the passengers.

8.88 When the duties of the Passenger Agent are assigned to him, he will be governed jointly by the rules and instructions of the Traffic and Accounting Department.

Passenger (Field) Agent

8.89 The Passenger (Field) Agent reports to and receives his instructions from the Operations Manager or designated officer. He must obey the instructions of the Traffic, Accounting and Treasury Departments. He must see that unauthorized persons do not have access to the offices under his jurisdiction.

8.90 He shall attend to the sales of ticket; the checking of passengers and their baggage; the weighing of baggage to determine excess; receive, deliver and forward mail, freight, express, and when necessary make collection for same; keep the accounts, and make reports and remittances; in the manner prescribed.

TRAFFIC DEPARTMENT – GENERAL RULES

10.01 The General Traffic Manager will have supervision over the traffic department of the entire TAT-MADDUX system, and will be held responsible for its operation, reporting directly to the President.

10.02 He shall be responsible for all advertising and publicity, and all traffic administration including expenses pertaining to the traffic offices and traffic personnel, appointment and handling of agents, approval of the issuance of tickets and refunds thereunder, and all matters pertaining to the sale of the service.

10.03 He shall be responsible for the handling of all passengers, freight, mail and express, except while in the air.

10.04 All provisions in General Memorandum No. 2, supplements thereto or reissues thereof, are hereby confirmed and made part of these general rules governing traffic employees.

10.05 Employees whose duties are in any way affected by General Memoranda of the Traffic Department, together with latest supplement in effect, should have a copy with them at all times.

10.06 Traffic Department employees must be fully conversant with the latest issue of the General Memorandum and latest supplements in effect. If in doubt as to their meaning, they should apply to proper authority for explanation.

APPENDIX

General Regulations for Traffic Department Employees
Chief of Transportation

11.01 Chief of Transportation shall report to and receive his instructions from the General Traffic Manager.

11.02 He shall be responsible for the proper handling of passengers, mail and express, except when in the air.

11.03 He shall work through the traffic managers of the various divisions.

11.04 He will cooperate very closely with the Operations Managers with regard to coordinating over the entire system in the handling of passengers and merchandise aloft.

Traffic Manager

12.01 The Traffic Manager of a Division shall report and receive his instructions from the General Traffic Manager.

12.02 He shall be responsible for the solicitation of all traffic within the territory of his division and shall be further responsible for the ground handling of passengers and merchandise, and other functions of the traffic department as described herein or in other general orders and general traffic orders over his division.

12.03 It shall be his duty to see that fights are cancelled or consolidated when there is not sufficient traffic to justify their operation.

12.04 He shall be responsible for all expenses incurred in connection with the operation of his department and for the discipline of the forces engaged therein.

12.05 The Assistant Traffic Manager of a Division shall report to and receive his instructions from the Traffic Manager.

12.06 He shall be responsible for and must discharge all duties of the traffic manager when the latter is off line.

Agents

13.01 General Passenger Agents, General Mail and Express Agents, Division Passenger Agents, District Traffic Agents, District Passenger Agents, Passenger or Express Agents, City Ticket Agents, Traffic Representatives and Solicitors shall report to and receive their instructions from the traffic manager or other designated officers.

13.02 Passenger Agents must obey the instructions of the Accounting and Treasury Departments.

13.03 Passenger Agent in charge of a station must see that unauthorized persons do not have access to the office under his jurisdiction.

13.04 He shall attend to the sale of tickets, validating of same, preparation of manifests, checking of passengers into and out of ships, weighing of baggage and collection of excess therefore, if any issuance of receipts therefore when collected, proper handling of passengers' baggage, and will receive, deliver and forward mail, freight and express when necessary, making collection for same, keeping proper accounts and making reports and remittances in the manner prescribed.

13.05 He must cooperate with the field manager in the proper maintenance of the company's property, the proper discharge of duties by other employees coming under his jurisdiction, and should report to his superior officer any misconduct or violation of the company rules or the rules of the Department of Commerce.

13.06 He must not sell tickets to persons who are blind and cannot ravel alone, or to persons who are intoxicated or otherwise incapacitated.

13.07 He must see that passengers are handled courteously, and above all see that proper protection is given to passengers when loading and unloading ships.

13.08 When requesting passengers to board airplane, he should announce the flight number (the section if there is more than one), the destination of the ship, and the name of the next airport stop as shown on the time table.

13.09 He is responsible for placing in the hands of the Mate the manifest showing the list of passengers as issued by the traffic department, and in particular be thoroughly conversant with special rules for forwarding passengers on interrupted flights. In this connection he should keep himself thoroughly informed with regard to all possible rail connections in his territory which can be made for the expeditious forwarding of passengers when occasion arises.

Special Rules for Forwarding of Passengers on Interrupted Flights

14.01 When ship descends short of destination at a regular company airport and flight is cancelled account bad weather or mechanical defect, station passenger agent will immediately contact passengers in endeavor to hold them over with ship at their expense until conditions permit ship to continue flight.

14.02 If, however, there are those passengers who prefer to proceed by rail through to destination or to point where they can again connect with another one of our flights and thereby save time, through rail and Pullman tickets should be furnished these passengers in line with their desires and convenience. Form E05 should be used for such rail and Pullman transportation with one order drawn on the initial railroad to cover both rail and Pullman.

14.03 Important Exception: Under no circumstances will rail or Pullman transportation be furnished passengers to point beyond final destination shown on TAT-MADDUX ticket.

APPENDIX

14.04 Upon issuance of rail and Pullman transportation to passenger, station passenger agent will endorse on back of passenger's ticket ate, points between which ticket was actually used in flight, reason for ship being grounded (either weather or mechanical difficulties) and points between which rail and Pullman transportation were furnished, returning this ticket with endorsement to passenger and reporting transaction to the Accounting Department in proper form as prescribed by them.

14.05 Where passengers are forwarded by rail, their names, Pullman space occupied, and point to which moving by rail should be immediately communicated by teletype to traffic manager of division to which destined

14.06 When ship descends short of destination at other than a company airport and Captain reports situation to nearest traffic representative under Rule 7.07, such agent should suggest to Captain most expeditious means of forwarding passengers by rail and wherever possible arrange to contact passengers en route, or have some other company representative do so, for purpose of helping passengers in every way possible.

14.07 When Captain so reports emergency landing and traffic agent instructs him as to best means of forwarding passengers, Captain will see that Mate issues necessary E05 forms for rail and Pullman transportation, and procedure is same insofar as circumstances permit as is laid down under above rules to station passenger agents for forwarding passengers from regular company airport.

Train Couriers

15.01 Train couriers will report to and receive their instructions from the District Traffic Agent at Port Columbus.

15.02 They will be responsible for the proper handling of the train manifest and correcting all mistakes therein after train journey has started. They will contact each air-rail passenger on the train, examining their transportation to see that it is in proper order, tagging all passengers' baggage to final destination, filling out passengers' names and permanent home address on such tags, as well as indicating flight number thereon. They should also ascertain if passenger will permit baggage stickers to be placed on their luggage and affix same when permission is granted.

15.03 Train couriers will be responsible for courteous handling of air-rail passengers en route and should keep themselves thoroughly informed in regard to all scheduled tariffs and practice on the line, as well as connecting air lines, so that complete travel information may be given to passengers desiring same.

15.04 Train couriers will be expected to make an effort to sell any unsold space wired them on the train by the district passenger agent.

15.05 Train couriers must cooperate in every way with the passenger agent in the handling of passengers and their baggage in the train to plane transfers and reverse operations.

Porters

16.01 Porters will report to and receive their instructions from the station passenger agents.

16.02 Porters must cooperate in every way with the passenger agent in the handling of passengers and their baggage and extend every possible courtesy toward passengers.

FLYING CARPET TIMELINE

1930

Grand Central - Kingman	December 22,
Kingman – Winslow	December 23
Winslow – Albuquerque – Amarillo	December 24
Amarillo – Oklahoma City – Fort Smith	December 25
Fort Smith – Memphis	December 26
Memphis – St. Louis	December 30
St. Louis – Indianapolis	December 31

1931

Indianapolis – Columbus - Wheeling, WV	January 1
Wheeling – Pittsburg – Ebensburg	January 2
Ebensburg - Philadelphia	January 3
Philadelphia – Washington	January 5
Washington – Philadelphia – Long Island	January 10
Long Island – Newark	January 28
Loaded on board the Majestic	January 30
Majestic departs	February 5
Majestic arrives in Southampton	February 10
Southampton – London	February 14
London – Paris	February 22
Paris – Lyon - Avignon	March 23
Avignon – Perpignan – Barcelona	March 24
Barcelona – Los Alcazares - Malaga	March 25
Malaga – Tangiers -Rabat	March 26
Rabat – Fez	March 27
Fez – Oran	April 1
Oran – Colomb Bechar	April 6
Colomb Bechar – Adrar – Reganne	April 17
Reganne – Gao	April 18
Gao – Timbuctoo	April 23
Timbuctoo – Gao	April 26
Gao – Colomb Bechar	April 29
Colomb Bechar – Oran	May 6
Oran – Sidi bel Abbes - Fez	May 14

Fez – Casablanca	May 17
Casablanca – Fez	May 18
Fez – Marrakech	May 20
Marrakech – Mecknes	May 21
Mecknes – Marrakesh	May 29
Marrakesh – Rabat - Seville	May 31
Seville- Lisbon	June 2
Lisbon – Madrid - Biarritz	June 5
Biarritz – Poitiers – Paris	June 6
Paris – Geneva	August 3
Geneva - Milan	August 6
Milan – Venice	August 7
Venice – Vienna	August 15
Vienna – Budapest	August 18
Budapest – Belgrade	August 21
Belgrade – Bucharest	August 22
Bucharest – Constantinople	August 26
Constantinople – Konich – Aleppo	August 28
Aleppo – Homs	August 29
Homs – Palmyra - Damascus	August 31
Damascus – Jerusalem	September 7
Jerusalem – Cairo	September 8
Cairo – Amman	October 26
Amman – Maan	October 27
Maan – Amman	November 4
Amman – Rutbar Wells	November 7
Rutbar Wells – Baghdad	November 8
Baghdad – Kermanshaw- Tehran	November 24
Tehran – Bushire	December 5
Bushire – Djask	December 21
Djask – Karachi	December 22
Karachi – Jodhpur	December 23
Jodhpur – Delhi	December 24
Delhi – Agra – Calcutta	December 30

1932

Delhi – Siliguri	January 6, 1932
Siliguri – Darjeeling	January 7

APPENDIX

Darjeeling – Mt. Everest – Calcutta	January 9
Calcutta – Akyab	January 16
Akyab- Rangoon	January 17
Rangoon – Bangkok	January 18
Bangkok – Prachuabkirikhan – Alor Setar	January 19
Alor Setar – Singapore	January 20
Singapore – Banca Island (Palemburg)	March 23
Banca – Pontianak	March 24
Pontianak – Kuching	March 25
Kuching – Sibu – Dyak Village	April 13
Dyak Village – Sibu – Brunei – Sandakan	April 17
Sandakan – Jolo	April 28
Jolo – Zamboanga	April 29
Zamboanga – Cotabata	April 30
Cebu – Lake Buluan	May 1
Lake Buluan – Lake Taal - Manila	May 2
President McKinley departs Manila	May 10
President McKinley arrives in San Francisco	May 31
San Francisco – Grand Central	June 2

EXTRA PICTURES

Moye and Dick participated in the 1928 Fox film 'Air Circus'. Above the star, Arthur Lake, reviews a scene with Dick. Katy Ranaldi photo; Advertisement below - author's collection.

Above, actor Wallace Beery frequented Clover Field and loved the camaraderie shown him by the other pilots. Below, Leo Nomis behind the camera in one of the many films for which he supplied pilots and planes. Photos courtesy of Katy Ranaldi.

Dick Ranaldi took over Moye's job when he returned for school. Dick poses with Allan Hancock in front of his Stearman. Below, Dick and Hancock's personal pilot Pat Fleming. Katy Ranaldi photos.

Dick stands in the cockpit of Hancock's Lockheed Vega shaking hands with Fleming. Below, a group of TAT pilots create a snow rescue at Kingman. Dick and Moye are on the right. Photos courtesy of Katy Ranaldi.

Above, TAT had a large sum of money invested in Kingman and wanted to make sure the public was aware of their services. Middle photo show TAT 'shuttle' van to deliver passengers to their hotel or the train station. Mohave Museum of History and Art photo. Below, TAT terminal and hangar in Winslow, Arizona. Katy Ranaldi photo.

Above, Dick and Moye having fun in an automobile in front of Northrop's headquarters. Barbara Connelly photo. Below, state-of-theart helmet for Moye to test fly the N-1M. Jack Northrop is leaning on the prototype. Western Museum of Flight photo.

ENDNOTES

ABBREVIATIONS
Airport Owners and Pilots Association Magazine (AOPA)
Halliburton's Flying Carpet (FC)
Halliburton's His Stories of His Life's Adventure (RH)
Hatfield's Los Angeles Aeronautics (LAA)
Society of Experimental Test Pilots (SETP)
Transcontinental Air Transport (TAT)

CHAPTER 1
1. Gates, 219.
2. Guinn, 762 – Albert Stephens' biography; www.calarchives4u.com – Los Angeles County Bar Association.
3. Real estate prospectus courtesy of Steve & Cathy LeFevre.
4. Moye F. Stephens interview.
5. Lussler, 6.
6. Wynne, 2, 6.

CHAPTER 2
1. Ronnie, 1; Hatfield, *LAA*, 12-17 – airport information; Waterman, 144 – Pacific Airplane & supply purchase.
2. Wynne, 30; Hatfield, *LAA*, p. 45.
3. Waterman, 134-135 – Whitney.
4. Davis-Monthan Register, Waterman, 313 – Budwig; Phillips - Hoyt

CHAPTER 3
1. Levi – provided an excellent source to further depict the Kramer Dance School.
2. Hatfield, *LAA,* 90.
3. *Indianapolis Star*, 28 July 1924, 1.
4. www.alphadeltaphi.org; Hoagland, 47; Dziemianowicz, 176-182.
5. Ship passenger lists *President Taft*, *City of Los Angeles*.
6. Hatfield, *LAA*, 96.
5. Waterman, 192.
6. Corn, 12-13.
7. www.youflygirl.blogspot.com/2008_03_01_archive - female exhibitionists

8. An artist, Otie Carter, spent the majority of his time painting signs and doing lettering. The tenants of Clover Field provided much of his income.

9. In 1925, Arrigo Balboni damaged his Jenny in a forced landing in mountainous country north of Los Angeles. Al Wilson offered him $50.00 for the ship if he would dismantle it and truck it to Clover Field. Balboni decided he would be better off if he sold the plane part by part to Jenny owners in the Los Angeles area. The procedure netted him many times more than the $350 he paid for the ship. This led to the establishment of a highly successful business of buying wrecked airplanes and selling salvable parts. Balboni became known as the *Flying Junkman*. Hatfield, *LAA*, 11.

CHAPTER 4

1. Shaffel; Rasmussen, B-3 - Julian; Corn, 36 – information on Powell.
2. Wynne, 36 - *Corporal Kate*; Hatfield, *LAA*, 63 – Fisk.
3. Hatfield, *LAA*, 153.
4. Cinnabar is a major ore for the production of Mercury. Most mercury is used for the manufacture of industrial chemicals and for electrical and electronic applications.
5. Kennedy, 23.
6. Dwiggins, 208-209.
7. *Master Plan of Airports*, 78-79; unidentified newspaper clipping – Ranaldi collection.

CHAPTER 5

1. Hoaglund, 82 – Alexander; Davis-Monthan Register – J. B. Alexander.
2. Hatfield, *LAA*, 22 – LaJotte.
3. Hatfield, *LAA*, 118-119; Conant, 1.
4. Hack, 69.
5. Waterman, 172-177 – Big Bear Airlines.
6. www.santamaria museum, smmof.org; hancockcollege.edu
7. Fox movie advertisement, author's collection.
8. Davis-Monthan Register – Moye Stephens record.
9. Dwiggins, 27 – Goddard's death.
10. Verification from the Stanford Registrar's office

CHAPTER 6

1. TWA: *The Making of an Airline*, 22; Hatfield, *LAA*, 134-136; Larkins, 60-64.

2. Bunker, 4; TWA: *LL*, 24; John & Jim Fritz interviews
3. Keys held controlling interest in Curtiss in 1920. He remained president of Curtiss until the 1929 merger with Wright Aeronautical Corp. to form Curtiss-Wright Corporation, whereupon he became president of the new company. During his tenure as president of Curtiss (1920-1929) and its successor, Curtiss-Wright Corp. (1929-1933), Keys brought the company from the brink of bankruptcy to a position as one of the leading aircraft manufacturers in the world. Curtiss also became the center of a group of aviation-related companies which served to market and operate Curtiss aircraft. At the same time, Keys expanded his own holdings until he was at the head of twenty-six corporations; these included aviation holdings companies, such as North American Aviation and National Aviation Corp., as well as the first American transcontinental air service, Transcontinental Air Transport, later Transcontinental & Western Airline.
4. Hatfield, *LAA*, 81; Underwood - *Grand Central Air Terminal.*
5. Unidentified magazine article, Vance Breese collection; Lane, 1208.
6. Estes, 20-24.
7. Nichols, 34-55; Beltran, 188-196.
8. Dutch Flats was a small dirt strip located just north of where the San Diego International Airport now operates. Ryan Aeronautical Company used it to test their aircraft. Most notable was Lindbergh's Spirit of St. Louis.
9. Haine, 297.
10. Waterman, 201 – Professional Pilots Association.
11. www.worldwar1aeroplanesinc.com – Quiet Birdmen.

CHAPTER 7

1. *Mohave County Miner* – 25 May 1928, 1 June 1928, 3 August 1928
2. *Mohave County Miner* – 17 May 1929, 14 June 1929, 21 June 1929, 28 June 1929
3. TAT Memorandum 30 September 1929.
4. Davis-Monthan Register – Burford.
5. In 1930, Boeing Air Transport was the first to hire women as stewardesses. Most airlines followed their example.
6.   Bunker (*Memories of KC*), 1 - Rockne crash; Bunker (*Da Lindboigh Line*), 7 – Montee.
7. TAT Memos # 22, 25.
8. TAT Memorandum #19
9. *Mohave County Miner*, 6 September 1929.

ENDNOTES

10. TAT Memorandum, 5 November 1929.
11. TAT Memorandum #42, 22 October 1929; *AOPA*, 42 – Moye quote; Waterman, 326.
12. TWA: *LL*, 117 – Fritz interview.
13. Allen, 14.
14. Allen, 14; Anderson, 8, 10.
15. Allen, 20-21.

CHAPTER 8
1. Cole, 46-47.
2. RH letters, 305.
3. Dickson; RH letters, 307 – Halley; Gilliam notes, 2 – Halliburton's flying lessons.
4. www.goldenageair.com – Velie Monocoupe.
5. Root, 172-173 – Halley.
6. *AOPA*, 42.
7. *Los Angeles Times,* 20 November 1930, A2 – Halliburton announced his choice of a pilot at the Los Angeles Breakfast Club.
8. *AOPA*, 45.
9. Ibid, 45.
10. Juptner, vol.1: 143.
11. Briody, 15; Oklahoma Historical Society – Earle Halliburton; RH, 307-308 – Durant.
12. Charmov, 1.
13. Max, 239
14. Rich, 122.
15. Cole, 48; *Los Angeles Times*, 25 August 1930, A3 – Erickson's company.
16. Flying Carpet Logbook – Princeton Collection
17. Cole, 49 – fuel tanks; *AOPA*, p.45 – hidden compartment
18. RH, 310
19. www.sandiegohistory.org/journal/84winter/ensenada.htm; De Novelo, 1.
20. Whitlock, 113.
21. Hoagland, 133 – Hadley; *Los Angeles Times*, 30 March 1931,3 – Hadley's world tour; *Los Angeles Times,* 11 December 30, A2 - "Flying Carpet Ready to Go."

CHAPTER 9
1. *National Cyclopedia*, C, 298 – Ferber; C, 366 – Norris; E, 168 – Hurst.
2. Waterman, 201 – APA.
3. www.oceanliners.com – R.M.S. Majestic.

4. Root, 179.
5. RH letters, 312.
6. Frank, G10.
7. Blankenship, 40.
8. Gordon, 281.
9. *Flight*, 12 May 1927, 286.
10. RH letters, 312.
11. *Flight,* 27 February 1931, 191.
12. *New York Times*, 5 May 1921; de Sibour, *Flying Gypsies*; *Flight*, 20 September 28, 822; 25 July 29, 807.

CHAPTER 10

1. Gordon, 215.
2. Gilliam, 3.
3. FC, 293.
4. Woolman, 149-152.
5. Seabrook, *Air Journey*, 21-24.
6. Ibid.
7. *Los Angeles Times*, 4-29-31, 4-25-1931 – Arrival in Timbuktu.
8. Kryza, xi-xiii.
9. Norwich, 158 - salt mines; Kryza, 231 – Islamic schools
10. Seabrook, *White Monk*, 63.
11. Ibid, 240 – name; 21-26 – history of White Fathers.
12. Ibid, 64; *Air Journey*, 59 – Salama.
13. Walton interview courtesy of Sabine Muller; Lebow, 277-278 - Mellie Beese.
14. Beinhorn, *Five Continents*, 7, 18; Beinhorn, *Flying Girl*, 9-36.
15. Beinhorn, 52-69.
16. Cortese, 126.
17. Centenaire de la Legion Official Program, Princeton Collection.
18. Russia issued Wiley Post and his navigator Harold Gatty a permit one month later which enabled them to complete a world flight in eight days. They covered 15,474 miles in F.C. Hall's Lockheed *Vega* with six stops in Russia. The difference in Post receiving a permit and Richard not receiving one appears to be related to their itineraries submitted to the Russian government. Post submitted specific landing sites and a landing schedule for his flight. He wanted to set a record, not sight-see. Richard's travel plans would have specified particular areas but the duration of his stay would have been indeterminate. A substantial fee might have accompanied the application as well. www.acepilots.com – Post/Gatty Flight.

19. FC, 112 -115.
20. Root, 231; Schwartz, 170.
21. McGuiness, 216.
22. Mercer, 244; Porch, 309, 467.
23. Cole, 55-56.

CHAPTER 11

1. FC, 129.
2. www.harrysbarvenezia.com;cipriani.com
3. FC, 322.
4. Simarski, 1 – Homs.
5. Robinson, 63-67 – Palmyra.
6. Robinson, 3-9 – Baalbek; RH, 324 – Sea of Galilee swim.
7. Patton, 75.
8. Bluffield, 65.
9. Cole, 57-58.
10. "A Brief History of Petra" (subject),www.brown.edu/petra
11. www.sacredsites.com – Jerash; Moye's letters.
12. McGregor, 1; de Sibour, 96.
13. McGregor, 1.

CHAPTER 12

1. Rogers, 44-50– ban in Persia.
2. RH, 330 – Dr. W. McGovern.
3. Abidi, 3.
4. FC, 238
5. FC, 239-240; Actual photos in the Halliburton Collection at Princeton clearly define the size of the two princess and Richard sitting in the airplane with the smaller of the two.
6. www.histaviation.com – Rasche, Etzdorf (Beinhorn history – beginning flying)
7. Beinhorn, *Flying Girl*, 4-5.
8. Gilliam, 4.
9. Beinhorn, 4-5.
10. Ibid, 85-91.
11. De Sibour, 184.
12. Beinhorn, 102.
13. FC, 294.

14. The Governor of Bengal, Sir Stanley Jackson, opened the Bengal Flying Club on February 2, 1929, at the Dum Dum Aerodrome with the support of the Indian government in order to foster civil aviation. *Flight*, 7 March 1929, 192.
15. FC, 282-3.
16. Griffiths, 330; www.guardian.co.uk, 3 January 1932; RH, 333.
17. FC, 284.
18. Gilliam, 4.
19. Lewis, 86-101.
20. *Reno Evening Gazette* 11 January 1932.
21. RH, 334.
22. Beinhorn, 133-135.
23. Sabine Muller interview – Elly's visit to California.
24. Sabine, copy of original note; Beinhorn, 7.

CHAPTER 13
1. FC, 304-305.
2. Gilliam, 5 (May 2004).
3. Eade, 76, 174-175.
4. Ibid, 57-60.
5. FC, 310.
6. FC, 312.
7. FC, 318.
8. Cole, 56.
9. Ibid, 56.
10. Cortese, 126.
11. *Flight*, 6 May 1932, 403; *Los Angeles Times*, 21 April 1932, 10.
12. AOPA, 45; *Los Angeles Times,* 27 April 1932, 9.
13. *Flight*, 1 July 1932, 610; *Los Angeles Times,* 3 June 1932, II,. 8; *Hollywood Citizen News* 1 June 1932, 7; *Herald Express* 3 June 1932, 12.
14. FC, 339.
15. Cole, 69-70; RH, 346.
16. Max, 214-224.

CHAPTER 14
1. *Los Angeles Times*, 8 July 1932, H18.
2. *Los Angeles Times*, 12 June 1932, D4.
3. Braly, 17, 204, 216; *New York Times.com*/1989/03/18/obituaries/edwin-janss; Hughes, 285.
4. *Los Angeles Times,* 30 November 1932, A6; 6 November 1932, B5 – wedding announcement; *Nevada State Journal*, 27 November 1931, 3;

Los Angeles Times, 4 December 1932, B5; 11 December 1932, B6 - wedding.

5. Parks, p. 5, 11.

6. Ibid.

7. *Los Angeles Times,* 15 May 1934; *Nevada State Journal*, 13 July 1934; Louise married Lieutenant James Halliburton Young of the British Navy on December 8, 1939. She met him while on holiday in Malta - *Los Angeles Times*, 8 December 1939 , A5; Louise married John F. Fay in 1960 – *Los Angeles Times,* 8 March 1960.

8. Sheriff's Aero Squadron, 12; informal materials from the Los Angeles County Sheriff's Aero Bureau Museum received 9-26-1995; *Los Angeles Times,* 3 November 1934, A5; 14 April 33, A1; 5 March 1934, A4; 1 October 1935, A7.

9. *Los Angeles Times*, 3 December 1935, A5.

10. aviationcountryclub.org/Historymain.htm; notes/ minutes forwarded by Ed Madigan 17 November 2008; *Los Angeles Times*, 19 January 1936, D1; 12 March 1936, A7.

11. *Los Angeles Times*, 28 May 1936, A1.

12. *Los Angeles Times,* 22 March 1937, A6; 18 April 1937, F6.

13. Lovell, route displayed inside the front and back covers as well as in text; Gillian interview with Moye, 4 August 1993.

14. *Los Angeles Times*, 12 August 1935, 7 – marriage; *Flight,* 4 July 1929, 542; 6 December 1929, 1292 – Hadley's European tour.

15. Hoagland, 133 – Hadley.

16. Lebow, 279 – Ferrario; *Los Angeles Times*, 22 May 1932, E4 – Inez's pilot's license; John Underwood, 16 May 2010.

17. Hussong's Cantina (subject), www.bajainsider.com/baja-california-travel/baja-destinations/ensenada/hussongs-cantina.htm; Gilliam interview tape, June 1993.

18. Gilliam interview tapes, June 1993, 1994.

19. *Los Angeles Times,* 29 October 1937, A5

20. *Northrop News,* 27 March 81; Coleman's unpublished notes.

21. Coleman unpublished manuscript, M.W. Stephens Collection.

22. Allen, 1-6; Coleman unpublished notes; www.century-of-flight.net

23. Coleman, 58-59.

24. Allen, 114.

25. Northrop, 14

26. Breese interview; Forden, 163.

27. Davis-Monthan Register

28. Davis-Monthan Register; Breese interview.

29. Waterman, 390.

30. Northrop, 27; Allen, 124.
31. Notes courtesy of Society of Experimental Test Pilots (SETP).
32. *New York Times*, 10 February 2008, 10; *Northrop News,* 16 August 1944, 6.
33. SETP interview.
34. Wolford interview.
35. Coleman, 61.
36. Coleman, 73.
37. *AOPA*, 45.
38. *Northrop News,* 16 August 1944, 6-9; Coleman, 91-92 — both sources review Northrop pilot histories; Ranaldi- logbook entry.
39. Hatfield Collection, undated letter.
40. Moye's notes.

CHAPTER 15

1. Coleman, 173.
2. Ibid, 173-180.
3. *Pasadena Star News,* 3 September 1974; Judith Mackel interview
4. *AOPA,* 46; Moye's father passed away in 1937 from complications following surgery.
5. *Pasadena Star* News, 3 September 1974.
6. *Los Angeles Times*. 31 July 1951, A9.
7. *Los Angeles Times,* 4 June 1936, 22 March 1937, 26 September 1937, 6 May 1938, 20 November 1938, 18 May 1939, 6 December 1939, 30 January 1940, 2 July 1940 — Social events Moye and Inez attended.
8. Unidentified newspaper clipping, Moye's papers.
9. Ranaldi, information courtesy of Barbara & Katy Ranaldi; Davis-Monthan Register
10. Moye interview
11. Moyito interview
12. Ranaldi daughters' interviews; Davis-Monthan Register; Moyito interview — reaction to Dick's death.
13. www.sandiegohistory.org/journal/84winter/Ensenada.htm
14. Moyito interview
15. www.OX5.org
16. Letter courtesy of SETP
17. Letter dated 2/8/1982; courtesy of SETP

BIBLIOGRAPHY

Abidi, Azhar. "The Secret History of the Flying Carpet." *Southwest Review,* v. 91, no. 1, 2006.

"Airy Epigram." *Time Magazine,* September 24, 1928.

"Airisms from the Four Winds." *Flight*, July 1, 1932; May 6, 1932.

Airreporter. "The Widow." *The Northrop News,* August 16, 1944.

Allen, Richard . *The Northrop Story 1929-1939.* Atglen, PA: Schiffer Publishing, Ltd., 1994.

Alpha Delta Phi (subject). www.alphadeltaphi.org.

Anderson, Fred. *Northrop: An Aeronautical History.* Los Angeles: Northrop Corporation, 1976.

Aviation Country Club (subject). www.aviationcountryclub.org

Beinhorn, Elly. *Flying Girl.* London: Geoffrey Bles, 1935.

Beinhorn, Elly. "Five Continents – One Airplane." *Airwoman*, March 1935, 2, no. 4.

Betts, Ed. "Moye W. Stephens." *TARPA TOPICS.* March 1996, 39-42.

Blankenship, Michael. "A Fellow Traveler: The Gay Adventures of Richard Halliburton Finally Come to Light (1900-1939)." *The Advocate,* 18 July 1989, 39-43.

Bluffield, Robert. *Imperial Airways: The Birth of the British Airline Industry 1914-1940.* Surrey, England: Ian Allan Publishing, 2009.

Braly, John Hyde. *Memory Pictures, An Autobiography.* Stanford: Stanford University Press, 1912.

Briody, Dan. *The Halliburton Agenda.* Hoboken, NY: John Wiley & Sons, 2004, 15.

Bunker, Wes. " Da Lindboigh Line (1930-1938)." *Contrails,* posted 2 February 2004. www.twaseniorsclub.org.

Bunker, Wes. "Memories of KC & TWA (1930-1938)." *Contrails*, posted 13 March 2004.

Centenaire de la Legion Official Program 1831-1931. Sidi Bel Abbes: R. Rodiot, 1931 (Princeton Library, R. Halliburton Collection)

Charnov, Bruce, *Amelia Earhart, John M. Miller, and the First Transcontinental Autogiro Flight in 1931.* www.aviation-history.com/airmen/earhart.Aurtogiro.htm. (Charnov quoted the source for the telegram as belonging to the Michael Manning Collection.)

Cole, Martin. *Their Eyes on the Skies.* Glendale: Aviation Book Company, 1983.

Coleman, Ted. *Jack Northrop and the Flying Wing*. New York: Paragon House, 1988.

Conant, Jane Eshleman, *Pioneer Pacific Flyers Wrote Tragic Chapter in Air History*. www.sfmusem.org/hist.10/27dolerace.htm.

Corn, Joseph J. *The Winged Gospel*. New York: Oxford University Press, 1983.

De Novelo, Maria. "The Hotel Riviera del Pacifico." San Diego Historical Society Quarterly. Spring 1983: 29, no.2.

De Sibour, Violette. *Flying Gypsies*. London: G. P. Putnam's Sons, 1930.

Dickson, J. Ron. "United Airport." *Aviation History in the San Fernando Valley*. www.godickson.com

Dwiggins, Don. *Hollywood Pilot: The Biography of Paul Mantz.* Garden City, NY: Doubleday and Company Inc., 1967.

Eade, Philip. *Sylvia, Queen of Headhunters.* London: Weidenfeld & Nicolson, 2007.

Ellenberger, Allan R. *Ramon Novarro: A Biography of the Silent Film Idol, 1899-1968.* Jefferson, NC: McFarland & Company, Inc., 1999.

Estes, Richard G., "The Development of Thoroughbred Horse Racing in Southern California" (Master's Thesis) USC, 1949.

Gates, Robert. "Sixth Tennessee Infantry." *Military Annals of Tennessee Confederate*. Compiled and edited by John Berrien Lindsey. Nashville, TN: J.M. Lindsley & Co., p. 204-227 1886. Reprint, Wilmington, NC: Broadfoot Publishing Co., 1995

"Gandhi Arrested." *Guardian.co.uk,* 3 January 1932, www.century.guardian.co.uk/1930-1939/Story/0,,126284,00.htm.

Gilliam, Ronald R. "Richard Halliburton and Moye Stephens: Traveling Around the World in the 'Flying Carpet." *Aviation History*, May 2004: 14, 22-26.

_____ "Moye Stephens Piloted More than 100 types of Aircraft and Flew around the World in the Flying Carpet." *Aviation History,* July 1999: 9,   issue 6.

_____ "Heroes Among Us." *Baja Sun,* December 1993.

Frank, Ann, "Pilot Recalls Flight with Halliburton." *Los Angeles Times*, 15 June 1954, G10.

Gordon, Dennis, *The Lafayette Flying Corps: The American Volunteers in the French Air Service in World War One.* Atglen, PA: Schiffer Military History, 2000.

Griffiths, Sir Percival. *The British Impact on India.* London: Macdonald & Co., 1952.

Guinn, James Miller, *A History of California Vol. II.* Los Angeles: Historic Records Company, 1915.

BIBLIOGRAPHY

Hack, Richard. *Hughes, The Private Diaries, Memos and Letters.* Beverly Hills: Millenium Press, 2001.

Haine, Edgar A. *Disaster in the Air.* Cranbury, NJ: Cornwall Books, 1994.

Harry's Bar (subject). www.harrysbarvenezia.com; www.cipriani.com.

Hancock, Captain Allan G. (subject). Santa Maria Museum of Aviation, www.smmof.org

Hatifield, David D. *Pioneers of Aviation – A Photo Biography.* Inglewood, CA: Northrop University Press, 1976.

_____ *Los Angeles Aeronautics – 1920-1929.* Inglewood, CA: Northrop University Press, 1973.

History of California Vol. II, Los Angeles: Historic Record Company, 1915.

Hoagland, Roland W. editor. *The Blue Book of Aviation.* Los Angeles: The Hoagland Company, 1932.

Hughes, Edan. *Artists in California 1786-1940.* Sacramento: Crocker Art Museum, 2002.

Hyatt, G.W. *The Great 1927 Trans-Pacific Dole Race.* CafePress.com, 2009.

_____ *The Davis-Monthan Register.* www.dmairfield.org

Kennedy, Arthur R. *High Times.* Santa Barbara: Fithian Press, 1992.

Kryza, Frank T. *The Race for Timbuktu.* New York: Harper Collins Publishers, 2006.

Lane, D.R. *The Human Element in Flying: How Maddux Airlines Solve the Safety Problem.* Unidentified publication, no date, 1208

Lebow, Eileen F. *Before Amelia.* Brassey's Inc.: Dulles, Virginia, 2003.

Levi, John Newmark Sr. "This Is The Way We Used To Live." *Western States Jewish Quarterly*, October 1971: 4, no. 1.

www.homepage.mac.com/lindalevi/personalAW/Father.htm

Lewis, Jon E. *The Mammoth Book of Eye Witness Everest.* NY: Carroll & Graf Publishers, 2003.

A Comprehensive Report on the Master Plan of Airports for the Los Angeles County Regional and Planning Districts, 1940. Los Angeles: Regional Planning Commission.

Los Angeles County Sheriff's Aero Bureau History. Sheriff's Relief Museum. Unpublished documents received 26 September 1996.

Lovell, Mary S. *The Sound of Wings: The Life of Amelia Earhart.* NY: St. Martin's Press, 1989.

Lussler, Tim. *Daredevils of the Air: Three of the Great – Wilson, Locklear, & Grace. www.silentsaregolden.com*/articles

Max, Gerry. *Horizon Chasers.* Jefferson NC: McFarland & Company, Inc., 2007.

McGregor, Alan. *Flying the Furrow.* Saudiaramcoworld.com, 4 March 1002: 52, no. 1.

McGuiness, Justin. *Footprint Marrakech and the High Atlas Handbook.* London: Footprint Books, 2001.

Mercer, Charles. Legion of Strangers. New York: Holt, Rinehart and Winston, 1964.

National Cyclopedia of American Biography. NY: James R. White & Company, 1930.

Nichols, Chris. *The Leisure Architecture of Wayne McAllister.* Santa Barbara, CA: Gibbs Smith Publisher, 2007.

Northrop, Jack. "The Northrop Flying Wing." *The Norcrafter*, December 1941: 2, no. 7, 17-19.

Norwich, John Julius. *Sahara.* London: George Rainbird Ltd., 1968.

Nugent, John Peer, *Black Eagle.* New York: Stein & Day, 1971.

Pape, Gary. *The Flying Wings of Jack Northrop.* Atglen, PA: Schiffer Military/Aviation History, 1994.

Parks, Walter P. *The Famous Wall of the Mission Inn.* Orange, CA: Infinity Press, 2004.

Patton, Lewis Bayles. *Jerusalem in Bible Times.* Chicago: University of Chicago Press, 1908.

Pedersen, Jeannine L. *Catalina by Air.* San Francisco: Arcadia Publishing, 2008.

Perraudin, Michael, *German Colonialism and National Identity.* New York: Routledge, 2009.

Phillips, Edward H. "Floyd Stearman – Aviator, Engineer, and Kansan." *Barnstorming Wichita's Past.* nd. www.wingsoverkansas.com/Phillips.

Pire, G.H. *Air Empire: British Imperial Civil Aviation, 1919-1939.* Manchester: Manchester University Press, 2009.

Porch, Douglas. *The French Foreign Legion.* New York: Harper Collins Publishers, 1991.

Rasmussen, Cecilia. "Early Black Pilot Found Racial Equality in the Sky", *Los Angeles Times*, 5 November 2000.

Rich, Doris L. *Amelia Earhart: A Biography.* Washington, D.C.: Smithsonian Institution Press, 1989.

Robinson, David M. *Baalbek Palmyra.* New York: J. J. Augustin Publishers, 1946.

Rogers, Howard. "Britain, Persia, and Petroleum". *History Today*, May 2008: 58, no.5.

Ronnie, Art. "Wilshire & Fairfax: Aviation Center." *Westways,* January 1960.

Root, Jonathan. *Halliburton: The Magnificent Myth.* New York: Coward-McCann, Inc., 1965.

Schwartz, David M. "On the Royal Road to Adventure with *Daring Dick*". *Smithsonian Magazine*, March 1989: 19, no. 12.

Seabrook, William. *Air Adventure: Paris – Sahara – Timbuctoo*. New York: Harcourt, Brace and Company, 1933.

_____ *The White Monk of Timbuctoo*. NY: Harcourt, Brace & Company, 1934.

Shaffel, David. "The Black Eagle of Harlem." *Smithsonian Magazine*. 1 January 2009, www.airspacemag.com/history-of-flight/The-Black-Eagle-of-Harlem.html

"Sheriff's Aero Squadron." *The Pilot*, June 1935.

Simarski, Lynn. "The Lure of Aleppo." *Aramco World Magazine,* July-August 1987.

Stephens, Moye and Hiatt, J.M. "Flying Dutchman of the Air". In *100 Ghastly Little Ghost Stories*, edited by Dziemianowicz, Stephan R.,   et al, New York: Barnes and Nobel Books, 1993. First appeared in *Weird Tales*, June 1926.

Stephens, Moye W. *Whither the Wild Blue Yonder*. np, 1984.

"Stephens Recalls Old Days." *Northrop News,* March 27, 1981.

Szurosy, Geza. *Wings of Yesteryear: The Golden Age of Private Aircraft*. Osceola, WI: Motorbooks, 2004.

"The Hotel Riviera del Pacifico: Social, Civic and Cultural Center of Ensenada." *Journal of San Diego History*, Spring 1983: 29, no. 2.

Thomas, Lowell. *The First World's Flight*. Boston: Houghton Mifflin Company, 1924.

TWA, *The Making of an Airline*. Trans World Airlines Publisher, 1971.

TWA, *Legacy of Leadership*. TWA Flight Operations Department, 1970.

Underwood, John. *Grand Central Air Terminal*. San Francisco: Arcadia Publishing, 2006.

_____ *Madcaps, Millionaires & "Mose" – The Chronicle of an Exciting Era When the Airways Led to Glendale*. Glendale: Aviation Books, 1984.

Waterman, Waldo D. *Waldo: Pioneer Aviator*. Carlisle, MA: Arsdalen, Bosch, and Co., 1988.

Whitlock, Flint and Barnhart, Terry L. *Capt. Jepp and the Little Black Book*. Superior, WI: Savage Press, 2007.

Windrow, Martin. *French Foreign Legion 1914-1945*. Oxford: Osprey Publishing Co., 1999.

Woolman, David S. *Rebels in the Rif*. Stanford: University Press, 1968.

Wynne, H. Hugh. *The Motion Picture Stunt Pilots*. Missoula, MT: Pictorial Histories Publishing Co., 1987.

INTERVIEWS

William Alexander, phone interview, September 1991
Michael Blankenship correspondence 1990
Bob Cardenas June 1998
Barbara Connelly 5-15-2010
John Ferguson 3-24, 25, 26-2010
John and Jim Fritz 8-16-2010; 9-5-2010; 10-5-2010; 11-3-2010
Linda Hendrickson, 4-4-2010
Steve LeFevre, 11-12-2008, 9-29-2009, 3-8-2010
Judith Mackel, 8-25-2010
John Meyers, Lancaster, CA 10-21-1998
Sabine Muller, 8-11-2009, 1-26-2010, 4-5-2010
Katy Ranaldi, 5-17-2010; 10-25-2010
Rosina Schulse, 9-7-1991
Max Stanley, 10-1998
Moye F.and Cecile Stephens 1996-2010
Moye W. and Inez Stephens June 24-26-1989; August 16, 1989
John Underwood 1997-2010
Roy Wolford, 10-19-2009, Ranch Palos Verdes

COLLECTIONS

Hatfield Collection, Museum of Flight, Seattle
Eugene Biscailuz Collection, University of Southern California
TAT Collection, Mohave Musem of History and Arts, Kingman, Arizona
Richard Halliburton Papers; Manuscript Division; Department of Rare
        Books and Special Collections; Princeton University Library
John K. Northrop-Richard W. Millar Aviation Collection, Occidental College,
        Glendale, California

INTERNET

www.acepilots.com
www.aerofiles.com
www.aviation-history.com/airmen/earhart-autogiro.htm
www.bajainsider.com
www.calarchives4u.com/history/losangeles/social890-784.htm
www. century-of-flight.com
www.civilwarhome.com/stephensshilohor.htm
www.encyclopedia.jrank.org/articles/pages/4337/Julian-Hubert

BIBLIOGRAPHY

www.esparacing.com/Aviation%20history.jet%20age/Northrop%20
www.fembio.org/biography
www.flightglobal.com/pdfarchive
www.godickson.com
www.goldenageair.com
www.guardian.co.uk
www.hotlinecy.com/interview/doolittle.htm
www.tngenweb.org/civilwar/csainf/csa6.htm
www.oceanliners.com/ships/bismarck.asp
www.oldbeacon.com/beacon/airlines/usa/maddux.htm
www.opencockpit.net/moye.html
www.ovpm.org
www.roynagl.0catch.com
www.sacredsites.com
www.sandiegohistory.org/journal/84winter/ensenada.htm
www.time.com/time/magazine/article/0,9171,928059,000.htlm
www.trainsofturkey.com/maps
www.wingnet.org/rtw/rtw002c.htm
www.worldwar1aeroplanesinc.org
www.youflygirl.blogspot/2008_03_01_archive.html

NEWSPAPERS & PERIODICALS

Appleton Post-Crescent
*The Chillicothe Constitutio*n (Chillicothe, Missouri)
Croydon Weekly Notes
El Paso Herald-Post
Flight Magazine
The Frederick Post (Frederick, MD)
Herald Evening Express
Herald Express
Hollywood Citizen News
Indianapolis Star
Ironwood Daily Globe (Ironwood, Michigan)
Laverne Leader
Lincoln Star Nebraska
Los Angeles Times
Montana Standard, (Butte, Montana)
Nevada State Journal, (Reno, NV)
New York Times

FLYING CARPETS, FLYING WINGS

Northrop News
Oakland Tribune
Pasadena Star News
Reno Evening Gazette
Reno Gazetet
San Francisco Chronicle

INDEX

Abbreviations:

Airport Owners and Pilots Association Magazine (AOPA)
Halliburton's Flying Carpet (FC)
Halliburton's His Story of His Life's Adventures (RH)
Hatfield's Los Angeles Aeronautics (LAA)
Society of Experimental Test Pilots (SETP)

INDEX

Stephens, Trowbridge 5-6, 16, 88
Stephens, William Henry 2-3
Stout, William B. 82
Stowe, J. B. 104, 108-109, 112

T
Thirteen Black Cats 42
Thomas, W. E. 16, 249
Tibbit, Lawrence 117
Timm , Wally 56, 245
Tomick, Frank 39, 57, 59
Tomlison, D. W. 96, 111-112, 128
Turner, Roscoe 90, 282

U
Unger, Ivan 39, 40-41, 42, 50
United Airport 124, 132

V
Von Karman, Theodore 254, 259
Von Stroheim, Eric 116
Vultee, Jerry 79

W
Warren, Roman 71
Waterman, Waldo 72-73, 99, 256-257, 282
Webster, Jim 13-14, 21-24, 37, 88
Wedemeyer, Art 63
Wharton, Bill 267
Whitmarsh, Phillip 277-278
Whitney, Frederic C. 18, 33, 65-68, 129
Wilde, Arthur 255
Wilson, Al 10, 39, 40, 56, 60-61
Wolford, Roy 263-264

Y
Young, T. C 15, 63

FLYING CARPETS, FLYING WINGS

THE AUTHOR

Barbara Schultz lives with her husband Phil on Little Buttes Antique Airpark north of Lancaster, California. She is a pilot and a member of the Ninety-Nines, Women In Aviation International, the Women's Air and Space Museum, and the Experimental Airplane Association. For the last 20 years, she has been involved in documenting aviation history. Her research has revealed the intricate and continuous connections between events and the early pioneers that expedited the early development of flight. The Dominguez Air Meet in 1910 inspired many young men and women to make their marks in the sky. Jimmy Doolittle, William Boeing, Roscoe Turner, Moye Stephens, and Pancho Barnes were among them. Each one has a story that should be told respectfully and factually.

The author and Vance Breese had a wonderful time talking about his father. Vance's autogiro "Predator" is a great background for the picture. Phil Schultz photo.

340